W9-BUX-611

3 1702 00054 1800

GRIC ITH991
10.95

THE CHEYENNE INDIANS

DANCERS WITH WILLOWS, MEDICINE LODGE

THE
CHEYENNE INDIANS

THEIR HISTORY AND
WAYS OF LIFE

BY

GEORGE BIRD GRINNELL

*Photographs by Elizabeth C. Grinnell
and Mrs. J. E. Tuell*

VOLUME ONE

UNIVERSITY OF NEBRASKA PRESS
LINCOLN AND LONDON

EDITION STATEMENT

The Bison Book edition is reproduced from
the first edition published by Yale University Press
in 1923. The contents of Volume II,
which includes the index for both volumes are

War and Its Ways
Warrior Societies
Religious Beliefs
Disease, Healing, Death
Useful Plants
Ceremonial
Medicine Lodge
Massaum Ceremony
The Culture Heroes
Appendixes A, B, C

International Standard Book Number 0–8032–5771–6
Library of Congress Catalog Card Number 23–17688

First Bison Book printing: October 1972
Most recent printing shown by first digit below:
5   6   7   8   9   10

Manufactured in the United States of America

PREFACE

MY first meeting with the Cheyenne Indians was hostile, and after that, though often in the country of the Cheyennes, I never knew them until their wars were over.

My first visit to their camp was in 1890 when, at the invitation of my old schoolmate and friend, Lieut. Edward W. Casey, 22d Infantry, who had enlisted a troop of Cheyenne scouts, I visited him at Fort Keogh and made their acquaintance. Lieutenant Casey was killed in January, 1891, and his scouts were disbanded a little later.

From that time on, no year has passed without my seeing the Cheyennes in the North or in the South, or in both camps. I have been fortunate enough to have had, as interpreters in the North, William Rowland, who married into the tribe in the year 1850, and later his sons, James and Willis. In the South, Ben Clark helped me; and until his death in 1918 George Bent, an educated half-breed born at Bent's Old Fort in 1843, who lived his life with his people, was my friend and assistant. He was the son of Owl Woman and Col. William Bent, a man of excellent intelligence and of extraordinary memory.

After a few years' acquaintance, the Indians began to give me their confidence, and I have been able to some extent to penetrate into the secrets of their life. On the other hand, I am constantly impressed by the number of things about the Indians that I do not know.

In describing the life, the ways, and the beliefs of the Cheyennes, I have gone into details which may sometimes appear superfluous; but after all, if one is to understand the viewpoint of the Cheyennes, this seems necessary. These primitive people in certain ways live more in accordance with custom and form than we do, and a comprehension of the motives which govern their acts cannot be had without these details.

I have never been able to regard the Indian as a mere object for study—a museum specimen. A half-century spent in rubbing shoulders with them, during which I have had a share in almost every phase of their old-time life, forbids me to think of them except as acquaintances, comrades, and friends. While their culture differs from ours in some respects, fundamentally they are like ourselves, except in so far as their environment has obliged them to adopt a mode of life and of reasoning that is not quite our own, and which, without experience, we do not readily understand.

It is impossible for me to acknowledge all the kindness that I have received during my long association with the Cheyennes. My Indian friends have always been cordial and helpful. To my interpreters, Ben Clark, George Bent, William Rowland and his sons, as well as to Mr. and Mrs. J. R. Eddy and to Mr. and Mrs. A. C. Stohr, I owe much.

The illustrations shown are a few of the many photographs taken by Mrs. Grinnell and by Mrs. J. E. Tuell, who have kindly permitted their use. They picture some of the old-time practices and ceremonies, never to be seen again.

Rev. Rodolphe Petter has been most generously helpful to me on the linguistic side; and finally, my friend, Frederick W. Hodge, so well equipped with general knowledge of American Indians, and the first living authority on the Indians and the history of the southwest United States, has performed for me the great service of reading over my manuscript. George E. Hyde has helped me with the index. To all these persons, past and present, my thanks are due.

G. B. G.

New York
August, 1923.

CONTENTS

CONTENTS

ILLUSTRATIONS

EARLY CHEYENNE HISTORY

DIVISIONS, NAMES, GENESIS, MIGRATION

THE Cheyennes are one of the westernmost tribes of the great Algonquian family. They formerly lived far to the east of their present range, in fixed villages and cultivated the soil; but moving west and southwest, becoming separated from their kindred of the East, they at last thrust out into the plains beyond the Missouri, and secured horses. In later days they were a typical Plains tribe of buffalo hunters, possessing energy and courage, and taking rank as one of the most hardy and forceful tribes of the great central plains.

The Cheyennes today are settled in two divisions: the Northern Cheyennes in Montana, where in 1921 they numbered 1411 individuals, and the Southern Cheyennes in Oklahoma, numbering in the same year 1870, giving a total for the tribe of 3281 persons. The arbitrary and modern division into Northern and Southern sections means nothing more than that a part of the tribe elected to reside in one region, and a part in another. The separation began about 1830. At first the movement was slow, but the building of Bent's Fort in Colorado in 1832 hastened it. Constant intercourse has always been carried on between the two divisions, and they regard themselves merely as two different camps of the tribe. Until the white occupancy of the plains made this impossible, Northerners moved south from time to time and remained there, and Southerners moved north. Often members of the same family lived, some in the North and others in the South. Frequent visiting still goes on by way of the railroads, and there are still changes of location by individuals or families.

I

The Cheyenne tribe, which we know is made up of the descendants of two related tribes, the *Tsĭs tsĭs' tăs,* or Cheyenne proper, and the *Suh' tai,* who are said to have joined the Cheyennes after they crossed the Missouri[1] and perhaps not much more than two hundred years ago, or in the early part of the eighteenth century. The Cheyennes were also called *Nĭ ŏm ă-hē' tăn iu,* the Sandhill Men.

For years during our first knowledge of the tribe, the name Cheyenne was supposed to be derived from the French word *chien,* "dog," and this appeared to receive confirmation from the fact that an important soldier society of the tribe was called Dog Soldiers. The tribal name is now known to be an abbreviation of the Sioux terms *Shā hĭ' yē na,* or *Sha hĭ' ē la,* "red talkers," meaning "people of alien speech"—those who talk a language which is not intelligible. The Sioux speak of people whose language they understand as "white talkers," and of those whose language is not understood as "red talkers." Thus Sha ia = *shā,* "red," and *ĭ'a,*[2] "to speak," or "words," means

[1] James Mooney states that the Suhtai crossed the Missouri River before the Cheyennes, but the Cheyennes, some of them of Suhtai descent, do not tell it so. Those whom I have questioned, both Northern and Southern Cheyennes, all declare that the Cheyennes crossed the Missouri before the Suhtai. Ben Clark and William Rowland, men of good intelligence, married into the tribe and residing with them for from thirty to fifty years, tell the story as the Cheyennes relate it. These men, through their long association with the tribe, in the course of which they must have heard the tribal traditions over and over again, are much more likely to have received a correct idea of the general Indian belief than any brief sojourner among them.

Yet it is but fair to say that there may be here a misunderstanding and that the present-day Cheyenne traditions may mean merely that the last meeting— we are told of others much earlier—took place on the west side of the Missouri River. Since the movements of the tribes were by individual camps and in no sense as a tribal body, it is, I think, impossible to learn that any camp of either tribe first crossed the Missouri. Each tribe might well enough have assumed that the other was a newcomer in the region. Up to the end of the eighteenth century there were camps of Tsistsistas and Suhtai on the Missouri River as well as far west of it.

[2] The interpretation of the word Cheyenne is probably as given, yet today many of the Sioux declare that the term was applied to the Cheyennes because when the Sioux first met them, the Cheyennes were painted red over the whole body and their clothing was painted red. The same thing is said of the Crees, who in early days also painted the whole body red. Among the names applied

"to speak in a language not understood." Among several Plains tribes the name for the Cheyennes is a variant of the Sioux name, as for example, when the Arikaras and the Pawnees call the Cheyennes *Shar' ha*. This term obviously suggests the word Chaa, applied by La Salle in 1680 to a group of Indians that visited him at Fort Crèvecœur, not far below the present site of Peoria, Illinois. Only a few days before this visit, some *Ma tou tĕn' tas* came to La Salle.[3] If the Matoutentas were Otoes, it may have been from them that La Salle secured the name of his visitors, for at that time the Otoes were near neighbors of the Cheyennes.

The tribe does not use the name which we have given them. They call themselves Tsistsistas, which the books commonly give as meaning "people." It probably means related to one another, similarly bred, like us, our people, or us. The Rev. Rodolphe Petter has pointed out that it may be translated "cut people," "gashed people," for the two words are nearly alike. This last meaning is practically that given them on the prairie in early times by whites and Indians alike, and evidently comes from the distant sign which they used to designate themselves, which means "cut arms." If one is speaking by signs to a Cheyenne close at hand and asks his tribe, he will make on the back of the left forward-directed forefinger two or three diagonal cross lines drawn toward his body with the right forefinger, and this is often explained as "striped feathers"—referring to those used on the arrows. The sign at a distance is, as

to the Crees by certain Missouri River tribes are some that resemble that applied by the Sioux to the Cheyennes. Maximilian gives the Hidatsa name for Cree as *Scha hi;* Matthews as *Sha i ye;* Hayden gives the Sioux name for Cree as *Shī ē ah la,* or as *Shī ē ya.* Mooney and Thomas say that these last are Assiniboine names meaning "enemies," "strangers." They may well mean strangers in speech, speaking a strange, unknown tongue.

The Cheyennes today consider the Crees to be related to them, and many years ago William Jackson, who had been brought up among the Crees, told me that the Cree name for the Cheyennes was *Ka nea hea wăs' tsĭk,* which was said to mean "they talk a little Cree," meaning that the Cheyenne language somewhat resembled the Cree.

[3] Margry, Découvertes, vol. II, p. 54.

said, that for "cut arms," but that sign has been misinterpreted by the Blackfeet, who have mistaken it for the somewhat similar sign for "spotted," and call the Cheyennes "spotted people," a designation which seems without appropriate meaning. It has been said that the terms "gashed or cut people," and "cut arms," were applied to them from their old practice of cutting strips of skin from their arms and other parts of the body to offer in sacrifice, to bring good fortune. The name "Black Arms," supposed to have been a designation of the Cheyennes, may also have arisen from a misunderstanding of the sign.

The early history of the Cheyennes, like that of all of their neighbors, is vague. Their movements may be traced back for more than two hundred years, but beyond that the investigator comes to a point beyond which all is conjecture. From their own traditions and from the fact that they are of the western Algonquians, whose current of migration was in a general westerly and southwesterly course, we may conclude that the Cheyennes came from the Northeast or East, but whether they reached the upper drainage of the Mississippi River along the southern shores of the Great Lakes, or along the northern shores and around the west end of Lake Superior, it would seem now impossible to learn.

Previous to the year 1880, certain Cheyenne traditions bearing on the earliest tribal wanderings were gathered at Fort Reno, Oklahoma, from a number of the oldest Southern Cheyennes, by the late Ben Clark, and the country described in these accounts as the primitive home of the Cheyennes seems to suggest the region lying north of the Great Lakes and toward Hudson Bay, rather than that south of the lakes.

According to one of these tales, the Cheyennes formerly lived under the ground. They were in a great cave; it was dark, but a distant light was seen, and traveling toward it they found an opening and came out upon the earth. At first the light hurt their eyes, but it was not always light. There were night and day. They found themselves in a new country, rough and strange, where rocks and stones were strewn all over the ground. Small animals with long ears—rabbits—were seen, and killed for food, and for a long time these were their only support. Their robes, or coverings for warmth, were made of rabbit-skins,[4] and their shelters were made of the stones which were so abundant. They journeyed on and came to a large river on which timber grew. Here a star fell from the sky and set fire to the timber, and in this way the Cheyennes learned of fire, to cook by and for warmth. They continued to travel and came to the shores of a great water where were found many things showing that other people had camped there. Hammers and axes of stone were found hidden in the soil, and wooden tent-pins were standing in the ground, even to the water's edge. The Cheyennes remained here for a long time.

When again they began to travel, they moved westward and at length reached a country which was very level. There they were attacked by the *Ho' hē*, or Assiniboines, who already possessed guns. The Cheyennes were finally driven westward and reached the Missouri River—*Ē o' mǐ tā ǐ*.[5]

Clark credits this information to such men as Bull Tongue, Many Magpies, Stone Calf, and others, who were living between 1865 and 1875. A considerable portion of what he gives

[4] Robes of woven strips of rabbit-skin have always been used by the Indians of the North. Mackenzie (Voyages, p. 44, London, 1801), found the Hare Indians clad in hare-skins. Note the suit of hare-skin in the Museum of the American Indian, Heye Foundation, New York.

[5] Eomitai is variously translated and there are various explanations of the name. One meaning is, "It gives fat." The word is often translated "greasy." It is said that long ago, when the Cheyennes first reached the Missouri River, they found on its banks many recently drowned fat buffalo. They named the river from this welcome food supply. Some of the Southern Cheyennes say that when they first saw the Missouri it was rising, and that great masses or lumps of froth were floating down. This froth resembled the foam which formed on the water in their kettles, when boiling pounded bones to extract the grease; and the name was given to the stream from these masses of greasy looking foam (*American Anthropologist*, N. s., vol. VIII, 1906, p. 16). After this paper appeared, Mr. R. Petter wrote me that "fatty foam" or "greasy foam" is the true meaning.

I have never heard. The story of the Cheyennes having emerged from under the ground may perhaps have been borrowed by them from the Arikaras or the Mandans, with whom for many years they were closely associated.

The Northern Cheyennes tell of having lived for a long time on the border of some great water, the winter home of multitudes of migrating wild fowl. Each autumn these birds passed over them in great flocks and alighted in this water, where they spent the winter, and when spring came and the first thunders were heard, the wild fowl rose and flew over them and away, to disappear in the North. The climate of this country must have been mild, because, at that time, it is said, the people wore no clothing.

From this great water they started on their journey toward the West. They tell of moving from some distant land by boats, which they cannot describe. They were poorly equipped with weapons, and were unable to capture large animals, except occasionally in snares. Their flesh food consisted largely of small animals—skunks are particularly mentioned—and the water fowl which bred in the lakes found everywhere in that region. When the birds came in spring and built their nests, the people gathered great quantities of eggs for food, and when the old birds shed their flight feathers many were captured, and when the young were partly grown these were killed.[6] Thus so long as the fowl remained they subsisted chiefly on them.

Their movement from the Northeast brought them to the edge of some large body of water which it became necessary to cross. The distance between shores was great, and landmarks could not be distinguished, or perhaps wild rice, rushes, or

[6] "The Indians were much fatigued, having been employed in running after wild fowl which have lately cast their feathers." (Mackenzie, Voyages, p. 26, London, 1801.) Geo. H. Wilkins says: "During the summer [near Kellett Point, Banks Island] the white geese especially can be driven about in flocks when they are molting, and killed like sheep. At this time of the year they are not so very fat and are much better if killed earlier in the season," i.e., before molting. (III Report on Topographical and Geographical Work, Canadian Arctic Expedition, p. 55, Ottawa, 1917.)

6

other growths were so high above the water as to obstruct the view; at all events it was needful to learn what course was to be followed. Young men were sent forward to discover what lay beyond this water, and in order to mark the route followed they placed in their canoes poles, which, as they advanced, they thrust into the mud of the bottom and left standing. They reached the other shore and found themselves in a flat country, which seemed to be flooded, for as they went forward in their canoes trees stood all about them in the water. At length they turned about, and following the sticks standing in the water, readily found the way back to their people. When the whole tribe advanced, the marked way was again followed.

Where this was we do not know, nor where the Cheyennes went from here. They speak next of a very flat country in which grew a tall red grass which they gathered and tied in bundles to use for fuel, for in that land there was little or no wood. Up to this time they are believed to have lived in shelters made by setting poles in the ground in a circle or oval, bending them over toward a common center to form a roof, and building up the sides with grass, earth, and sods; in other words, in permanent earth lodges.

It is told by the Cheyennes of today that soon after they reached the flat country of their tradition, they were attacked by the Hohe, or Assiniboines, and perhaps by the Crees. These possessed firearms—guns presumably obtained from the Hudson Bay Company or from still earlier traders on Hudson Bay. These attacks of the Hohe drove their tribe in a southwesterly direction until they reached the Missouri.

Some years ago Mr. F. W. Hodge edited a manuscript dated about 1660, by Dr. Thomas Hutchins, then physician at York Factory, at which time, as was inferred from the manuscript, many Crees went there to trade. This manuscript is, or recently was, in the London Archives of the Hudson Bay Company.

The earliest Indians that came to trade to the shores of Hudson Bay appear to have been the Crees, for according to the

7

Jesuit Relations for 1657-1658 there was some small traffic to the shores of the bay as early as that time. Mention is made of a Cree having spent the winter with the traders there and promising to return in the spring with many of his countrymen. This was presumably at Port Nelson.[7]

Soon after this the Assiniboines who lived about the Lake of the Woods, and the Crees who occupied the country of the Kaministiquia River, came to fighting. The Crees were the first to receive arms from the English by way of Hudson Bay, and fought the Assiniboines, their nearest neighbors. These, finding themselves the weaker, asked for peace, took Cree wives, and later joined the Crees against the Sioux.[8] However, this peace between the Crees and the Assiniboines may have been broken from time to time, for Raudot, writing from Quebec in 1710, says that the Assiniboines would readily come to trade on the shores of Lake Superior if they were not at war with the Christenaux (Crees).[9]

On the other hand, Lewis and Clark state[10] that in 1806 the Cheyennes declared that they had been driven from the Red River country by the attacks of the Sioux, and the Sioux tradition recorded by Dr. Riggs states that the Sioux and Ojibwas both attacked the Cheyennes and drove them to the Missouri, where they formed a new village and planted on the east bank of the river. After a time the tribe crossed to the west bank and had a fortified village there. In 1804 the ruins of a Cheyenne village were pointed out to Lewis and Clark by an Arikara chief.[11] As I shall try to show, these statements as to hostilities between the Cheyenne and the Sioux are unsupported by any evidence from either tribe.

The Cheyennes now came into touch with two tribes of the Missouri, the Mandans and Arikaras. Mandan tradition given

---

[7] Jesuit Relations, Thwaites ed., vol. XLIV, p. 239 *et seq.*, Cleveland, 1899.
[8] Margry, vol. VI, p. 82.
[9] *Ibid.*, p. 14.
[10] Original Journals of Lewis and Clark, vol. VI, p. 100.
[11] Also Ordway Journal, Wis. Hist. Colls., XXII, 1916, p. 154.

to Maximilian tells us that they were attacked by the Cheyennes soon after that tribe arrived on the Missouri, and that a war ensued;[12] but peace was at length made, and for a long time the two tribes were on terms of close friendship—as they were in the days of Lewis and Clark. This tradition of war between the Cheyennes and Mandans I do not trust. No present-day Indians have ever heard of it, though stories are often told of fights with the Arikaras. In these friendly relations the Arikaras also were usually included, and the oldest Cheyennes of the last generation—1890-1900—often spoke of the time when the two tribes lived together at the mouth of the Moreau or Owl River; the Arikaras lived farther down, near the Cheyenne River.[13]

After the Cheyennes had crossed the Missouri River and a part had worked their way out on the plains to or near the Black Hills, they met with a numerous company, the Suhtai, who spoke a dialect of the Cheyenne language—rougher, harsher, and more guttural. Cheyenne tradition says that long, long ago, very far back, long before they began their westward migration, the Suhtai had been their enemies. They used to fight with them, but at last the two tribes discovered that they spoke the same tongue, and so were related. When this was learned they became friends and made an alliance. Later, still in the North, they separated and for a long time did not meet. Some informants have been told that the two tribes came together and separated three times. When the Suhtai joined the Cheyennes in the Black Hills country they were at once recognized by their speech, which was so similar to the Cheyenne tongue that it could be understood, though many words differed from those used by the Cheyennes.

[12] Maximilian, Travels, vol. II, p. 369 *et seq.*, Paris, 1841.
[13] Renaudière found the "Rickaras" on the Missouri, ten leagues above the Mahas in 1723 (Margry, VI, p. 392); just below Cheyenne River, Lewis and Clark (Orig. Journ., vol. I, p. 176) passed a Ree village which may have been abandoned about 1750, and another near Owl River perhaps abandoned about 1796.

For many years after crossing the Missouri River, the Suhtai lived near and in association with the Cheyennes.[14] Yet they retained their tribal organization and spoke their own dialect as late as the year 1832, when William Bent, going north from the recently completed fort on the Arkansas to find the Cheyennes, came upon the Suhtai camp, and by them was told where to look for the Cheyennes. Bent, who spoke Cheyenne, declared that he had difficulty in understanding the speech of the Suhtai. Not very long after this, the Suhtai appear to have joined the Cheyennes permanently and to have become a part of the tribe, regularly camping and living with them. When this took place the old Suhtai dialect began to be lost. Though it was still spoken by the old people, the children who were born and reared in the Cheyenne camp naturally spoke the dialect of their fellows, and today few old men or women remain who can recall any of the old Suhtai who spoke that dialect.

The old-time beliefs and ways were more enduring, and a multitude of customs of the Suhtai, handed down to their children, are practiced in the tribe today. One of the important mysteries of the Cheyennes is the so-called buffalo hat, *Ĭs' sĭ-wŭn*, which it is believed was brought to the Suhtai by that tribe's culture hero.

Nothing is known of the Suhtai before they reached the plains. Perrin du Lac, who saw some Cheyennes before the earliest American explorers, speaks of them as in three bands— Chaguyenne, Ouisy, and Chousa—terms which suggest Cheyenne, Omissis, and Suhtai. Mr. Petter, however, our first authority on the Cheyenne language, is quoted as referring these names to *Hēv' ă tăn iu, O mĭss' ĭs,* and *Ho tăm' ĭ tăn iu*— but the last-named group is a soldier organization, not a division.

In the year 1905 I requested the late Dr. William Jones, who was then investigating the Ojibwa and other Algonquian tribes in Minnesota and Manitoba, to make inquiry concerning the

---

[14] Ben Clark, MS., *circa* 1880.

Suhtai, or any tribe whose name might suggest that word. He wrote me:

The nearest I can find to your Suhtai is *Shō' ta wī ni' ni wŭg*. The last part of the word, *"i ni ni wug,"* is the plural of *"i ni ni,"* which means "man," but no one seems to know what *Shota* means. The word was given me by the chief of the Bear Island Pillagers, in answer to my question about Suhtai. He said it was the name of a people who used to live east of this place, meaning between Leech Lake and Lake Superior, but that he had never heard of them—*i.e.*, of their present existence—nor where they went. The man who told me this is Madcigado, who claims to be seventy-five years old.

It would seem therefore that there is a tradition of a people locally known as Shohta, who in early times lived west of the western end of Lake Superior, and perhaps before the Ojibwa had worked as far west as this point.

The full name of these people, Shotawininiwug, is now used by the Ojibwa to designate the Hebrew race; the fact that it ever applied to a tribe of Indians having apparently been forgotten.

It is perhaps worth noting in this connection that a very aged Cheyenne woman who was once the wife of Charles Auterbees always spoke of the Suhtai as Sōh' ta.

The early French traders and Lewis and Clark considered the Suhtai—as in fact at that time they were—a tribe distinct from the Cheyenne, and called them Staĭtan, which seems to be the answer made by some Suhtai, who, when asked who he was, replied, "Sūh' tai hē tăn," meaning, "I am a man of the Suhtai."

When the three allied tribes, Tsistsistas, Suhtai, and Arapaho, camped together, the Suhtai village was to the north, the Cheyennes next to them, and the Arapahoes to the south. For this reason, perhaps, one of the Cheyenne names for a division of the Arapahoes is *Nŭm o sĭn' ha nhĭ' a,* "build their fires to the south." This relative situation of the camps may possibly have some reference to the order in which the three tribes crossed the Missouri River.

At the present day the Suhtai remain among the Cheyennes merely as the name of a division. The old dialect has disappeared. The meaning of the name is not known. Tangle Hair believed it was derived from *ĭssŭht'*, "ridge," which suggests that it may mean "dwellers on the ridge."

Even after the Cheyennes had reached the Missouri River, while some of them stopped there, others still seemed disposed to roam. Information from different men—one of whom himself remembered a time when some Cheyenne still lived on the Missouri River—shows that after they had come to that stream and settled there to cultivate their crops and live their lives, there was a tendency among some of the more restless people to go farther, to work out on the plains, where buffalo were abundant. A part remained in different camps on the Missouri River, sedentary, and occupying permanent houses, and a part began to wander out onto the plains. Elk River (born about 1810) says that one band that remained on the Missouri River moved down below the Standing Rock, and then, changing their minds, moved again and went on farther down, established a new village, there planted their corn and tobacco, and raised crops for many years. His mother's statement will be given farther on.

The people who began to wander out on the plains at first merely made hunting journeys, and returned with their meat to the village; but gradually these hunting excursions lasted longer and longer, until a time was reached when they practically lived on the plains and visited the river. Wandering farther and farther, those who had left the Missouri River reached the Black Hills, about which they lived, and which for generations was the center of their wanderings. Elk River declared that it was that division of the tribe that first reached the Black Hills which first met the Arapahoes there, and gave Curly as the name of the head chief of that tribe at the time.

The streams running from the Black Hills were pleasant to live on. Food was abundant, and after the Cheyennes had made successful killings of buffalo, the people, when they visited their relatives on the Missouri River, were accustomed to carry back quantities of dried meat and present it to those who were farming there. The accounts of the visitors, confirmed by the gifts of food which they brought, formed a constantly increasing temptation to those who still lived on the Missouri River; and the ultimate result—though it may have taken generations to bring it about—was that most of the Cheyennes moved out to the plains, but the final exodus probably did not take place until the early part of the nineteenth century.

Lewis and Clark speak of the Cheyennes as established in 1804 in two places, of which the explorers knew, for they speak of them as the Sharha, people on the other side, and the Wee-hee-skeu, people on this side.[15]

SETTLEMENTS IN MINNESOTA AND THE DAKOTAS

In their progress through the new western country, the early travelers found here and there camps of Indians, and heard of other camps which they did not see. Accustomed to the sedentary habits of white people, the explorers seem to have taken it for granted that any place or point occupied by a tribe of Indians was the home of that tribe and that it remained permanently in that tract of country—had always been there, and always would be there. Writers who followed the early travelers shared that belief and copied their statements.

Such permanence of occupancy is not likely ever to have been true of the Plains Indians. The conditions of their lives and the difficulties of obtaining food were such that they were seldom all together. Usually they were scattered out over a wide extent of territory, each little group endeavoring to find some place where enough food to support them could be had.

It is true that certain tribes of Plains Indians which depended largely on agriculture occupied permanent villages and

[15] Orig. Journ., vol. I, p. 190.

were to some extent sedentary. They made periodical hunting trips, in summer and in winter, which lasted for two or three months, when the tribe returned to its permanent villages. Yet from time to time, through scarcity of food, attacks by enemies, or from unknown causes, these sedentary tribes modified or even entirely changed their ways. In historic times some tribes of Pawnees abandoned their permanent villages, moved away, and built new ones far from the old. Aged Sioux men—Santees in recent years located at the Standing Rock Indian Reservation—have declared to me that their fathers had told them that, many years before, their people lived in permanent (earth) lodges[16] and that it was not until they had commenced to move out onto the plains and toward the Missouri River that such permanent villages were abandoned and skin tipis exclusively adopted.

While the permanent houses of the Mandan, Hidatsa, Arikara, and Pawnee endured to very recent times and have been described in many books, those of the Cheyennes are known only from tradition and from the suggestions of early writers; and soon after the beginning of the nineteenth century the greater part of the tribe had probably abandoned permanent houses, had to a great extent lost attachment for certain particular localities, and had become wanderers, as they continued to be until the end of the Indian wars. Notwithstanding this change of habit, they still cultivated the ground and raised crops.

From the statements of the oldest Cheyennes, and from what we know of Indian character and ways, it is probable that at the time when some of their villages were permanently situated at certain points, a part of the Cheyennes were still pushing westward, and that the tribe was partly migratory and partly sedentary, some established in one place and some moving about. It is possible that the permanent villages on the Yellow

---

[16] Winchell, N. H., Habitations of the Sioux in Minnesota, *Wisconsin Archaeologist*, vol. VII, no. 4, p. 155.

Medicine River in Minnesota, and on the Sheyenne River in North Dakota, and perhaps others, were occupied during the same period, that even at this time there may have been a settlement of Cheyennes on the Missouri River, and that other groups may then have been wandering on the plains after the buffalo.

In the last of the eighteenth and in the early part of the nineteenth century, camps of the Cheyennes were found over a wide territory extending from west of the Black Hills to the Missouri River on the east, and from the Little Missouri River toward its mouth, south at least as far as the Arkansas River, and perhaps still farther. There is mention of Cheyennes in New Mexico before the beginning of the eighteenth century. Of this tribe, as of others, but—so far as I know—more of this tribe than of most others, it may be said that they were scattered over a very wide area.

As already noted, La Salle saw the Chaa (? Sharha) in 1680 when they told him that they lived about the head of the Great River. There is extant also a letter written by De Vargas, in May, 1695, in which he says that certain Apaches from the east, "who are called Chiyenes," had recently come to Santa Fé.[17] Just who these people may have been is uncertain. It is not said that they called themselves Chiyenes, but were called Chiyenes. The term Apache is said to signify enemy, a person not one of the Pueblo tribes and presumably hostile. Mr. F. W. Hodge believes the term was applied by the Spaniards of New Mexico to any non-sedentary tribe, one at enmity with Pueblo Indians and Spaniards alike. A common Spaniard term for hostile, or wild, Indians was *gentiles*.

Mr. Hodge thinks the Vargas reference to the Chiyenes not doubtful, and that he could not possibly be mistaken in the name. It may well be that even at that early date a party of Cheyennes had drifted far southwestward after buffalo. The Comanches made their appearance in New Mexico in 1700.

[17] Twitchell, New Mexican Archives, vol. 1, p. 265.

Carver, in 1766, mentions the Schians as found in the great camp that he visited on the Minnesota River. The Schianese, he says, live farther to the west. Nearly one hundred years later Riggs and Williamson repeat Sioux traditions which declared that in earlier times the Cheyennes had lived on the Minnesota River, but had moved westward.

Two points of permanent occupancy seem generally accepted: (1) the earth-lodge village on the Sheyenne River, a tributary of the Red River from the west, near the present Lisbon, in North Dakota, and (2) the two neighboring village sites on the Missouri passed by Lewis and Clark in October, 1804, which an Arikara chief told them were formerly occupied by the Cheyennes.

In the Smithsonian Report for 1871, Dr. Comfort describes his investigations into certain mounds which he found near Kettle Lakes, west of Lake Traverse, which he speaks of as made by the Cheyennes.

Disregarding the earliest and very vague traditions of the Cheyennes with regard to their most ancient wanderings, and treating Tsistsistas and Suhtai as a single group, we find that there still remain in the tribe accounts of a time when they lived on the borders of large lakes in a region which was wholly timbered. This country was presumably in the present state of Minnesota, or to the northeast of that. Later they speak of a blue water, or river, flowing through a "blue earth" country, near which they lived for a long time. This was perhaps the Minnesota River country.

Dr. T. S. Williamson[18] records among the "common and most reliable traditions" of the Sioux, one which states that when the ancestors of the Sioux first came to the Falls of St. Anthony the Iowas occupied the country about the mouth of the Minnesota River, and the Cheyennes dwelt higher up on the same stream. He states also that the Cheyennes formerly

[18] Minn. Hist. Soc. Colls., vol. I, p. 242.

VALLEY OF LAME DEER RIVER

TONGUE RIVER INDIAN AGENCY, MONTANA

planted on the Minnesota between the Blue Earth River and Lac qui Parle.

Writing about 1850, Dr. Riggs[19] says that "two hundred years ago or thereabouts the Cheyennes had a village near the Yellow Medicine River in Minnesota, where are yet visible old earth works; that from there they retired to a point between Big Stone Lake and Lake Traverse, where they had a village, and then moved to the south bend of the Sheyenne River, a tributary of the Red River of the north." This last village is the one near Lisbon, North Dakota. From the site on the Sheyenne River the Cheyennes are assumed to have moved toward the Missouri River, and when they reached it are said by Riggs to have had a village on the east side and afterward to have crossed the river and to have lived with or near the Mandans.

Dr. Comfort, in his account of Indian remains[20] (near Fort Wadsworth, west of Sisseton, South Dakota), speaks of the occupancy of the region by the Cheyennes as well known, and states that "the Cheyennes about one hundred years ago were dispossessed of the soil by the Dakotas." The village referred to by Dr. Comfort is not the Lake Traverse village said by Riggs to have been occupied next after that on the Yellow Medicine, but Comfort speaks (p. 398) of mounds and earthworks on the shores of Lake Traverse which might be the traditional site referred to by Riggs.

Rev. Dr. T. S. Williamson[21] says of the return of the Sioux to the Minnesota River, perhaps many years after their first visit:

The Cheyennes were then in the upper part of the valley; and near the Yellow Medicine a fortification is still plainly visible, which it is said was made by them near a good spring of water; and in 1853, when the first plowing for the Sioux was done in that region, large quantities of muscle shells were turned up near the remains of this fortification, indicating that the ground had been cultivated. The

[19] S. R. Riggs, contr. to *North American Ethnology*, vol. IX, p. 193.
[20] Smithsonian Report for 1871, p. 402, Washington, 1873.
[21] Minn. Hist. Soc. Colls., vol. III, p. 284.

Sioux who expelled the Iowas, a kindred race, made a league with the Cheyennes, who, though of a different origin, have ever been counted a part of the Dakota nation.

Of the settlement on the Yellow Medicine, Dr. Riggs says:

The excavation extends around three sides of a somewhat irregular square, the fourth being protected by the slope of the hill, which is now covered with timber. After the filling up of years, or perhaps centuries, the ditch is still about three feet deep. We found the east side in the middle of the ditch to measure thirty-eight paces, the south side sixty-two and the west side fifty. The north side is considerably longer than the south, the area enclosed is not far from half an acre. On each of the three excavated sides there was left a gateway of about two paces.[22]

An early reference to the village on the Sheyenne River appeared in 1863, from the pen of the same author.[23] He says:

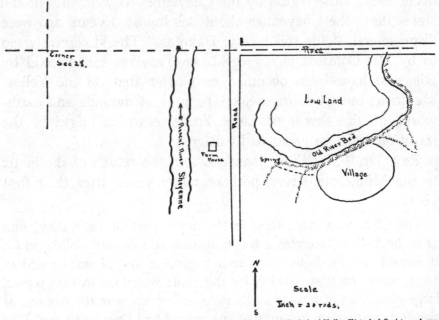

Cheyenne Village Site. Described by Geo. F. Will, *Proceedings Mississippi Valley Historical Society*, vol. VII.

[22] Minn. Hist. Soc. Colls., vol. I, p. 119.
[23] *St. Paul Daily Press*, August 5, 1863.

The village stood on the southeast side [of the river] on a high piece of land abutting on a swale which contains springs of living water. More than fifty years have passed since its abandonment by the Cheyennes, but the fortifications are all easily traced. The ditch that encircled the village proper is now, in places, three feet deep. It terminates at either end at the bluff bank, and is the shape of a half-moon, a little gibbous. It includes between two and three acres of ground. This place was thickly settled with houses. Some sixty or seventy of these houses stood inside the fortifications. Then outside the city were suburban residences, but they were not sunk into the ground nearly so much as those on the inside.

In 1850 the stream on which this village site stands was still called by the Sioux *Shā ī' ē na wo jŭ' pĭ*, "Where the Cheyennes Plant."

Later Dr. Riggs wrote:

Dakota tradition says that it was for a great many years successfully defended by the Cheyennes against the hostile Sioux, that many bloody battles were fought there, the Sioux often being driven back with great slaughter.

In a periodical entitled *The Monthly South Dakotan* (vol. II, no. 4, August, 1899) is a description of the village by the Hon. A. L. Van Osdel of the Sibley Expedition of 1863—the one that Dr. Riggs accompanied. The account possesses a certain interest, but apparently the writer has endeavored to make it vivid by suggesting that the site had been recently abandoned. In fact, in one place he says: "Several old dirt lodges were still standing, delapidated and in the lost [*sic*] stages of decay. These old structures were built in a circular form and were from fifteen to twenty feet in diameter." Interesting, however, is the fact that this writer has hit upon the truth as to the enemies with whom the Cheyennes fought, and declares that the battles of those who formerly occupied this place were with the Assiniboine Sioux. This he repeats more than once, and in this he is right, for the fighting of the Cheyennes was with the Assiniboine Sioux, and not with any other Sioux.

The village on the Yellow Medicine was of small extent and could have been occupied by only a small number of people. One-half an acre of land—Dr. Riggs' estimate—would have

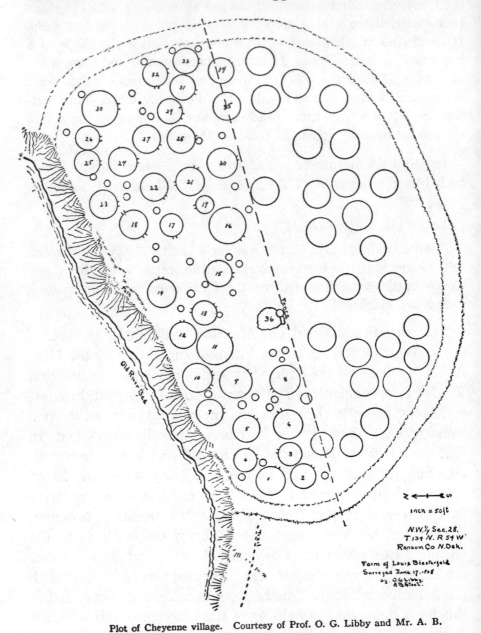

Plot of Cheyenne village.   Courtesy of Prof. O. G. Libby and Mr. A. B. Stout.

held but a few lodges. The village on the Sheyenne River was much larger, yet its 60 or 70 lodges would hardly have housed more than 500 or 600 inhabitants.

Dr. Riggs and Dr. Williamson seem to assume that the different village sites in Minnesota and North Dakota were occupied successively, but I believe that this was not the case. It seems more probable that several of the various villages were occupied at the same time and were merely different permanent, if scattered, camps or villages of distinct bands of Cheyennes, just as, a few generations ago, different sections of the Pawnee tribe occupied their permanent villages at distances one from another in portions of Kansas and Nebraska.

Although, so far as known, the Cheyennes were never a large tribe, yet as long ago as 1820 Morse[24] gave their numbers as about thirty-five hundred, and this did not include the Suhtai, then not identified with the Cheyennes. In none of the known settlements of the Cheyennes east of the Missouri River could such a number of people have been accommodated.

I have no doubt that for a long time a number of contemporary Cheyenne villages were scattered along the Minnesota River and to the westward, and that some of these, after they had been occupied for a generation or two, were abandoned and new locations sought. At all events the trend of tribal movement was westward, and this at last brought the Cheyennes to the Missouri River.

In the movement of a group of Indians, a camp or village followed its own ideas as to where it wished to go, and usually did not consider the movements of other camps. It moved independently. There was no contemporaneous tribal migration. The different camps did not unite in a forward movement. The trend of the tribal movement being westward, a group moved on, established itself at a point, and remained there for a time —perhaps for many years, perhaps for a generation or two.

[24] Report to the Secretary of War of the United States on Indian Affairs, pp. 251, 254, 366, New Haven, 1822.

Later, some village behind it moved forward, passed the first village and stopped somewhere beyond. The gradual westward progress consisted of a succession of such movements, the tail of the long procession often becoming the head, and the different camps or villages moving on successively and passing each other. Since for all the people the important question was that of subsistence, it is evident that when a place was found especially favorable for the procuring of food, the camp would remain there longer than it would in a place where subsistence was less easily had—would be likely to remain, in fact, until food became difficult to obtain. Thus in the tribal movement westward the rearmost camps of the migrating Cheyennes were constantly moving onward and passing those in advance of them.

Most early writers who mention the Cheyennes speak of them as having been driven southwest by the Sioux, but I believe that these statements are due to misunderstanding. Although Lewis and Clark, 1804, the Rev. Mr. Riggs, 1850 or thereabouts, and W. P. Clark, 1884, all repeat the same story, I am convinced that it is misleading. Long-continued inquiry among the Cheyennes reveals no account of any wars with those tribes which we commonly called Sioux—that is, the southern branches of the Dakota group. Carver speaks of the Cheyennes as camped in 1766 with the Nadouwessi of the Plains; Trudeau, 1795, speaks of Sioux as associated with the Cheyennes; and Henry, 1806, speaks of Sioux and Arapahoes as in company with the Cheyennes when they visited the Hidatsa to make a binding peace with them. The western Sioux today declare that they have always been friends of the Cheyennes, and Rev. T. S. Williamson says, as previously stated, that the Cheyennes "have ever since [their first meeting] been counted a part of the Dakota nation." John Hay,[25] in his notes on Capt. Mackay's Journal, writing of the years 1794 and

25 Extracts from Capt. Mackay's Journal and others, Proceedings State Historical Society, Wisconsin, 1915, Separate no. 171, p. 208.

1795, says that the Cheyennes, or Shayen,—who formerly lived on the tributary of the Red River of that name,—"were so harassed by the Assiniboine and Sious" that they had to leave their village and go to the Missouri River.

The Hohe—the Assiniboines—however, are constantly spoken of by the Cheyennes as enemies, and inquiry among the Yankton, Hunkpatina, and Teton Sioux, now settled on the Missouri River in North Dakota and South Dakota, seems to show a general agreement that the Assiniboines were their enemies also, while the Cheyennes were their friends. The Assiniboines used to make war journeys against Sioux and Cheyennes alike. This hostility is spoken of by Henry in 1806. I believe that the Cheyenne tradition of their being driven south refers to early attacks on them by the Assiniboines, perhaps in company at first with the Crees and later with the Ojibwa. That there may have been occasional individual quarrels between Cheyennes and Sioux and between Cheyennes and Mandans is possible and even likely, but I believe nothing in the nature of a general war.

Through Dr. A. McG. Beede, of Fort Yates, North Dakota, I learned that the Teton Sioux, now allotted and scattered over the Standing Rock Indian Reservation, declare that on the west bank of the Missouri River, not far from Fort Yates, there were formerly two Cheyenne villages, and with Dr. Beede I visited these sites.

The more northerly of the two is situated on a bluff above the Missouri River on the south side of Porcupine Creek, less than five miles north of Fort Yates. The village has been partly destroyed by the Missouri River, which has undermined the bank and carried away some of the house rings, but many remain. A few are still seen as the raised borders of considerable earth lodges, the rings about the central hollow being from twelve to fifteen inches above the surrounding soil, and the hollows noticeably deep; usually, however, the situation of the house is indicated merely by a slight hollow and by the peculiar character of the grass growing on the house site. The house rings nearest both Porcupine Creek and the Missouri River stand on the bank immediately above the water, and some of those on the Porcupine may also have been undermined and carried away by that stream when in flood.

This settlement must have been large. It stands on a flat which slopes slightly toward the river, and the houses were close together. Many of them were large, one being sixty feet in diameter. Besides the large houses there were many smaller ones, probably occupied by small families, by old people living alone, or used as menstrual lodges, or perhaps even for dogs. We counted more than seventy large house sites, taking no account of the small ones. The houses extend several hundred yards back from the river, that is, toward the west, and 150 or 200 yards north and south. It is probable that once they were much more numerous, and they may even have extended a long way down the river. Two miles below are evidences of another village, said by the Sioux also to have been a Cheyenne village. On the site of this last old village, many years ago, a group of Standing Rock Sioux built a number of log houses, the foundations of which have largely obliterated the evidences of the earlier Cheyenne village. This log-house village was known locally as "Slobtown."

On the gently rising land to the west of the Porcupine village the Cheyennes are said to have planted their corn, as also on the flats on the north side of the Porcupine River. The village site now stands on the farm of Yellow Lodge, a Yankton Sioux, who stated that he had always been told by the old people that this was a Cheyenne village, and that in plowing he had often turned up pottery from the ground. Most of this pottery was broken, but he had found some pots that were perfect. He had turned up also glass beads, which he described as like the charms or beads which we know the Cheyennes used to manufacture—in later times perhaps from pounded glass like those said to have been made by the Mandans.

In company with Dr. Beede, I visited the village site at the farm school, less than fifteen miles south of Fort Yates, said by the Sioux to be of Cheyenne origin. This is just over the boundary line between North Dakota and South Dakota, perhaps three miles south of the mouth of Blackfoot Creek and a mile below what I suppose to be Eagle Feather Creek. It is east and a little north of the Cheyenne Hills.[26] Just above Blackfoot Creek and on the state boundary line is an old village site with three mounds and many house sites, said by the Sioux to be Mandan.

The farm school buildings are in the middle of the old Cheyenne village. To the south and southeast of the school are a dozen or twenty house rings, and to the north, close along the river, are others. Within the boundaries of the school are three low mounds. From one of these, excavated to make a root cellar, a considerable quantity of pottery fragments were thrown out. On another mound stands the Roman Catholic Chapel; and a low mound almost within the school enclosure is partly occupied by one of the office buildings of the school. Here were found a few pieces of pottery, one of them ornamented.

This village was large, and the way in which the houses at its border were placed suggests that attacks by enemies were not anticipated. The cultivation of the soil, the erection of the school buildings, and the westward movement of the Missouri River, which continually undermines the high bank and causes it to drop into the river, have greatly reduced the area of the village.

The Sioux told of a Cheyenne village site on Grand River about seven miles below the post office of Bull Head, and near the camp where Sitting Bull was killed in 1890. The Sioux and Cheyenne name for Grand River signifies Ree River.[27] Old

[26] See War Dept. map, Capts. D. P. Heap and William Ludlow, 1875, and sectional map of South Dakota, Rand, McNally & Co., Chicago, 1889.
[27] War Dept. map, Capts. D. P. Heap and William Ludlow, 1875.

Cheyennes used to tell of the days when the Cheyennes camped on the river of Big Round Rocks—the Cannonball—and of when they lived on the Ree River, *Onō' ni o' hē.*

There is still extant among the Cheyennes a song in which Ree River is mentioned. A young girl fond of a boy sings a song asking him if he intends to go to Ree River to marry. It is supposed that the boy was in the habit of leaving his home camp where lived the girl who made the song, to visit the village on Ree River, and she suspected that he was fond of some girl in that village.

There was no difficulty in finding the village site on the north side of Grand River, a mile or a mile and a half below Sitting Bull's camp. Here were a few house rings, within one of which was a hollow,—a cache which had fallen in,—and a few hundred yards farther down the river, on a higher bench, many more house sites, some of them forty feet in diameter. They were often overgrown with low bushes. The village was large and the houses ran back nearly a half mile from the river. Sometimes they stood close together, and the general plan of the village reminded me much of the old Pawnee village on the Loup River in Nebraska. On a sandy ridge near the river bank were found a number of large caches, apparently distant from any house sites. Some of these occurred in pairs—two deep holes rather close together. According to Sioux tradition some of the lodges here were so large that the Cheyennes took their horses into their houses at night for protection.

The account given by Mackenzie[28] of his visit to the Cheyenne camp south of the Hidatsa in 1806—although he says nothing as to the direction in which he traveled on his way to that camp—mentions crossing the "Clearwater," Heart, and Cannonball rivers, and suggests that the Cheyenne camp of 220 lodges that he visited was on what we know as Grand

[28] Les Bourgeois de la Compagnie du Nord-Ouest, 1st Ser., p. 376, Quebec, 1889.

River. In 1811, the Astorians[29] under Mr. Hunt found on "Big River"—*i.e.*, Grand River—a large camp of Cheyennes.

Sioux tradition declares that the village on the Porcupine River was established about 1733 or a little earlier, perhaps 1730; they fix the date as about one hundred years before the star fell—1833. It was occupied for fifty years or more, and then the people abandoned it and moved over to a point on Grand River twenty miles above its mouth. The date of the removal is given as about the time of the great flood at this point, which, it is said, took place about 1784. The Cheyenne village remained on Grand River for a long time, probably as late as 1840, for Red Hail, a Sioux (born 1833), often told Dr. Beede of visiting the village as a small boy, six or eight years of age, and eating green corn there.

The Cheyennes who settled on the Porcupine are said by the Sioux to have been the first of the tribe to reach the Missouri River at that point, though long before this there were Cheyennes west of the Missouri. The story is that they came from some village described as being on the Minnesota River, near where Mankato now is, near the mouth of Blue Earth near the old Sioux Crossing,—Traverse des Sioux,—perhaps in the locality referred to by Williamson and Riggs. At that old village, according to Sioux tradition, there are mounds built by the Cheyennes, and there they raised their crops.

From this Minnesota home these Cheyennes had journeyed westward, had passed by the Cheyenne village on the Sheyenne River, and gone beyond that to a small flat on the headwaters of Maple Creek, west and a little south of the present town of Kulm, North Dakota.[30] At that point—near Kulm—they had built a village and had lived there for a few years. Dr. Beede tells me that he has seen there the remains of houses and some

---

[29] Irving, Astoria, vol. II, p. 69, London, 1836.

[30] General Sully marched over this ground in 1863, and in September fought the battle of Whitestone Hills not far from where Kulm now stands.

small mounds. This village was soon abandoned and they moved on westward.

Some time after the Cheyennes had established their village on Porcupine Creek—still according to Sioux tradition—another group of Cheyennes made their appearance on the Missouri River, crossed it to the village of their friends on Porcupine Creek, remained there for a time, and after no very long stay moved south to a point a short distance south of the present North Dakota and South Dakota boundary line, where they established a village a little up-river and northeast of the Cheyenne Hills—the farm school Cheyenne village, which the Sioux call the Cheyenne Plantings. This group of Cheyennes is said to have been the one that long occupied the village on the Sheyenne River, near the present Lisbon, North Dakota. It is possible that these Sheyenne River Cheyennes may have built and for a time occupied the village two miles below the Porcupine on the site of which "Slobtown"—already referred to—was afterward built. They lived at the Cheyenne Plantings —the farm school site—for about twenty-five years, and then moved up Grand River to Dirt Lodge Creek, where they built a village of earth houses. This is some distance west of the point on Grand River where the Cheyennes of the Porcupine River settled.

The winter count of Blue Thunder, a Sioux historian still alive, records that it was 127 years ago, or in 1795, that the Cheyennes left the farm school village and moved up to Dirt Lodge Creek. The Sioux say that the Cheyenne village, near the present Lisbon, had been there for a long time, and the village was very old. It had often been unsuccessfully attacked.

According to Sioux traditions there was a Cheyenne village on the east bank of the Missouri River, opposite the farm school village and one on the Little Cheyenne River in South Dakota, near the former town of Forest City. This settlement on the Little Cheyenne, referred to by Riggs,[31] is one of the

---

[31] Contr. to *North American Ethnology*, vol. IX, p. 194.

many places still known to the Sioux by the name of *Shā hī'-ēn a wō jū*. It was occupied for a long time, and from it the people moved south. Old Sioux today talk about the village near Forest City, opposite the present Cheyenne River Indian Agency,—*i.e.*, on the Little Cheyenne River—and of the fences, made of sticks set up in the ground criss-cross, and filled in with brush and weeds, which enclosed the corn-fields at that place. Of late years, if a Sioux builds a fence where the carelessly set posts lean—are not upright—or are placed too close together, the Sioux in derision say it is like the fence about Shahienawoju, referring to this old village on the Little Cheyenne. (See Appendix A.)

It seems probable that the last of the Cheyennes left the Missouri River and moved west toward the Black Hills more recently than is generally believed. They were at the mouth of White River not long before the advent of Lewis and Clark, and there planted near their village corn and tobacco, which they returned to harvest at the beginning of the autumn.[32]

This was precisely the method of the Pawnees. They planted and cultivated their corn in the spring and early summer, and then set out on the summer buffalo hunt, from which in early autumn they returned to harvest the crop. It was perhaps mere accident that Lewis and Clark did not come upon an occupied Cheyenne village.

Near the end of the eighteenth century—if we may believe Cheyenne accounts and confirmatory traditions of the Sioux—several Cheyenne and Suhtai villages were still occupied along the great river and its tributaries.

In the year 1877 Little Chief's band of Cheyennes, while being taken south, was for some time detained at Fort Lincoln, North Dakota, and among them were the mother of old Elk River and part of her family. During their stay at Fort Lincoln,

[32] Perrin du Lac, Voyage dans les deux Louisianes, etc., Paris and Lyon, 1805, p. 259: "Sement pres de leur village du mais et du tabac, qu'ils viennent recolter au commencement de l'automne."

this old woman took her daughter-in-law and granddaughter[33] about to various localities not far from the post, and with laughter and tears pointed out to them the well-known places where, as a girl, she had played and worked. She said that at the time of which she then told, her group of Cheyennes lived in a permanent village on the east bank of the Missouri River and planted there. In the large houses of this village, the grandmother said, there were often a considerable number of people —two or three or four families. The small house circles seen in the villages were where menstrual lodges had stood, or those occupied by old women who lived alone, as often they did when they were old, and believed that they had not long to live. Elk River was a Suhtai.

White Bull, a Northern Cheyenne (born 1834), declares that in 1832, when High Backed Wolf, Limber Lance, and Bull Head returned from Washington—the first Cheyenne delegation to visit the seat of government—the Cheyennes were still farming on and near the Missouri, and this confirms the Sioux tradition. It was soon after the death of High Backed Wolf in 1833[34] that an increasing number of the Missouri River Cheyennes began to take to a wandering life and some of them to go south. Up to this time many Cheyennes and many Suhtai were planting on the Missouri River. The different camps of Cheyennes, and of Suhtai, were sometimes on one side of the Missouri River and sometimes on the other. Yet, according to Cheyenne and Sioux tradition, there were Cheyennes far west of the Missouri River 150 years before that time.

The original map sent back by Lewis and Clark in 1805, and

---

[33] This daughter-in-law and granddaughter I knew well. The granddaughter is living.

[34] Donaldson in his Catalog of the Catlin Indian Gallery says, p. 88, that Catlin painted Wolf on the hill—High Backed Wolf—in 1834, but this appears to be an error. Donaldson's map of Catlin's routes does not agree with this date. The Cheyennes, including High Backed Wolf's two daughters, say that he died in 1833, and fix the date by the star shower of that year. They knew that High Backed Wolf had been painted by Catlin. It used to be said that the stars fell from the sky because of the death of so important a man.

perhaps quite forgotten until unearthed by the late Arnold Hague and published in *Science,* November 4, 1887, shows Cheyennes, Suhtai, Kiowas, Kiowa-Apaches, and Comanches all scattered about the Black Hills, camped in localities where they might have been in Verendrye's time.

Much of the information shown on this map concerning territory away from the route of travel along the Missouri River came from Indian and early Spanish and French trader sources, but the map is remarkably accurate so far as the region east of the Rocky Mountains is concerned. So far as it goes, it confirms statements made by the Cheyennes and other tribes of the traditional recent entry of the Dakotas into the Plains country. The map is dotted with names of tribes, but north of the Platte River, except for the Poncarars on the head of the Niobrara, no Dakota names seem to be found west of the Missouri River, though there are a number on that stream. The Brulé Sioux were on the Missouri between the mouth of White River and the Teton, and the Okandandas Sioux just below the mouth of the Cheyenne River. There were other tribes of the Dakotas on the river farther up toward the Cannonball, but most of the Sioux were still on tributaries of the Mississippi.

On the head of the North Fork of the Cheyenne River, that is to say, north and west of the Black Hills, were the Cheyennes, a group of *Nĭ′ mou sĭn* (Comanches), a camp of *Do′ ta īne* (Kiowas), a group of *Ca ta′ ka* (Kiowa-Apaches), while on the heads of the South Fork of the Cheyenne River and White River were the *Staĭ′ tan,* or Kites (?), the Suhtai.

On the tributaries of the North Platte, or at its head, were two camps of Arapahoes, and a little south of them, another camp of Kiowas. In other words, according to the earlier maps and the independent testimony of the Indians met with by Lewis and Clark, there were few Sioux west of the Missouri River, which is just what all the oldest Cheyennes have declared.

The Assiniboines, who were then the westernmost of the Dakotas, seem to have been on the north side of the Missouri River, along the Assiniboine River and its tributaries, and the White Earth River, while north of them were the Crees.

Not a few traditions exist among the Cheyennes of the first appearance of Sioux immigrants toward the Black Hills country. One of the early meetings told of was at some point on the plains west of the Missouri River. A party of Cheyennes met a party of Sioux, but each group was suspicious of the other and they did not approach closely, but at a distance talked by signs. From each party, at the request of the other, an arrow was shot over, which, taken back to the home village, should bear witness to the truth of the statements made by each. This comes from White Frog (born 1840), and the story was told by his grandfather, who died before White Frog was born, said to have been one hundred years old—so old, according to the accounts, that for a long time before his death he was too feeble to walk. These Sioux were met, according to the statement, when the grandfather was a young man, about twenty years of age. This would make the date of meeting about 1760.

On another occasion a small party of Sioux, poor and on foot, were discovered by some Cheyennes. There was much discussion as to whether they should be allowed to come into the camp or should be killed, but since they carried a buffalo head, which represented food, it was finally decided to receive them as friends.

The Sioux remained with the Cheyennes for some months and when they went away the Cheyennes gave them two colts, for the Cheyennes then had a few horses; not everyone in the camp had a horse, but here and there a man had one or two.

The Sioux were not seen again for two or three years. Then they returned to the Cheyenne camp, and with them came a few more Sioux. They stayed for a time and were given more colts.

After that they began to come in greater numbers. They are

A FASHION OF OLD-TIME DRESS

supposed to have gone back to their village in the East and reported there, "We have found a tribe of people who have animals that they can ride and that carry things on their backs, while we have only dogs and must walk, and ourselves carry our possessions."

This tradition was commonly known by all old Cheyennes twenty years ago, and has been told me by such men as Old Little Chief, Spotted Wolf, Bull Thigh, Iron Shirt, and others, —all men born in the early years of the nineteenth century.

CONTACT WITH THE WHITES

The Cheyenne tradition of their first meeting with the whites is vague as to time and place. The usual account is substantially that given by Clark.[35] Once long ago a man in a starving condition wandered into the camp. When they saw him, the people said to one another, "This is one of the persons that Sweet Medicine told us we should meet," for the man had hair all over his face and his skin was white. The Cheyennes took him into a lodge, gave him food and clothing, and nursed him back to health. He remained with them for a long time—so long that he learned to speak their language—and explained that he had been with two or three other men in a boat which had upset and that his companions had been lost. He told them that his home was far off toward the sunrise and that he wished to return to it, but he said, "Some day I will come back and will bring you things that will be useful to you."

The man went away, and one day, a long time afterward, the people heard a noise like thunder—the report of a gun. Everyone went out from the camp in the direction from which the sound came to see what it was, and there they saw, coming, this white man and others with him. He had with him guns, knives, flint-and-steel, needles, and many other things which he gave them in exchange for skins.

[35] Indian Sign Language, p. 98.

With pieces of iron that he brought, he made arrowpoints which they at once saw were better than theirs of stone or bone, so that all who could procure it used the iron for arrowpoints. With these arrows they could kill animals much more easily than with those made of stone. They, therefore, threw away their stone points.

This man who had first come among them remained with the Cheyennes until he became old, and at last he died. Sometimes he made journeys to the east and took back with him in a boat the furs for which he traded. Of the first white men that came among them some, they say, could write, but they did not write on paper, but on a black rock—no doubt slate. Some of the old men have heard that this first white man was a Spaniard. There is no hint as to whence he came, nor of the situation of the camp that he reached.

Another account says that the first Frenchman came to the Cheyennes where they were farming on the Missouri River. Some say that this was at the mouth of the Cheyenne River. This man is said to have carried his property on a sort of low two-wheeled cart, all tied up with rawhide and with solid wheels. The rims of the wheels were wrapped with rawhide. The cart made a loud squeaking or screaming noise, and was hauled by dogs. Long before the man arrived they heard a loud sharp sound, and wondered what it was. When the man reached them they made signs to him, asking what caused this strange noise. He pointed to a long stick—a gun—that he held in his hand, and indicated that this made the noise. They asked him to do it again, and he loaded the gun and fired a shot, and some of the children and women and men thought it was the thunder and fell down on the ground. All were much frightened and ran away. The man remained with them for a time and then went away, saying that he would return. He did come back, but in a boat. They looked down the river and could see the flag and the boat under it, coming very slowly.

Standing All Night stated that in his early days most of the

Sioux were still east of the Missouri, and that it was from that direction also that the Arapahoes had originally come. He said too that once on the other (east) side of the Missouri he and some other Cheyennes met two white men—people with fair faces and with beards. When they saw them, the Indians were frightened and ran away, for they thought that they must be mysterious people, who perhaps had come out from the ground or out of a hill. The white men motioned to them to approach, but the Indians ran off and moved their camp away from the locality. In other words, these particular Indians had not before seen white men.

Elk River believed that the first white men the Cheyennes saw were the French, *Mai vĭ' hĭo,* "red white men." They were good friends to the Cheyennes. It was from the French that they got their first guns.

Cheyenne tradition, known to all the older men, declares that in early days, probably long before the Cheyennes met the French, wandering Mexicans were accustomed to make frequent journeys north to trade with all the northern Indians, who at that time lived about the Black Hills—Kiowa, Comanche, Cheyenne, Crow, and Arapaho. These Mexicans went as far north as Tongue River and the neighborhood of the Big Horn Mountains. The *ciboleros,* or buffalo hunters, spoken of in books on the early West, were no doubt the last of these. They brought with them for trade, the Cheyennes tell us, a certain dry, hard bread, of which the Indians were very fond, salt, arrowshafts, bows and partly manufactured bows, and sheet iron for arrowpoints. Indeed, many of the oldest men among the Northern Cheyennes believe that it was from these Mexicans that the Cheyennes procured their first metal arrowpoints. The dog-drawn cart before referred to is quite suggestive of a diminutive *carro* of New Mexico in earlier days.

The articles brought by the Mexicans were exchanged for dried meat, parfleche, robes, back-rests, moccasins, and various other things, which the Indians had in abundance. It was from

one of these Mexican traders that the so-called "iron shirt"—
a coat of mail—was obtained by an Arapaho or a Flathead and
finally passed into the possession of the Cheyennes, who retained it until the year 1852, when Alights On The Cloud, who
was then wearing it, was killed and the shirt was captured by
the Pawnees and destroyed.[36]

Alexander Henry the Younger,[37] in speaking of the Cheyennes at the time of his visit to the Mandans, July, 1806, says,
"Many of the European dresses I saw were of Spanish manufacture." He says also that "last fall two Spaniards came up
the river which runs to the S. in a wooden canoe or a boat,
loaded with goods, who passed the winter among them, disposed of all their property, and sold very cheap, giving a large
double handful of gunpowder and 50 balls for one beaver."
The river that runs to the south was perhaps the Platte River.

The French had been meeting the Cheyennes in the Black
Hills country long before the advent of Lewis and Clark. Margry gives a letter[38] stating that a certain Frenchman had gone
with the Pawnees to visit the Arikaras before 1734, that he had
found mines there, and was likely to return for further investigation. If this Frenchman went to the Arikaras, he no doubt
saw the Cheyennes, and he or some one of his companions may
have been the Frenchman spoken of by the Verendryes as
being in the country which they reached.[39] It may well be that
when the Verendryes passed southwest from the Mandan village they met the Cheyennes, though this is suggested merely
by the name *Gens du Serpent* in the Verendrye account given
to a tribe not then identified. After the Cheyennes, or a portion
of them, had moved out on the plains toward the Black Hills
and the Little Missouri, they met in that region the Comanches,
whom they called Snake men (*Shǐ shǐ nǐ wī hē' tǎnǐu*), an

[36] The Fighting Cheyennes, p. 75, N. Y., 1915.
[37] Henry, New Light on the Early History of the Greater Northwest,
Coues ed., vol. I, pp. 383-384.
[38] Margry, Découvertes, vol. VI, p. 453.
[39] Margry, *ibid.*, p. 608.

equivalent of the Verendryes' *Gens du Serpent,* made unmistakable by the sign for snake.

The Cheyennes use the name *Sŭs' so ni* for the mountain tribe called by the whites Snakes or Shoshonis. They recognize their close relationship to the Comanches but call them by a different name. Lewis and Clark called the Comanches *Gens du Serpent.*

Mr. Will believes[40] that the Verendryes met the Cheyennes, who he intimates were the *Gens de la flèche collée,* which he says was the name commonly used for the Cheyennes by the French. I have not understood this to be the case.

The Verendryes had no interpreter and probably communicated with the Indians by signs, and evidently the sign for a particular tribe would be common to all tribes of the region. The Cheyennes, Kiowas, and Arapahoes all apply an equivalent of the name "Snakes" to the Comanches. The term as denotive of enemies or an enemy people was employed by many Algonquian tribes, and may have that meaning here.

Lewis and Clark speak of the French as with the Cheyennes in the Black Hills. John Valle, who wintered on the Chien River, under the Black Mountains,[41] was familiar with the region and described the animals found there and some of the birds. Lewis and Clark hired "a Canadian Frenchman who had been with the Cheyenne Ind. on the Cote Noir last summer descended thence the Little Missouri"—Baptiste Le Page, who took the place of Newman, who had been discharged.

Perrin du Lac saw Cheyennes at the mouth of the White River in 1802, and says that most of them had never seen a white man, yet the French had been with some of the camps for years. He speaks of them as wanderers, but says that they sow near their village maize and tobacco, which they harvest in autumn. I have already referred to Indian testimony that about the beginning of the last century there were Cheyenne villages along the Missouri River in the present North Dakota and

[40] *American Anthropologist,* vol. xix, p. 291.
[41] Lewis and Clark, Orig. Journ., vol. i, p. 176.

South Dakota, and to the testimony of a daughter of Elk River, whose grandmother, born about 1786, pointed out to her, in 1877, places not far from the mouth of Heart River, where in the grandmother's girlhood her people had cultivated their crops.

One of the early Frenchmen among the Cheyennes, whom he called Chaguiennes, was Jean Baptiste Trudeau,[42] who was among the Arikaras in 1795, and whose trading house, "the House of Troodo where he wintered in '96," mentioned by Lewis and Clark, and later by Chittenden, was situated on the left bank of the Missouri River, a little above and opposite the site of Fort Randall.

Early in July three Cheyennes came to Trudeau, reporting to him that the Kiowas, the Arapahoes, and Pitapahotoes were camped near their village, and that these three men had come on to investigate the report that strange white men with much powder and merchandise had come to the Arikaras. Trudeau says that these Cheyennes came from a village called Ouify (Ouisay), or Omissis. A little later, Trudeau sent back the Cheyenne messengers with tobacco and presents for the inquiring tribes as evidence that the white man was actually there.

Trudeau's mention of the Kiowas as camped on the Cheyenne River, and as coming in a wholly friendly way to the Arikara village, is complete confirmation—if that were needed —of the Cheyenne tradition of the existence of the Kiowas at the beginning of the nineteenth century in the country between the Missouri River and the Black Hills, while the Lewis and Clark map and statements of Perrin du Lac[43] as to the battle of the Cheyennes with the Halitanes, in what is perhaps the same region, confirm similar statements as to the Comanches.

Lewis and Clark speak of the Cheyennes as very shy and unwilling to have to do with the whites, and state that one head

42 Proceedings Missouri Historical Society, vol. IV, p. 46, 1912.
43 Perrin du Lac, Travels through Two Louisianas, p. 72, London, 1807.

man, to whom a medal had been given, after a time returned it, being afraid to keep it.

Old men among the Cheyennes have always declared that they have been told that, when the whites first came into their country, the chiefs advised all their people to have nothing to do with the newcomers, but to avoid them, and that usually this instruction had been followed. This may perhaps refer to the prophecy made by the culture hero, *Mot si i u*, who, when he left his people, warned them that only harm would come to them by association with the whites. A few years later, however, the Cheyennes had become somewhat accustomed to seeing white people.

A group of Cheyennes was met by Major Long's expedition to the Rocky Mountains in 1819-1820, and by Glen's trading camp, as noted in the diary of Jacob Fowler. They were living in association with a mixed camp of Arapahoes, Comanches, Kiowas, Kiowa-Apaches, and other Indians; and according to their own statements and those of Bijeau, one of Major Long's interpreters, they had been with these bands for at least three years prior to 1820.

Inquiry among the Southern Cheyennes fails to identify this band. All the oldest Southern Cheyenne men and women declare positively that no Cheyenne ever lived south of the Platte prior to 1826, and that it was in that year that the Cheyennes and Arapahoes began to move south to the Platte to live. Left Hand Bull, who was eighty-four years of age in 1900, and so was born about 1816, said that when he was small, "just a little boy," the Cheyennes and Arapahoes were living in the Black Hills, when thirty or forty lodges of Gros Ventres and twenty of Blackfeet came down from the North and joined them. These Blackfeet were a war-party on their way to steal horses from the Kiowas and Comanches. He saw the Blackfeet march through the camp in a long line, singing a song to the effect that they knew better how to go to war than anyone else. They kept on south and took a large herd of horses from the

Kiowas and Comanches. This made the Cheyennes and Arapahoes jealous, and soon afterward the Arapahoes and part of the Cheyennes moved down to the Platte and began to make raids on the Kiowas and Comanches. Left Hand Bull fixed the date of this movement to the Platte as 1826. The Cheyennes who went south with the Arapahoes at this time were mostly Hair Rope people (*He'v a tan iu*), and their leaders were Yellow Wolf, Medicine Snake, and Afraid Of Beavers. The Cheyennes are said to have met the Bent brothers on one of their first expeditions south, and the building of Bent's Fort on the Arkansas in Colorado resulted from this meeting, said to have been in 1827. Except for the building of that fort the movement of the Cheyennes toward the Arkansas would probably have been much slower than it was.

Black Moccasin (born about 1807) is reported to have stated that these northern Indians, the Gros Ventres and a few Blackfeet, joined the Cheyennes and Arapahoes near the Black Hills, and that a few years later they left the Cheyennes and Arapahoes on the Platte and returned north. It may be noted also that the Cheyennes state that the Gros Ventres were camped with the Cheyennes and Arapahoes at the time when the Crows came down there to make peace with the Cheyennes after the great Crow battle about 1820.[44] As recently as 1890 I found among the Southern Cheyennes two men of Blackfeet blood who had married Cheyenne women, and were living in the Cheyenne camp. This suggests that notwithstanding the more or less frequent wars between the two tribes, some friendly intercourse was occasionally kept up between Cheyennes and Blackfeet. The Arapahoes and Atsena came together at frequent intervals.

The oldest Northern Cheyennes, however, have stated that in early days some camps of their people were accustomed to procure British and American goods at the Arikara and Mandan villages on the Missouri, and to make journeys west and

[44] The Fighting Cheyennes, p. 29, and Bent letters to George Hyde.

south to meet the Arapahoes, Kiowas, and other Indians to barter their goods for horses and Spanish goods from the south. One such story especially tells of a camp that went south to the Arkansas River at the beginning of the last century, and sounds very much like the account quoted below as given by James. At all events among the Northern Cheyennes up to recent times there has been a clear memory of such early trading journeys by their people, in large parties or small. It appears also that some of the French traders of those times had the confidence and even the affection of some of the young Indians. Elk River used to tell of two young men who, against all the persuasions of their tribe, joined a party of white traders and went away with them, and were not seen for years. Later, still with the traders, they returned to the tribe and were urged to abandon their white friends and to remain permanently with the tribe. The young men refused to do so, declaring that the whites had treated them well and that they preferred to live with them. These two young men went away with the whites and never returned.

At another time three other Cheyennes went off with French traders and never came back to stay, though once or twice they returned in company with the traders. One of these men was named Hair Newly Cut—the name referring to the ancient practice by the Cheyennes of cutting all the hair off the head except a little on the top.[45]

James' narrative of Long's expedition to the Rocky Mountains gives us the first definite account of the Cheyennes south of the North Platte River. The narrative seems to refer back to the year 1815, though the date is variously given as winter of 1814-1815, 1815, and 1816. The story was told James by the interpreter Bijeau, who had been one of the trappers of the Chouteau and DeMun party in 1816-1817. This man, Joseph

[45] A custom perhaps borrowed from the Sioux. See Carver, Travels, p. 226, London, 1778.

Bissonet, signed an affidavit made by some of Chouteau and DeMun's men in St. Louis, September, 1817.

James says:

About four years previous to the time of our visit there had been a large encampment of Indians and hunters on this creek [Grand Camp Creek]. On that occasion three nations of Indians, namely Kiawas, Arrapahoes and Kaskaias or Bad-Hearts, had been assembled together, with forty-five French hunters in the employ of Mr. Choteau and Mr. DeMun of St. Louis. They had assembled for the purpose of holding a trading council with a band of Shiennes. These last had been recently supplied with goods by the British traders on the Missouri and had come to exchange them with the former for horses. The Kiawas, Arrapahoes, &c. who wander in the fertile plains of the Arkansa and Red [i.e., Canadian] River have great numbers of horses which they rear with much less difficulty than the Shiennes, whose country is cold and barren.[46]

The British traders commonly supply the Minnetarees or Gros Ventres of the Missouri with goods; from these they pass to the Shiennes and Crow Indians, who in their turn barter with remoter tribes; in this manner the Indians who wander near the mountains receive their supplies of goods and they give a decided and well founded preference to those which reach them by this circuitous channel over those which they receive from any other source.

In another place James says that this mixed group of Indians formerly carried on a limited trade with the Spaniards of Mexico, with whom they exchanged dressed bison skins for blankets, wheat, flour, maize, &c., but their supplies of these articles are now cut off by a war which they at present are waging against that people. They also at distant periods held a kind of fair on a tributary of the Platte near the mountains (hence called Grand Camp Creek), at which they obtained British merchandise from the Shiennes of Shienne River, who obtained the same at the Mandan village from the British traders that frequent that part of our territory.

[46] James, Long's Expedition from Pittsburgh to the Rocky Mountains, vol. I, p. 502, Phila., 1823.

This passage seems to imply that the Cheyennes had been supplying these bands with British goods for a number of years after the old trade in New Mexico had been broken up because of hostilities.

The description of the South Platte given by James makes it difficult or impossible to locate Grand Camp Creek. He says that on July 6 the party marched up the Platte and halted at 11 A.M. near the mouth of Defile Creek, which is perhaps the modern Plum Creek. Of other days' journeyings we are told that the party marched until 11 A.M. and camped after making about sixteen miles along the Platte Valley, and it is perhaps safe to assume that they made this distance July 6, and that their camp of that day was about five miles below Clear Creek, which James calls Medicine Lodge Creek. Grand Camp may be either the modern Bear Creek or another stream near to it. On the other side of the mountains, in the southern part of Carbon County, Wyoming, there is a Grand Encampment Creek, tributary to the North Platte. The James' Grand Camp Creek was on the South Platte.

As already stated, we know nothing definite as to who these Cheyennes were, when they came south and when they returned to their own tribe. Bijeau told James that the Cheyennes had come south—about 1816—to trade with the Kiowas and other Indians on Grand Camp Creek, and it may be inferred that Bijeau was present during this trading fair. We may believe that these Cheyennes were the same that Long's party met on the Arkansas in 1820, for from what Bijeau said to Mr. Say, several of them were recognized by Bijeau.[47]

On another page James says:

The Shiennes or Shawhays, who have united their destiny with these wanderers [the Arapahoes, Kiowas, and others, met on the Arkansas in 1820], are a band of seceders from their own nation; and sometime since, on the occurrence of a serious dispute with their

[47] James, *ibid.*, vol. II, p. 197.

kindred on Shienne River of the Missouri, flew their country and placed themselves under the protection of the Bear Tooth.[48]

In another place[49] Bear Tooth is spoken of as the great chief of the Arapahoes; his word was law, not only to his own people, but to the other tribes which usually camped with his band. This man was farther down the Arkansas and does not appear to have been met by Long's people.

Of these people with Bear Tooth James says:

These nations have been for the past three years wandering on the head waters and tributaries of Red River, having returned to the Arkansa only the day which preceded our first interview with them [July 26] on their way to the mountains, at the source of the Platte River. They have no permanent town, but constantly rove, as necessity urges them, in pursuit of the herds of bisons in the vicinity of the sources of the Platte, Arkansa and Red Rivers.[50]

Further on he writes:

These nations are at war with all the Missouri Indians as far down as the Osages, who are also included amongst their enemies, and it was rumored that hostilities had recently commenced between them and the Shiennes upon the river of the same name.[51]

This last statement was probably not fact, for at this time (1820) the Cheyennes and Sioux were actively engaged in fighting the Crows, and the oldest Cheyennes living in recent years have always given us to understand that the war between their tribe and the Kiowas and Comanches began about 1826.

The remains of large Indian camps seen on the Arkansas by Long's party in 1820, and extending from the canyon and Fountain Creek down to and below the Huerfano in Colorado, were no doubt old camps of these Indians. The descriptions of some of them indicate that they were winter camps.

48 James, *ibid.*, p. 186.
49 *Ibid.*, p. 367.
50 *Ibid.*, p. 187. James always calls the Canadian, the Red River, from its color of course.
51 James, *ibid.*, p. 368.

There were perhaps Comanches with these, for in the winter of 1819-1820 a fight took place between a large war-party of Skidi Pawnees and a greatly superior force of mounted "Ietans, Arrapahoes and Kiaways," among whom were these Cheyennes. The Indians met by Major Long told the party the detailed story.

A war-party of ninety-three Skidi Pawnees went south on a horse-taking expedition against these Indians, were discovered, and a desperate fight ensued. The Pawnees, caught in the open plain, were surrounded, but after hard fighting a remnant of them succeeded in breaking through the mounted enemies and reached a small timbered creek. They left fifty-three of their men, including all their leaders, dead or wounded, on the ground, and of the forty men who reached the shelter all but seven were wounded. The attacking party now drew off and the surviving Pawnees began their homeward journey. On going into the fight they had, as usual, discarded all their clothing, and during the homeward march had nothing to wear except the green hides of a few buffalo that were killed. Those of the party too severely wounded to walk were placed on pole drags, which were drawn by the unwounded and the slightly wounded men.

It was from Captain Bell, attached to Long's expedition, that Jedidiah Morse received his information about the Cheyennes who had "attached themselves to the Arrapahuys."[52]

None of these earlier accounts seem to mention the Suhtai, except Captain Bell, in whose statement, published in Morse (1822), is given the number of Staitan or Kite Indians who roved from the headwaters of the Platte to the Rocky Mountains.

In the *Journal of Jacob Fowler*[53] it is stated that his party met a large group of Indians, said to have included Arapahoes,

[52] Morse, Report to the Secretary of War on Indian Affairs, New Haven, p. 254, 1822.
[53] Journal of Jacob Fowler, pp. 54-55, N. Y., 1898.

Kiowas, Comanches, Kiowa-Apaches, Cheyennes, and Snakes, amicably traveling together. These Indians were then at war with the province of San Antonio, now Texas, in northeastern Mexico, but were at peace with the Spaniards of New Mexico. A similar state of things existed at a much later date. Though these tribes were then at peace, a few years later bitter war existed between the Kiowas and Comanches on the one hand, and the Arapahoes and Cheyennes on the other.

Not long after Jacob Fowler met these Cheyennes, they began to get liquor and were soon greatly affected by it. In the North alcohol had for many years been one of the chief articles of trade with the Indians, and it now began to make its entrance into the southern country. A few years later, in 1833, the Rev. Moses Merrill reports that two men who had come into his missionary station near Bellevue, Nebraska, declared to him that half of the furs purchased in the Indian country were obtained in exchange for whiskey. "They also stated that the Shiennes, a tribe of Indians on the Platte River, were wholly adverse to drinking whiskey, but five years ago; now— through the influence of a trader, Capt. Gant[54] who by sweetening the whiskey induced them to drink the intoxicating draught—they are a tribe of drunkards."

One has only to read the younger Henry's account of his daily life, or Larpenteur's story of his experiences,[55] or the Rev. Moses Merrill's diary, to see how almost universal, where the Indians could obtain it, the use of alcohol had become. Accounts of the wars between Cheyennes and the whites have been given in an earlier volume.[56]

[54] Gant's post on the Arkansas was on the north bank of the river, six miles below Fountain Creek. The post was built in 1832. It is mentioned by Col. Henry Dodge and by Sage.

[55] Larpenteur, Forty Years a Fur Trader, Coues ed., N. Y., 1898.

[56] The Fighting Cheyennes, N. Y., 1915.

OLD-TIME WAYS

WE have some accounts—at second-hand to be sure of the manner of life of the Cheyennes in the early days, four or five generations ago. These reports came from people born about the middle of the eighteenth century and were made to men who now are old.

In 1869 died Standing All Night, an old Arikara who from young manhood had lived with the Cheyennes. At the time of his death he supposed that he was more than one hundred years of age. As far back as extended the memory of men who then were old, he had always been regarded as an old man. During the last years of his life he was feeble, toothless, and subsisted on fluids. Men still living testify to his high reputation in the tribe, and even in 1919 he was spoken of as a person exceptional for his trustworthiness and for his knowledge of the tribal lore. By men who knew him well—Two Crows, Little Hawk, Porcupine, and George Bent—I have been told much of what Standing All Night related as to certain customs in vogue in his youth.

In early life he lived in an earth lodge on the Missouri River with the Mandans, and had married a Mandan woman. At that time a group of the Cheyennes occupied a village near to the Mandans and adjacent to the Arikaras. The date, if the statements about the age of Standing All Night may be trusted, would be between 1750 and 1800. Even if he were much younger than he believed, he must have lived with the Mandans long before they saw Lewis and Clark.

Doll Man, who died in 1871, said to have been more than eighty years of age, declared that he was born on the Missouri

47

River in a camp of Cheyennes that dwelt permanently near or with the Mandans. These Cheyennes only occasionally went out on the plains to hunt buffalo. Doll Man also had married a Mandan woman. It may have been this man who accompanied the little party headed by White Thunder, which about 1835 visited the Pawnees in an endeavor to make peace and to recover the medicine arrows.[1]

Old women, born in the early years of the nineteenth century, used to relate stories which they had heard from their elders. These women were Twin Woman, Crow Woman, and Lightning Woman. Crow Woman was captured from the Crows as a child about 1820. These old people have told of many events of times long past—periods that cannot be identified. Some of them had heard that in old times canoes were made by hollowing out logs by fire, and that sometimes a family would work for a long time over a log, keeping the fires burning day and night, until the log was properly hollowed. It is possible that this story may have come in from some other people.

Of the early days north of the Missouri, when the Cheyennes were constantly in fear of the Hohe, it is related that early each evening the crier went about the camp and called out, directing the women to put moccasins on the children so that if during the night they were attacked and had to run out, they would not be obliged to go barefoot. Near by they had places selected to which they could run in case of an attack, and all about the camp were breastworks or places of defense, where young men watched all night to warn the people if an attack was threatened. These young men were armed with bows, and a few had lances, but they had no guns. Standing All Night used to say that in his time they had horses, but very few guns.

The same informant stated that they caught fish in devices

[1] *American Anthropologist*, N. s., vol. XII, p. 542.

BIG WOMAN

like nets, of parallel willow twigs, described elsewhere; made and used stone axes, and knives of flint and bone, as well as earthenware pots. These last were occasionally in use up to the middle of the nineteenth century.

In the old, old times, even before they had dogs, the houses were built of the shoots of a kind of willow, the twigs of which are reddish in color and very tough. These houses must have been tightly built, for it is said they used to moisten clay and mix it with pounded stone, so as to make a mortar, with which they plastered the whole outside of the house, leaving a round hole at the top. The lower walls leaned in, and the roof leaned in still more and was rounded over, making a structure which suggests those houses formerly used by the Sauk and Fox of Iowa. Sometimes, instead of using this plaster or mortar to cover the houses and to keep out rain and snow, they covered the dwellings with mats woven of rushes. When the warm weather came, the people moved out of their winter houses, and made summer shelters of woven willows, some peeled, and some unpeeled, which gave the houses an ornamental pattern. Such dwellings were not plastered. The houses were built together—in a town—from which the people often moved off on hunting excursions, returning as soon as they had obtained a supply of food.

The permanent houses described as occupied in that northern country by a big river, where it was very level, and where they used bundles of a tall red grass for fuel, were built of poles set in the ground, and brought together at the top. The openings between the poles were stuffed with grass, and over the outside they put sheets of bark to keep the grass from working out. Within, the houses were lined with dried hides with the hair on them.[2] The door of the lodge opened into a passageway, not straight, but zigzag, to keep the wind and snow from blowing

[2] Compare Life and Correspondence of Major Cartwright, vol. II, p. 309, London, 1826.

into the lodge, for in that country it was very cold. Houses such as these were built only in places where they intended to spend the winter. In such houses the floors were dug out, so as to give more head room; the doors were small, and in entering it was necessary to creep on hands and knees.

On making camp, when they were moving about, they thrust into the ground the ends of the short travois poles used for the dogs' loads and bent them over toward each other, to make a framework on which to support the covering of the shelter. Outside this framework bundles of grass were heaped up and were covered with bark. Into these houses many persons used to crowd for warmth and protection from the weather. Later they made better shelters for their journeyings, but not at all like the lodges of later times. They were still frames covered with hides, and when fires were lighted in them the hides were partly removed from the top, so that the smoke might escape.

Skin lodges were then unknown, and even after they had been devised, their adoption was slow. At first they were small and were few in number, and from various remarks that I have heard I am inclined to think that the skin lodge did not very long precede the advent of the horse. Aged women, still alive in 1915, spoke of a time when the possession of a lodge was the exception among the Cheyennes. The complete and comfortable lodges of modern times were the ultimate development from the windbreaks of undressed hides set up over a framework of poles. It was, they say, only after reaching the Black Hills and procuring long poles that they made their first big lodges. Old women long continued to use the old-time small lodges with short poles.

The first lodge of modern shape is said to have been suggested by a man who was handling a large poplar leaf, and quite by accident bent it into the shape of a cone—that is to say, of a lodge, such as are used today. As he looked at the leaf it flashed into his mind that a shelter like that would be better than those they then had. He showed it to the people, and they made lodges in the shape of this leaf, and have used them ever since.

Probably as recently as 1830 or 1840 the people used large stones to hold down the edges of the lodge covering. This was done in winter, when they could not drive pins into the frozen ground. This practice explains the stone circles often seen on the prairie. Wherever these circles of stones were found, we may feel sure that there was a winter camp, and frozen ground.

A Cheyenne friend once said to me: "In ancient times people used to camp on the tops of high bluffs. In such places we still find circles of stones where the lodges have been, with fire places and bed places marked out. Sometimes we can even see the place for the door. People seem to have been foolish then, camping as they did so far from water." I explained to him that these camps high up in the hills and far from the streams were, as a matter of fact, camps made in late winter and early spring, when water was found standing in every hollow of the prairie. At that time the people were not obliged to camp by the river or a spring, but could and did camp almost anywhere, because almost everywhere there was water.

In those times long ago when they lived near the lakes told of in the North, geese, ducks, cranes, coons, and skunks constituted a large part of their summer food. In winter, the whole camp, men, women, and children, and dogs, went out to surround deer and drove them into snowdrifts. Out in the tall grass prairie were stony hills, where skunks were abundant. Each fall when the skunks were fat, all the people in the camp moved out to these hills and hunted skunks. At the end of the hunt all the skunks were brought in and laid out in rows and then divided—a certain number to each family. Around these hills there was little or no wood. The people collected tall grass, tied it in long bundles, and used it as fuel. One end of the bundle was lighted and it burned for a long time.

On the shores of the lakes were found eggs and birds'

feathers, and while the waterfowl were laying there was a continual search for the eggs.

When the old birds had lost their feathers in the molt, they were killed, and as the young birds grew large they also were killed. Sometimes the young feathers on the growing birds were boiled, for the nutriment contained in the soft and swollen ends.

By means of devices elsewhere described, they caught many fish, and by boiling the fishbones secured a fine clear white oil. At this time it is said they made their clothing of the skins of small animals sewed together.

In those days their weapons were few. They surrounded animals and killed them with arrows armed with points of stone, bone, or horn. Some of these points were short, and some long. After they had killed large animals, they skinned them with knives of flint or bone. Some of these knives were small, hardly larger than arrowheads; but others were ten or fifteen inches long. The knives often had no handles attached to them, but had a rounded handhold which sometimes was wrapped with a piece of hide, or the stone cutting edge was sometimes attached to a handle of bone or of wood.

When the Cheyennes first found the buffalo they had no knowledge as to how to dress hides. Later, the Sioux on the east side of the Missouri showed them how to cut hides in two, dress them, and sew them together again. These they used as robes. After they had reached the Black Hills the Kiowas and Comanches taught the Cheyennes how to dress buffalo-hides in one piece, and also showed them the use of a mixture for softening the hide.

At this time, as in later days, they used the bone of the hock of large animals as a flesher. They ground down the dorsal spine of large animals on a stone, and with this sharp edge hacked the notches in the cutting edge of the flesher.

The details of buffalo hunting will be described later. The best time to kill buffalo, the old men say, was in winter, in the deep snow; for they used to make snowshoes, which supported them, while the buffalo sank deep in the snow, and the people could run up close beside the buffalo and kill them with their lances. Then they carried in the meat, or at a later time brought it in on the dog travois. But in early times, when snow was on the ground—if the snow was crusted or if a frozen stream was near—they spread out a hide, packed the meat in it, and lacing it up flesh-side out, dragged it into camp over the snow.

In the days before they had flint-and-steel, fire was often made, as among many people, with fire-sticks. The revolving stick was of some hard wood, and the piece, or hearth, which received its point, was of softer wood. Some men made a specialty of manufacturing fire-sticks, while others could not make them at all. After a set of sticks had been made, the maker held them up to the sun and prayed over them, asking that they might be blessed and might prove useful. Gentle Horse (born 1800) stated that the lower of the two fire-sticks (the hearth) was commonly cottonwood, while the upright or twirling stick was a straight shoot of greasewood.

A little white quartz sand was often put in the hole in the hearth, and powdered dry buffalo-chip, or dry white sage leaves, about the edges of the hole, to serve as tinder, and this readily caught fire. Sometimes in kindling a fire they rested the lower stick on a buffalo-chip, and the hot spark dropping from this stick ignited the dry chip, which would smolder for a long time. In modern times, fire-sticks were sometimes made from the central flower-bearing stalk of the soapweed (yucca). Both the twirling stick and the base stick were of this wood. In their war journeys not very long ago, probably between 1860 and 1870, the Southern Cheyennes used such fire-sticks if their matches became exhausted. The earlier sticks were as described by Gentle Horse. In using the soapweed sticks, the twirling stick was pointed, and a little hole made in the base stick to receive that point. With these it did not take very long to make a fire. The sticks were revolved between the open hands.

Elk River stated that in ancient times fire was often made by splitting a flint stone, and then placing the dry rotten root of soapweed on one surface of the flint rock and rubbing it briskly with the other. Sparks were obtained also by knocking together two hard stones.

As fire was difficult to produce, it was transported from place to place. Sometimes a dry buffalo-chip was ignited, and this burned slowly and lasted a long time, perhaps during the whole march to the next camp. Often fire was carried with them by means of a burning stick.

When the leaders of a traveling village reached the place chosen for the camp, the young men at once collected piles of wood; and as soon as anyone came in who carried fire, these piles were kindled and from them the different women procured coals for starting their individual fires.

In later times, however, they carried the living fire, smoldering, and often renewed, in a fire horn. I have explained[3] how the Blackfeet Indians did this; and the Cheyenne method was much the same, except their horns were smaller. In later times, after they obtained flint-and-steel, the fire horn was used for carrying the unlighted punk, to protect it from wet and wear. This punk was usually dry, rotten cottonwood, or box-elder wood, or the dry, rotted root of the soapweed. They cut off the end of the sheath of the horn, making a hole large enough to receive the stick of punk. The larger open end of the horn was plugged with a stopper of wood, and the stick of punk was of such length that, when put in the horn, the end for lighting met the wooden plug, and the fire was extinguished. Horns for carrying punk were in use up to about 1870. They were usually carried in a deerskin sack, sometimes in the ball pouch, or sometimes merely tied to the shoulder belt. The stopper in the

[3] Blackfoot Lodge Tales, p. 200.

small opening of the horn was not always tight, and sometimes leaked a little, so that in a storm, dampness or water might get into it, and the end of the punk get wet. When this took place, the end which became wet was the holding end, not the fire end.

The first flint-and-steel is said to have been obtained from Mexicans.

In those ancient times, when the people moved, they carried on their backs all their possessions, including the smallest children and their food. This was before they had dogs to help them. In the old-time dresses the shoulders were always naked, and carrying these heavy loads must have been hard, for the lines must have chafed their shoulders. To transport the meat to the camp a hide was cut in several pieces, and in each piece was packed as much meat as a man or a woman could carry. The hide was laced up, and the pack was put on the back, and held there by straps passing over the head and chest. In winter, however, they tied up their belongings in bundles, put them on a dried hide, and walked along, dragging the hide, which was thus like a loaded sled.

Strong Left Hand was told that when dogs were first seen they were wild on the prairie and were of different colors. This dog was different from the wolf, and seemed an animal that might be easily tamed. Sometimes the people fed the dogs, going out near to them and holding up a piece of meat so that they might see it, and then putting it on the ground and leaving it. The dogs would come up and eat it. In that way they began to grow tame, though at first very timid. At length, when a dog saw a person coming with a piece of meat, it ran up to him and wagged its tail, for it knew it was to be fed. Finally, they put strings on the dogs and led them into the camp. This happened long, long ago. After they got dogs these increased very fast. After they had many dogs it occurred to someone that the dogs might carry some of their things, so the dogs became a help to them in their moving, and a large dog was valuable. *Hōtăm'* means a full-grown dog.

Elk River (born about 1810) described these dogs in more detail:

These dogs, though big, were not like wolves. They were of different colors—black, white, yellow, and spotted. They had long bodies, and feet that turned out, though not like the little dogs of today that have crooked feet. Sometimes today one sees a dog built like these old-time dogs, though much smaller. They had these large dogs until after I was a young man. They were a great help to women in getting wood. Some women had ten or twelve dogs, and packed them all, for they carried packs on their backs, besides hauling the travois.

On the travois hauled by the dogs were packed chiefly small articles, the small lodges, and sometimes the children. Usually the dogs were led by the women, so that runaways were infrequent. These early dogs are said to have been so large and strong that one of them could haul two children on a travois.

In those days the women's dresses were very different from those worn today. They were made of buffalo-skin—sometimes of lodge covering (*mōh sĭh'' kŭn*), or of tanned deerskin. The dresses of the early part of the nineteenth century, of deerskin, reached down about halfway from the knee to ankle. Midway between the waist belt and the border of the dress there was a flounce about four inches wide. Such dresses, formerly ornamented with porcupine quills, later had two rows of blue beads running across the front above the belt (the waist), with ornaments of porcupine quills—knots, as it were—hanging down from them. The dress was held up by a strap which passed over the left shoulder, and the short sleeve was open above, so that the arm was bare. The right arm was covered by a short sleeve, nearly to the elbow, laced above, and tied at its lower end. Across the bare left arm the woman might paint a red stripe for every coup her husband had counted.

The most ancient dresses worn by the women, of which there is any recollection, are described as consisting merely of two rectangular pieces of dressed skin, tied together with strings which passed over the shoulders and supported the dress, and tied together also, at intervals at either side, with strings, and held by a belt or thong about the waist. In the same way the leggings of the men and the sides of their shirts were tied together with strings at what would now be the seams, for at that time the art of sewing was unknown. Carver's figure[4] of a Nadowessie woman, already referred to, shows a costume which suggests the Cheyenne women's dress, though it is shorter, barely reaching to the knees, but its support over the shoulders on either side seems to be a mere knot or string. Carver, it is to be remembered, mentions the Cheyennes as one of the bands of Sioux.

"In the time of our grandmothers," old women say, "perhaps a hundred years ago [1800], the dresses worn by women were longer [i.e., hung down farther] on the right side than on the left. The right arm had a short sleeve; there was a strap over the left shoulder, and the hide was doubled back, hanging down from the upper chest in a loose flap, ending in an edge which ran diagonally from the right shoulder in front around the body to below the left shoulder-blade."

The first belts were of parfleche tied together with tanned leather strings. The first ornamented belts were straps of parfleche, to which were sewed the little coarse beads that the Cheyennes had obtained. After these belts came straps of parfleche on which were placed flat brass buttons of various sizes, which they obtained from the Hudson Bay Company. Holes were made in the parfleche, and the eyes of the buttons were passed through the holes and fastened there with strings of deerskin.

At that time, women's leggings were fringed at the bottom

[4] Carver, Travels in the Interior Parts of North America, p. 230, London, 1778.

and up the sides, as they never have been in modern times. They were commonly painted yellow, and were often marked with horizontal black cross-lines around the leg. This painting continued to recent times.

The early moccasins, to be described later, were made of a simple piece of deerskin sewed in a single seam at the side, and a sole was afterward sewed on over the deerskin. Such moccasins were worn by old Suhtai within the memory of men still living.

Black Eagle, who gave me his ancient scalp shirt about 1906, said: "The man who put us on earth invented the fashion of these shirts. They come from the old people who lived on the Missouri River and in the Black Hills. This shirt was made by my wife's grandfather, Horn, who gave it to his son, Brave Wolf [often spoken of as Maple, or Box Elder], the father of my wife. When I was made a chief, at the age of twenty-five, the shirt was given to me, and I have had it ever since—more than forty-two years."

No man might wear a scalp shirt unless he was brave, and had counted one or more coups. The owner must be brave in fight, the first to advance and the last to retreat; he must pick up a dismounted comrade; should he fail in these things, he must give up the shirt and lose his honor. The cost of the ceremony of making the shirt was considerable, for it could be made only by a man who had worn one. In making a scalp shirt, men were called in who had counted coups, and a coup was counted for each scalp-lock put on. A scalp shirt and its obligations might be given away by the owner, but the gift did not carry with it the right to make one. The owner of a scalp shirt ranked as a chief; he must not get angry if his horses were stolen, and if his wife was carried off, or ran away, he must not seek revenge; if a man killed his relations he might not personally revenge them, but must leave this to other members of the family. If he gave away his scalp shirt, he abandoned those obligations, and again became as other men. People did not like to wear the garment, because of the cost of having one made and the customs to which the owner must conform. If a scalp shirt was captured by the enemy, the responsibilities which went with it were lost.

Arapaho Chief, a Northern Cheyenne (still alive in 1917), told Bent that his youngest wife took advantage of the fact that he was having a scalp shirt made to run away with another man. Little Wolf was counting his coup on the scalp shirt when one of Arapaho Chief's sisters came to the outside of the lodge and called to Arapaho Chief that his wife had run off. Arapaho Chief merely filled his pipe, smoked, and passed it to the other men, saying that he had no fault to find with her; no pipe or present was ever sent to him.

In the early days—say before the nineteenth century—the men wore no scalp-lock, but often wore the hair behind stuck together with pine gum in several or a dozen little strings, hanging down the back, and this continued down to and beyond 1850. In those days the Cheyennes were noted for their very long hair, and the old books speak of this. As a rule, today, these people have long, but not unusually long hair; yet occasionally an old Indian is seen whose hair, if free, would drag on the ground. Red Eagle, who lived on the Northern Cheyenne Reservation, wore his side-braids doubled up twice, yet they reached below his waist; while when he was sitting, a foot or more of his scalp-lock rested on the ground.

It is said that three or four generations ago the women used to braid the hair somewhat as they do now, and to wear as ornaments little fringed rolls of deerskin tied to the outside of the braids, close to the head. On the outer side of the deerskin rolls some women always tied sprigs of sage. Following this came a fashion in which the women doubled the braids up two or three times, and tied these bundles and the deerskin rolls behind the head.

Then came another method, which was practiced in 1830 or thereabouts and was remembered by women whom I knew well. This custom was to wear the hair, not hanging down as at present, but each braid was doubled up several times at the side in a little pack and fastened above and behind the ear, close to the head. Each bundle of hair was wrapped about with a little beaded or quill-ornamented rectangular piece of deerskin, so that on each side of the back of the head these bunches of hair stood up "like two little stub-horns." After the hair had been fixed in this way, the smooth hair on top of the head— not on the bunches—was painted with a red streak, from before backward, for every coup that the woman's husband had counted.

It is interesting to note that Carver[5] tells that the women that lived to the west of the Mississippi, namely, the Nadouwessie and the Assinipoiles, divided the hair in the middle of the head, and formed it into two rolls, one against each ear. Carver says, to be sure, that these two rolls stood at the front of each ear, and this may be a modification before or after the Cheyenne fashion, which old women who were living in recent years remember to have seen practiced by their grandmothers.

In those old times the Cheyenne men dressed their hair very differently from the modern fashion. They say that in times very far back—long before the memory of the oldest person— they cut off much of the hair of the head. Some wore a narrow roach, and some a wide one, while others had a circular crownpiece, on which the hair was long, the rest of the hair being pulled out, so that the head was elsewhere naked. This has been told by the very oldest people, and through them comes down to the present time. It was a fashion of long ago. In later times the men commonly cut off all the hair except a little on the top of the head. This way of wearing the hair is of course comparable with certain familiar fashions of modern times, when the Pawnees, Osages, Kaws, and others, wore such roaches.

[5] Carver's Travels, p. 230, London, 1778.

The figure of a man of the Nadowessie in Carver[6] shows him apparently without hair over most of his head, but with a crown-tuft of longer hair, in which feathers are tied.

Among Indians, as among white people, the fashions changed. After the practice of wearing the roach, or a tuft of hair, became obsolete, they used to cut the hair square across the forehead, and stiffen it with clay, so that it stood straight up; then, stringing little shells on deerskin strings, they tied them to the hair on the front of the head, so that two of these strings of shells hung down on the right side of the face. The men braided the back hair somewhat as they do now. The cutting of the hair across the forehead and stiffening it with clay is said to have been an old method of hairdressing practiced by the Crees.

By a later fashion the hair was cut off on one side only and left on the other; thus there was only one braid, and one ear was covered by the hair and the other exposed. The covered ear was usually not ornamented, but in the exposed ear often many holes were bored, each of which held an ornament. This practice may have been continued to some extent up to modern times, for the right ear of my friend, White Elk, had been many times pierced, while in the left ear there was only a single hole.

The old-time people wore rings in their noses. An old woman, now, or very recently, alive in the Cheyenne camp, can remember three old men who wore such nose ornaments. They took the shells of mussels and carved them into different shapes, and tying the shell to a deerskin string, passed the string through a hole in the septum of the nose. After the fashion of wearing shells passed out, they wore rings of metal in the nose, and after the nose ornament ceased to be fashionable, the practice arose of wearing earrings. These, up to the present time, were inserted in half a dozen holes cut in the cartilage of the ear, near its margin, but a long time ago—seventy-five or a hundred

6 Carver, *loc. cit.*, pl. 3, p. 230.

years—a long hole was cut in the cartilage near the margin, reaching from the top to the lobe; the hole was distended by a stick passed through it, until it healed, and then the margin of the ear was wrapped with beads strung on sinew. Adair and J. Long saw this fashion among other Indians in the eighteenth century. Big Woman told me that she remembered that, as a little girl, playing with her grandmother, she could put three of her fingers through each of the holes pierced in her grandmother's ears. This fashion must have disappeared about the middle of the last century. Big Woman's grandmother and her aunts were the last ones whom she remembers to have practiced it.

The first bracelets that women wore were of hoop iron, sometimes brightened with a file. After this came bracelets made of brass wire, wound around the arm. Other old women, however, say that among the earliest ornaments they had were blue beads, copper bracelets, and finger rings of wound wire.

VILLAGE LIFE

INCIDENTS OF A DAY

I F in imagination we can carry ourselves back sixty or
seventy years, to the time when the Indians wandered free
and before their lives had been greatly modified by the
influence of civilization, we may picture some of the features
of the daily life of the Cheyennes in the days of the buffalo.

The camp was pitched in a broad bottom, and the lodges
stood in a great circle whose diameter was half a mile or more
—three arrow flights from a strong bow, and as far as a man
can throw an arrow by hand. It was summer, and most of the
women had renewed their lodges, so that they stood white in
the dim light of the early morning. The sun had not yet risen,
but already the fires were kindled, and from the lodges gray
columns of smoke were rising through the still air. From all
quarters of the camp women were hurrying down to the stream,
or coming from it, carrying to the lodges water for the morning
use; for the Cheyennes did not use water that had stood all
night—they called it dead, and said that they wished to drink
living water. As the light grew stronger, men and boys—some
of them little fellows just able to walk—came from the lodges
and hurried down to the stream, to plunge into it; for the early
morning bath was a regular practice. This was done by all at
most seasons of the year; but some of them omitted the bath
in winter when the streams were frozen, while others broke the
ice and bathed in the cold water. This was for good health, to
make them hardy, and also to wash away all sickness. The
custom was peculiar to the men; women did not do it. The
practice was similar to that of the Blackfeet.

The rising sun looked down upon a camp full of moving people. The women were cooking the meals, the men and boys were returning to the lodges. The pot was removed from the fire, and with a sharpened stick the meat taken from it and put in wooden bowls, or in dishes made of buffalo-horn. Before eating, most of the boys rode out into the hills, and drove in the herds of horses, from which certain ones were selected to be tied in front of the lodges, to be at hand for any use, while those—usually the most valuable ones—which during the night had been tethered there, were turned loose and taken to the hills to graze, under the charge of a son or a nephew of the lodge, or perhaps of some poor orphan who lived there, receiving his food and clothing and in return performing the various small services that all boys were expected to render to older persons.

The morning meal ended, many of the men saddled their horses and started out to hunt; but before this the voice of the old crier was heard, shouting out to the camp the commands of the chiefs, the order of the day, or perhaps only some items of personal news. He commenced at the opening of the circle, which always faced the rising sun, and riding around, within but close to the lodges, first to the south, then to the west, then to the north, and so back to the east again, called out the news, repeating his announcement at frequent intervals. Perhaps it was that the camp was to remain in this place for one, two, or three days; perhaps that men were not to disturb the buffalo; perhaps that some soldier band was to have a dance that night; or merely that some warrior or chief had lost a piece of property, and people were notified of its ownership. At first the crier's voice came to the distant lodges merely as a faint, droning shout, without words, but it told the people that he was coming, and as he drew nearer, they began to listen, to distinguish what he was saying. A woman, eager for news, stepped out of her lodge to hear the better, and exchanged with some interested neighbor comments on the announcement.

USING SMOOTHER ON QUILLS

Now, some woman who was making a new lodge carried out and spread on the ground the dressed skins to be used in its construction. Before day came, she had sent a messenger to call her friends to come and help her sew it, and the lodge cutter was already standing over the skins, preparing them for the sewing. The women who were to help in the work, some of them carrying their bundles of sinew thread, began to arrive from various quarters of the camp. Many hands made light work, and before night the sewing of the lodge was completed.

Long before this the children had scattered out to play. Some of the tiniest, unless they had older sisters or cousins to take charge of them, stayed close by their mothers; but the older ones scattered to the river, where the boys were swimming and diving in the warm water, or were running races on the sand-bars, or perhaps burying each other, all except the head, in the sand, already heated by the strengthening sun. Other lads were busy near a mud-bank, modeling images of animals and people and lodges from the tenacious clay, and setting them in the sun to dry.

Some of the older boys and young men were practicing at shooting with the bow, or at throwing arrows, or were playing one of the wheel games, or sliding their slender, straight throwing-sticks far along the smooth ground.

Big girls, not yet old enough to work at dressing hides, gathered in groups to play the football game elsewhere described.

During the morning parties of women and young girls started off to get wood, perhaps only two or three together, perhaps fifteen or twenty. They were a merry group, laughing, joking, and playing tricks on one another. When the place was reached where they were to get wood, some gathered the sticks lying on the ground; others climbed up into the trees, breaking off and throwing down the dead branches, while those below trimmed and made them ready for the ropes. The wood was divided into even loads, and when all these were prepared, each woman took hers on her back, and, in single file, they set out for the camp, separating as they reached it, each turning off to her own lodge. In winter when there was snow on the ground, the companies of women made hard-beaten roads to and from the timber, where they gathered their fuel.

Other groups of women and young girls went out into the hills to gather roots, and were seen walking across the wide prairie, armed with their root-diggers, and then climbing the hills, and at last—mere dots in the distance—scattering out and occupied in their work.

The men left in the camp sat about in the shade of the lodges. Some smoked and gossiped; others worked at different implements which they were fashioning, a bow, arrows, a pipe, a pipestem, a whetstone, or what not. Old men discussed the happenings of past years, their war journeys, their meetings with other tribes, visits that they had received from white people, or mysterious events that had taken place within their knowledge. Sometimes, near groups of these old men might be seen two or three growing boys, seated at a little distance behind them, eagerly drinking in the talk that flowed from the lips of these wise elders.

Some young men devoted much time to their personal appearance, plucking out the hairs from eyebrows, lips, and cheeks, combing and braiding their hair, and painting their faces. After this had been done to the dandy's satisfaction, he dressed himself in his finest clothing, and a little later rode about the camp so that people might admire him.

For plucking out the hair, a pair of tweezers was used, called the "eyebrow plucker," from which we might infer that the Cheyennes practiced plucking the eyebrows before they removed the hair from the face by the same process. This last custom is still very generally practiced, although some men now allow the eyebrows and lashes to remain, more especially the eyelashes. At present some Cheyenne young men shave instead of plucking the hair from the face.

Before this some old women dragged out their green hides,

and spread them on the ground, and were hard at work over them. Others pounded berries under a shade; others still sewed clothing.

As midday approached, and the sun grew hotter, many of the people retired to the lodges; the lodge-skins were raised all about and they sat there in the shade, while a warm breeze blew through the lodge.

As the afternoon advanced, men were seen returning from the hunt, riding horses laden with meat. Each dismounted before his lodge, and his women took the load from the horse, and either turned the animal loose, or, if it was a fine running horse, took it down to the stream and washed from it the blood and dirt with which it was likely to be covered.

Suddenly, from a near-by hill, sounded the war-cry, and there was a little stir among the growing men of the camp. The women and girls who had been off to dig roots were announcing their return and signaling with their blankets, and a crowd of men rushed out to try to rob them of some of their spoils, while the women in the camp hurried out of the lodges to see the fun.

As they were returning to the camp, the girls who went out to dig bear-roots and turnips tied their roots in small bundles of five or six. Often some girl who was slow at digging, and had secured but few roots, might propose that they should divide into two parties and gamble for the bunches of roots. If all agreed, one of the women threw her root-digger as far as she could, and the others stood in a row and threw their root-diggers at the first one. If a woman's missile touched the mark, her side won. If a root-digger from each side hit it, the game was a draw, while if none of the root-diggers thrown hit the mark, it also was a draw. They competed as well by throwing the short root-diggers so that they should strike on one end and keep turning over, end for end, as they went. The farthest throw won. Some root-diggers would not go at all; they perhaps just stood in the ground, or bounded off to one side. In these contests, they tied the small roots in bunches of five or ten, and wagered these bunches, or a number of them.

In the same way, and for the same purpose, they threw the front marrow-bone of a buffalo, the metacarpal. It was thrown on the ground, so as to strike on its end, and then bound, turning over and over, end for end, to go as far as possible. Often, before betting, a woman might throw the bone, and then go to it and put her foot on it, and say, "If you do not win for me, you shall be pounded up and used to get grease from." This was a jocular threat, the expression of a hope that she might win.

Now, when the women were returning to camp with their roots, and when they had come within sight of the camp, they sat down in a line, and each woman put her roots a little way in front of her on the ground. Then some woman shouted the war-cry, and signaled to the camp with a blanket, as if a war-party were returning. When the people saw this, some of the young men took the parfleches used under the stone anvils on which meat and berries were pounded, and carried them as shields, while some had already made imitation shields of willow twigs. These young men mounted the oldest, laziest, ugliest horses they could find, and charged out on the women, who were busily gathering sticks and buffalo-chips with which to defend themselves.

When the two parties were close together, the girls pelted the men, who dodged and protected themselves behind their shields, and there was much confusion. Only a man who had been wounded in war, or had had his horse shot under him in real warfare, was permitted to take the roots away from the girls. Such men might do so, though before they secured their plunder they received a plentiful pelting. A man who was hit by a missile was supposed to be wounded, and out of the game. Other men might not dismount. However, after a time the men got some roots, and they retired to some hill to eat them, while the girls went on to camp with those they had saved.

The parties who had been gathering roots were made up of little girls, grown girls, married women, and old women. They were not so attacked when they went for berries or cherries, but only when they went for *pomme blanche*.

Among the Southern Cheyennes it is said that mounted men used to steal upon and surprise the women, and after counting a coup to take their roots. If the women discovered the men coming, they sounded an alarm, and all rushed together to defend themselves. With a root-digger they drew on the ground before them a little furrow to represent breastworks. It was understood that no man might pass that furrow to take roots, unless he had counted a coup or killed an enemy within breastworks. If none of the men had performed this feat, none might enter, and they rode about outside the circle, while the women hooted at and derided them. A man who had counted a coup within breastworks, however, dismounted and entered the circle, told of his coup, and took what roots he wished, sometimes loading himself down with them.

As the sun fell, and it grew cooler, people came out of their lodges, and the scene grew more active. Now the feast shout was heard, and children were seen going to and fro across the circle, carrying messages of invitation. Working women and working men had long ago put away their tasks; the evening meal was being prepared. From the hills, horses were driven in, and, followed by great clouds of dust, rushed down the bluffs and into the camp, where, after some had been caught, the others turned about and returned to the hills.

As darkness settled down, the bright firelight shone through the yellow lodge-skins; sparks came from each smoke-hole, as the fire was mended or fresh wood thrown upon it. For three or four hours the camp was a busy place. People were passing back and forth in all directions. Music began to be heard: songs for dancing from some lodge where young men and women were having a social dance; the quicker, more lively music of the gambling songs, from some home where the game of "hiding" was being played; the droning, minor chant of a doctor, whose song was a prayer to the favorable spirits for help; or the love notes of some boy, who was playing his flute on a hill away from the camp. To most of the songs time was kept by drumming; it might be on a large drum, for the dancers, or on a small hand drum, for the doctor; or perhaps only on a parfleche or on the ground, by the gamblers. Over all the camp there was the hum which always accompanied the assembling of a number of people, and this was broken by the neigh of a colt, the barking of dogs, the yelp of some sportive boy, the shout of some old man calling a friend to a feast, the musical laughter of the women, and in the distance the shrill howl of coyotes. Then suddenly the people seemed to grow fewer; one by one the fires burned down, and at last the camp was as silent as the prairie had been before the people moved in.

Long after the people had gone to bed, young people might be awake and stirring, and perhaps doing reckless things. One night, many years ago, Buffalo Wallow Woman, then a young girl, in company with another girl, her special friend, went out of the lodge late, after all the people were asleep. Lying on the ground near the lodge was a three-year-old colt that had never been ridden. He was fast asleep and his nose was resting on the ground. Buffalo Wallow Woman said to her friend, "I could ride that colt."

"Do not be foolish," said the other girl; "he would throw you off." Buffalo Wallow Woman gathered her blanket close about her, began to sing a song, and then jumped on the colt's back. She remembers how it sprang to its feet, and the first few bucks, but after that she must have lost her wits, and just clung to the horse.

The animal rushed about through the camp and frightened all the horses, which stampeded with a great noise. The people awoke and rushed from their lodges, and the horses dashed out of camp toward the hills. The next thing that Buffalo Wallow

Woman remembers is that the colt stopped at the edge of a cut bank, while she flew over its head and alighted in the willows below. She was frightened, and under the cover of the bluff and the darkness crept back into the camp. It took the people a long time to gather their horses.

At the breaking up of any large gathering, as the camp at the Medicine Lodge, or at the renewing of the arrows, there was a general presenting of gifts, chiefly of women's things. The women relations of a young married man presented to his wife or to his mother-in-law food, dishes, shawls, or blankets, which the wife or mother-in-law distributed among the girl's female relations. These, on their part, were likely the next day to bring similar gifts—sometimes even lodges and lodge-poles —which they presented to the girl or to her mother, and which by them were given to those relations of the husband who had made the other presents. At these large gatherings the well-to-do young men usually possessed large new lodges, like those owned by the chiefs and the heads of the soldier bands. Such lodges were especially visited by parties of serenaders who were looking for presents.

NAMES OF THE CHEYENNE MONTHS

Here are incorporated the names of the Cheyenne moons or months, with their respective meanings, the first list being that given by Wolf Chief, the other by Big Knife.

Ŏk sēy' ē shǐ hǐs, Hoop-and-stick game moon; January.

Mǎk ōk sēy' ǐ shǐ, Big hoop-and-stick game moon; February.

Pǔn ǔ mǎ ēs' sǐ nǐ, Light snow moon; also called *Shi iv i ne,* Dusty moon; March.

Kā ǔhk tsī' ūt sī, January.

Māh kōhk tsī' ūt sī, February. Big wheel moon. A few buffalo calves and colts appear, but it is still cold.

Pō ō tǎn ē' ǐshī, March. Buffalo-and-horses-begin-to-fill-out moon.

71

Măt sī' ŏ mĭ īsh' ĭ, Spring moon; April.

There is no name for May and June, but they are referred to as "the time when the horses get fat."

Hīvĭ ŭts ī' ĭ shĭ, Moon when the buffalo bulls are rutting; July.

The Cheyennes have no name for August, but it is referred to as "the time when the cherries are ripe."

Tō nō' ish ĭ, Cool moon; September.

Sē' in ĕ, Moon when the water begins to freeze on the edge of the streams; October.

Hĭk' ŏ mĭn ĭ, Freezing moon; November.

Māk hĭk ŏ mĭn ĭ, Big freezing moon; December.

Mähk ē ō mē' shĭ, April fat moon.

Hōhk tsī' ēt sĭ, April moon, when they play wheels. When high water comes, the wheels and the sticks are thrown into the stream and carried off by the water.

Ō ăssī' ŏ wāh' tŭt', May moon, shiny, or bright; ball game month; because during this month the sun shines bright.

June, July, and August moons are just summer; green grass is up, the hot weather comes, and they do not count the moons until the plums get ripe.

Wāh' kă nŭn ē ishĭ, September moon. Plum moon.

Hĭs' sĭ kē vĭn hĭs', October. Dust or dirt in the face, from the dry dust blowing.

Hē kōn in hĭst', November. Hard face, referring to the cold. Leaves falling, and a little ice formed at the edge of the rivers.

Mähk hē kōn in' ĭ, December. Big hard face. Strong cold.

CERTAIN CAMP CUSTOMS

IN the ordinary life of the camp there is much of custom and ceremonial, all of it interesting, but so great in volume that it is impossible to learn any great part of it, or, within any ordinary limits, to set down even the part that one has learned.

A good part of the life of home and camp was conducted after established forms which were supposed to be known to everyone, and the failure to observe these conventions was formerly regarded by Indians as an extraordinary proceeding, much, in fact, as a breach of good manners would be looked at by well-reared people in civilized society. Thus, in the old days it was a common remark among Indians that white men did not seem to know how to act—how to conduct themselves. Of course, in these later times, a long experience of the white man's ignorance and disregard of their methods and ways of life has more or less accustomed them to such violations, and they no longer feel their former sense of injury and indignation at what they regard as his bad manners.

In entering the lodge the visitor turned to the right, and paused or sat down. The owner was sitting on his bed at the back of the lodge—the west side, or perhaps farther to the south—and when he welcomed the person entering, he asked him to come back and sit down. The place of honor was at the left of and next to the owner, who with his family lived to the left of the door, though his sleeping place might be at the back of the lodge. It was not etiquette to go to that part of the lodge occupied by the family, nor to pass between the fire and the owner of the lodge; nor, indeed, was it good manners to pass between anyone sitting in the lodge and the fire. Well-bred people passed behind the sitters, who leaned forward to give them room.

In the lodge, as a member of the owner's family, there was often a boy or a young man who was not related to it. Boys from ten to fifteen years of age, orphans or young relatives who had no one to care for them, often lived in a man's lodge and herded his horses, and performed other small services. The lad received his food and clothing, and after a time, when the lodge owner thought best, he gave him a pony. When the boy was fifteen or sixteen years of age, he perhaps went on the war-path. If on this first war-path he did well, showed courage, or was so fortunate as to capture horses or to count a coup, he no longer herded horses when he returned, but he still lived in the lodge, hunted, and turned in his meat there, and remained a member of the family. Such boys did not make the fires, but they cut the tobacco, lighted pipes, and carried messages. The fires were lighted by the women.

In old times smoking was an important ceremony, which different men practiced in different ways. In some cases no one might leave or enter a lodge while the owner was smoking. Some men went so far as to tie up the door of the lodge. No one must stand up or walk about in the lodge. Certain men, who were very particular, when about to smoke took down everything that was hanging up in the lodge, on the back-rests or to the lodge-poles. When they smoked they began by ceremonially pointing the pipestem to the sky, to the ground, and to the four directions, in order, and saying: "Spirit Above, smoke. Earth, smoke. Four cardinal points, smoke." Then the man made his prayer for help. The smokes to the four cardinal points were offered to the spirits who dwell in those quarters.

The pipe when passed always went with the sun, from right to left, starting from the owner of the lodge. When the man sitting next to the door had smoked, the pipe might not be passed across the doorway, but was handed back all around the circle—no one smoking—to the man on the opposite side of the door. He smoked, and then the man on his left, and so the pipe went on to the owner, or until it was smoked out. In primitive times they had a native tobacco that they cultivated and used for smoking.

At present, in the South, they mix dried leaves of the sumach with the tobacco they smoke. In old times they put a little buffalo grease with this. In the North they use "red-willow" (cornel) bark with tobacco.

The Cheyennes think it unlucky to touch anything with the stem of the pipe while smoking. The pipe must be held straight up as it is passing from man to man, not passed across the body the stem or bowl first, but held upright, the bowl down. Still there are various individual ways of passing the pipe. Some hold it so that the neighbor can take hold of the top of the stem; others, so that he can grasp the lower part. Others point the stem downward, and others still—and this is more usual— rest the bowl of the pipe on the ground as it passes. Many men will not receive the pipe unless it is passed to them in what they consider the proper way.

Often they make a prayer as they take the first smoke— sometimes a very long prayer. In old times some men would not smoke unless a little powdered buffalo-chip was scattered on top of the tobacco when lighting it. This was only to make the fire catch more readily. Some would not smoke unless alone. Nowadays, old men when cleaning the pipe empty the ashes carefully into a little tin can, on which the cover is replaced. None will scatter their ashes after smoking, but keep them carefully in a little pile near the edge of the fire. This has some relation to the sacredness or solemnity of the act of smoking. When old men are smoking, nothing must be beaten in the lodge. There must be no sudden noise. No one must tap on a stick. Dishes must not be knocked together. No one should walk in front of the smoker; that is to say, between him and the fire. In old times, as a rule, only the older men smoked.

Young men were advised not to do so, as it would make them short-winded, so that they could not run long and far. In old times many men would not smoke if a woman was in the lodge.

In buffalo days men were continually calling to the feast. The crier was asked to go out and call the names of those invited, mentioning each man's name, and bidding him to the lodge of the host. If it was not a formal feast given to a large number, but only two or three men were invited, the host might send a boy or even a little child, who would go to the man's lodge and say, "My father calls you." The meal usually consisted of roasted ribs or boiled hump ribs, or boiled tongue, of the buffalo.

A feast was begun and ended with prayer, and before eating, a little from each kettle was offered to the spirits, the food being held up to the sky and then placed on the ground at the edge of the fire. Private persons did the same when eating, in the lodge or elsewhere. The food offered lay where it had been deposited by the fire till the lodge was swept. When it had been held up to the sky and then placed on the ground, it was supposed to be consumed, and no longer to be of any value.

At feasts were often related the stories and traditions of the tribe. A person might make a feast and ask a certain man or woman to come and tell a particular story. After the guests had eaten, he or she would tell the story, and at its close might possibly present the story to some individual in the lodge, and after this had been done that person might tell it. At such gatherings people who were well known as story-tellers were in great demand.

When a man desired to have stories told in his lodge for entertainment at night he sent to some old man well known as a story-teller a message asking him to come to his lodge and eat. A comfortable place was fixed for the guest to sit and lie, and food was prepared, but not cooked. Meantime the news that such a man was to tell stories at this lodge had gone through the camp and very likely many people gathered there to listen.

When the old man came in and sat down, a pipe was offered him, and he smoked. When he received the pipe he raised and lowered it four times, touching the bowl of the pipe to the ground four times, and after he had finished smoking he went through the ceremonial motions of passing hands over legs, arms, and head. This was a promise to tell the truth—that is, to relate the stories as he had heard them—and a prayer for help to do this. Then food was cooked and set by the side of the fire.

Many of the stories told by the Cheyennes were the property of particular families, and might be related only by members of these families, grandparents and parents carefully teaching the children these tales of the past. Such stories were often personal property, and only those to whom they had been presented might repeat them.

Certain stories were told in sections. A short story might be told, and at a certain point the narrator stopped and after a pause said, "I will tie another one to it." Then there was a long pause; the pipe was perhaps lighted and smoked, and a little conversation was had; then the story-teller began again, and told another section of the tale, ending as before. Such stories were often told in groups of four or six, and might last all night. At less formal gatherings a man might tell a story, and when it was finished might say: "The story is ended. Can anyone tie another to it?" Another man might then relate a story, ending it with the same words, and so stories might be told all about the lodge.

When a sacred story was to be told the people were called into the lodge, the door was closed, and everyone sat quite still. No one was permitted to enter or go out while the narrator was speaking. Playing children were told to keep away, because if any noise were made in or near the lodge, something bad would happen—someone might get sick or die, or might be killed.

Sacred stories were told only at night, for if they were related in the daytime, the narrator would become hunchbacked.

Speech-making, story-telling, and conversation were the usual forms of entertainment among the Cheyennes at their more or less formal feasts; but on some occasions feasts were given which were attended by the members of two of the soldier bands, for the purpose of determining which band had among its members the most men who had performed brave deeds.

When a competition of this sort took place, the two bands were ranged on opposite sides of the lodge, facing each other. Those present did not at first speak, except when asked. Some elderly man was chosen to preside, one who had no special affiliation with either party, and so was disinterested. He sat at the back of the lodge with the pipe lying on the ground before him, the bowl pointing to the south. The umpire had already thought over the list of brave deeds to be brought up. Before him were a number of counters, consisting of small sharpened sticks, which he thrust upright into the ground for the purpose of marking what had been related—the points gained by either party.

When all were ready to begin, he passed a counter to the man sitting at one end of the line. The counter passed from hand to hand until it reached the man for whom it was intended, and then the umpire asked, perhaps, "Which one of you ever counted coup on a man who carried a gun?" If the man holding the stick had not done this, he passed it to his next neighbor; and so it went from hand to hand until it reached one who had done this thing, when he narrated the circumstance, perhaps mentioning the name of some witness to the deed.

Sometimes most unlikely things were suggested by the umpire, as when the stick was passed for a man who, riding a spotted horse, had touched an enemy carrying a gun. Without a word the stick passed from hand to hand until it reached a man on the north side of the lodge, who said: "At such a time and such a place, when riding a spotted horse, I touched a Ute. He held his gun in one hand, and was trying hard to get away."

"Ah," said the umpire—Woman's Heart, a Kiowa,—"that will not do. He must have shot at you." So the stick went on, and no one claimed the deed. When one side had counted a coup, and received credit for it, the stick was passed again to that side. A man who had more than once performed the feat mentioned might ask to have a second or a third stick passed to him, receiving them up to the number of his coups of the kind in question. When the coup had been related, the stick which had been passed for it was returned to the umpire, who thrust it in the ground to his right or left hand, according as the winning was by the party to his right or left.

In case neither side had been able to count the coup suggested, or if both sides had counted it, so that they were even, the stick was passed alternately to one side and the other. After four passings of the stick, someone might suggest that the pipe be lighted, and for a time smoking and conversation followed. The partaking of this pipe was a pledge of the smokers' truthfulness; and the purpose of the pipe lying on the ground before the umpire was also to insure truth-telling. No one would venture to lie or to exaggerate under such circumstances.

After the pipe had been smoked out, the contest began again, and with intermissions for smoking was likely to last all night. Whichever side had the most sticks received a feast the next day from the losing side.

Young men who had not done much in war never took part in such a competition. It was participated in chiefly by those who had been to war many times.

Among the Cheyennes, just as among all people, civilized and savage, the belief prevailed that personal suffering was acceptable to the supernatural powers, and would be likely to secure their favor. Just as the devout Christian in a civilized community may, during certain seasons of the year, wear a hair shirt, refrain from eating meat or using tobacco, or may give up going to the theatre, in the belief that this sacrifice of self is acceptable to God, so the Cheyenne who wished for good fortune—for success in his undertakings, or to avert an evil chance—cut strips of skin from his body, or starved, or swung to the pole, believing that by this sacrifice of self he would gain the favor of the *Mai yūn'*, those mysterious powers which controlled the affairs of men, and brought good fortune or bad, according as they were reverenced or neglected. It has been said elsewhere that in old times men going on the war-path used to slice bits of skin from their arms in sacrifice, and in earlier days—at the time when they wore nose-rings—men used to take narrow cross-strips of skin from the arms, frequently from shoulder to wrist, and sometimes cut similar strips from the legs. These were offered in sacrifice—a part of the body given to *Hē' ămmă wi' hio*, to bring good fortune. Sometimes, in the same way, a narrow strip of skin was cut out, running in a spiral from the middle of the chest around over its surface, as large as a dinner plate. Besides this, there were many other forms of personal sacrifice, of which the suffering in the Medicine Lodge is that best known.

Many years ago, when they went on the war-path, and felt that they were in danger, young men used to promise the spirits that if they were saved from danger they would cause themselves to suffer.

In those old times, young men used to go off on the hills and fast for four nights. This was called *a wū wŭn'*, starving. They did this in order that they might be fortunate, and might not be hit in battle. When they slept, they lay on their faces, with their heads toward the east; they had no shelter and no covering. They might smoke three times each day—at sunrise, at noon, and at the going down of the sun.

The young man might ask an instructor to take him up on a

RETURNING TO THE CAMP

high hill, on the right-hand side of a river; that is to say, either on the south or the west side; or to a point of rocks on the right-hand side of a lake. The young man must lie there for four days without eating or drinking. Usually such young men took up with them white sage, to lie on as a bed, and a filled pipe. Sometimes, if the sun was very hot, the man stuck a bush in the ground to give him a little shade. Usually he made an offering to Heammawihio, which he left there when he went away from the spot. These votaries did not choose places which were especially dangerous, but went to the tops of hills, open to the view, from which they could see off over the prairie.

If the dreams which a man had during this ordeal were favorable, he usually remained for four days; but if unfavorable, he was likely to stop and to return to the camp. If he fasted to the end, after four days the old man went to him and brought him down to the camp. They did this only in summer. This is said to have been purely a sacrifice, and not an attempt to dream for power; but often those who lay there did have dreams, and what they dreamed surely came to pass. If the Maiyun came to the man and talked to him, and smoked the pipe, he would be successful. Not everyone starved, and to only a part of those who starved did the vision come.

In another form of personal sacrifice the suffering was more acute, though shorter lived. When a young man intended to sacrifice himself in this way, he went out in the afternoon and cut a stout pole to take up on the hill with him. To the top of this pole a rope was tied.

At daylight the next morning the young man filled a pipe and went to the home of a man who had done what he now intended to do. He entered this man's lodge and offered the pipe to him. The man took the pipe and smoked. When he had finished smoking, he said to the young man, "Well, friend, what is it?" The young man replied, "I wish you to go up on the hills with me."

When they started, the young man took with him the pole

he had cut, and when they reached the place the old man dug a hole in the ground and planted the pole there. He then took hold of the rope, and tested the pole to see that it was firm in the ground, and that there was plenty of room for the young man to swing.

The young man sat down, facing the east, holding his shoulders well back, and his arms and wrists at his side. The old man pinched up the skin of the breast on either side, ran a knife through it, and then taking two skewers, about three and a half inches long, he passed one through the cut on each side of the breast. From a knot tied in each end of the rope, two flat ends of hide ran out, and from these ends hung heavy deerskin strings, slit like a buttonhole. The eyelets of each string were slipped over each end of either skewer. Then the old man stepped behind the young man, lifted him up and drew him back, so as to see if the rope was tight and the pull on its two branches even. After that the old man said, "Now, walk up that way [to the right, *i.e.,* south] and back four times." He walked about one-quarter of a circle to the right four times and back. He might then walk one-quarter of a circle to the left, walking a half-circle in all. The pipe was left at the end of the quarter-circle to the right (at the southern limit of his walk), and it was there that he smoked three times during the day. All the time that he was walking, the man was sagging back on the rope, trying to tear the skewers through the skin of the breast. He never succeeded in doing this, however; the skin is too tough.

The man who had given the instruction then went back to the camp, and at sundown came again, and with a knife cut the skin across behind each skewer, so as to free it. The skin cut off was placed, with a prayer, on the ground at the foot of the pole and left there. He then untied the rope from the pole, rolled it up, and returned to his lodge, taking the young man with him. At the left of the back of the lodge the young man

82

found his food in a bowl, and some water. The old man offered these to him, and first he drank his water, then ate.

Men suffered in this way in order that they might be fortunate in war—might take horses, or might count a coup—or it might be done as the result of a dream.[7] It was often done just before going on the war-path. The same man might do it several times.

Sometimes this sacrifice was made in the night, in which case assistance was asked of some old man who had suffered in the night time. The boy or young man was obliged to find out for himself the name of one who had done this same thing at night. The sufferer was made fast to the pole just as the sun was setting, and was set free just as the sun rose.

If done at night, the young man contemplated the spirits, and often during these sufferings he saw wonderful visions. Men were pierced and swung to the pole at night in the same way as during the day. There were different opinions as to which form of suffering was the more acceptable to the Maiyun.

Sometimes in the day a young man might have several buffalo-skulls attached to slits cut in the skin of the back, over the shoulder blades, and drag the skulls up and down over the course where he walked. This was sometimes done at the camp, and after the circle of the lodges had been put up the young man might start at the opening of and within the circle, and go all around the circle to the point from which he had started. There the old man awaited him, and took off the skulls, which were placed in line in the opening of the circle, facing inward. In taking off the skulls, the drawn-out skin was cut off, and the old man held each piece to the sun, and down to the ground, and toward the four directions, and then buried it in the ground. This might be done at any time when the young man wished to pay his vow. Often it was done at the time of the Medicine Lodge, but might be done at any time.

[7] See "The Cheyenne Medicine Lodge," in *American Anthropologist*, N. S., vol. XVI, p. 245.

Besides offering the pipe to the instructor, the young man was obliged to make him a liberal payment.

Sometimes when the Medicine Lodge was being made, a young man might have a slit cut in his shoulder, and tie to the shoulder a shield, which he wore through the ceremony.

When, at the Medicine Lodge or at any other time, men swung to the pole in this way, if they broke away, then they stopped and retired.

Sometimes a young man might take a buffalo-skull to the top of a hill, and from sunrise to sunset stand on it without eating or drinking, all the time looking at the sun. Sometimes, toward evening, friends would go up to the place to bring him down to the camp, and would find him so stiff from standing on the skull all day in one position that he could hardly move. When he did this, he stood facing the east in the morning, and turned, following the sun until it disappeared in the west.

The young man might stand in the same way on the ground, motionless, except as he turned with the sun. He might rest four times during the day, sitting down for a little while. This was regarded as an easy thing to do.

A young man might ask an old man if he knew how to stand in the water. The old man, if he assented, took him to a stream, and led him into the water until it was about up to his chest, and there he must stand all night. While standing there, the man might see some good sign, or something that was bad. If what he saw portended evil, he usually gave up, and left the water.

Once in a Medicine Lodge ceremony the father of Stacey Riggs, looking at the top of the center-pole, saw there himself. His fingers were cut, and his head hair gone; he stopped dancing. His wife asked him why he had stopped, and he told her what he had seen. Afterward, when he was killed by the Utes— in 1864, not far from Bent's stockade, on the Purgatoire River —he was scalped, and his fingers were cut, just as he had seen himself in the Medicine Lodge.

Old Whirlwind, as a young man, sleeping on a high hill for four nights, without food or drink, had a vision in which he saw himself, but with gray hair. This was a sign to him that he should live until he was old—until his hair was gray. He did live until his hair turned gray, and died an old man. He was in the Sauk and Fox fight, and was in great danger there.

A friend who starved himself twice, once lying down and once standing up, prayed that he might be helped through his life, might live to old age, and that whenever they had war he might kill an enemy. It has been so up to this time. When he went up on the hill to perform this sacrifice, he was told to stand up, but that just at noon he might sit down for a short time. After he had been standing for nearly twenty-four hours he was so stiff and sore he could hardly sit down. Each man who went out to perform this sacrifice was instructed in what he must do by older persons who knew—who themselves had been taught, and had made this sacrifice. Such instructors were not necessarily possessed of spiritual powers.

SOCIAL ORGANIZATION

WE know little about the early relations of the different groups that make up the Cheyennes of today. That the tribe is composed of Tsistsistas and the Suhtai, who were later absorbed by them, we are quite sure, but some old men have declared that originally there was a third tribe, *Hĕts tsĭ o mĭs' tăne,* pipestem men. It has been suggested by one man that this last name was possibly the same as Ĭssĭ o mē' tăne.

Old people have told me that from 1845 to 1865 many Suhtai still lived in the camp and practiced their old-time ways. Their clothing differed somewhat from that of the Cheyennes. The men did not wear breechclouts, but wore flaps hanging from the belt in front. The men's leggings were made each one from a whole deerskin, drawn tight about the leg above the knee but very loose below, folded over double in front, and tied behind in a bow-knot. The moccasin was sewed on one side only, being all in one piece, with a parfleche sole sewed on outside.

The woman's dress in front came up to the chest, and then the skin of the dress was turned over and hung down in a flap. At the left shoulder the material of the dress was gathered in a bunch, and a strip of skin passed over that shoulder, to support the dress on that side. The arms and shoulders were bare. The Suhtai women did not sew their dresses, but tied them together at the sides with strings.

Short Old Man, one of the last of the Suhtai, could not endure the smell of coffee. He and his wife did not like to ride on horseback, but usually walked and led the horse. Once while

86

crossing the Arkansas River, Short Old Man fell off his horse. He said that the water sweeping under him made him dizzy. Once he was persuaded to go on a buffalo hunt on horseback, but as soon as his horse began to run, he fell off. When he and his wife became very old, the Cheyennes used to put them on a travois when the camp moved. This always made them sick. Short Old Man always smoked "red-willow" bark with his tobacco, and placed a little powdered buffalo-chip on the filling of the pipe. These two never wore blankets, but always buffalo robes; in winter with the hair on, and sheets, so called, tanned without hair, in summer. They bathed every morning, winter or summer, cutting a hole in the ice if necessary. After their bath they returned to the lodge and made the fire.

Short Old Man wore the Suhtai flap and leggings, and his wife wore a buffalo-skin dress painted red. The man wore his hair rolled up on his head and coiled in a peak on his forehead; his wife wore her hair loose. They painted themselves with old Indian earth paint, and never used the new colors that the Cheyennes traded for at Bent's Fort. Their ways must have been notably different from those of most of the Cheyennes, for old people now relate that as very little children they used to run away from these Suhtai through fear. The man carried a quiver of buffalo-skin. His left arm was cross-scarred from wrist to shoulder, showing where he had removed strips of skin in sacrifice.

Since the Suhtai existed as a separate tribe up to 1831, we may assume that not a few of the original tribe members survived up to the year 1870 or later; and in accounts of fights between white troops and Cheyennes, we sometimes read of the killing of old men or women whose dress suggests that they were of the original Suhtai. Such a woman was killed at the fight of Summit Springs in 1869.

After the tribal groups had coalesced, all the people of the whole Cheyenne camp usually met together at least once a year at certain important religious festivals. The great camp was arranged in a wide circle with the lodges three or four deep, the opening of the circle being to the east or southeast.

In those days there were ten groups or divisions of the tribes, which in 1902 I stated were clans, that is to say, bodies of kindred, supposed to be descendants of a common ancestor. Further investigation extended over a dozen or fifteen years has led me to modify this conclusion. Certain very old men have told me that they have always heard that in the earliest times of which anything is known there were the three divisions of the tribe, Hevataniu, Suhtai, and Omissis, and that all the others have split off from them. The statement made by Perrin du Lac, who spoke of these people as in three villages, Chaguy-enne, Chousa, and Ouisy, seems to point in the same direction. Yet this means little, for he speaks only of the villages that he met and heard of, while the traditions of Cheyenne, Sioux, and Arikara tell of a time after the Cheyenne had reached the Missouri River, when their villages were many and widely scattered.

Most old people who tell of these divisions or bands agree that they were ten in number, including the Suhtai, yet old men differ as to the position in the camp-circle occupied by these different groups, each of which had its own place in the circle, all its members camping together. These differences of memory seem to indicate that the group places in the circle were not firmly fixed and may have changed from time to time.

While there are differences of opinion as to the positions in the circle which the groups occupied, it is generally agreed that the group *Ī vǐs tsǐ nǐh" pāh* pitched its lodges immediately south of the opening of the circle, and the group Omissis camped immediately north of the opening. The four men quoted below for the order of these group positions were probably born between 1809 and 1835. Porcupine Bull was a Southern Cheyenne, Tangle Hair and Elk River were Northern Cheyennes, while White Bull was formerly in the South, but

88

spent his latter years in the North. This is the order given for the period 1850-1860 by these four men:

Porcupine Bull	Tangle Hair	White Bull	Elk River
1. Ĭ vĭs tsĭ nĭh'' pah	Ĭ vĭs tsĭ nĭh'' pa	Ĭ vĭs tsĭ nĭh'' păh	I vĭs tsĭ nĭh'' pa
2. Sūh' tai	Hō ĭv ĭ măn ah''	Ĭssĭŏ mē' tăn e	Hōn ĭs' kū (?)
3. Wŭh' tă pĭu	Hēv' ă tăn iu	Hōf' nō wă	Ōōhk to ŭn' a
4. Hēv' ă tăn iŭ	Ĭss ĭ ō mē' tăn iu	Hō ĭvĭ măn ăh'	Sūh' tāya
5. Hō ĭv ĭ mă nāh'	Wŭh' ta piu	Māh sĭh'' kō ta	Ĭs sĭ o mē' tăn e
6. Ĭs' sĭ ō mē' tăn ē	Ōhk' tō ŏn' a	Ōhk tŏ kŭn ah'	Ma sĭh'' ko ta
7. Hōf' nō wā	Hōf' nō wa	Wŭh' tă pĭū	Wŭh' ta pi u
8. Ōhk' tō ŏ nă	Sūh' tai	Hēv' ă tăn ĭū	Tŭt o' ĭ ma nah' (?)
9. Māh sĭh'' kō ta	Māh sĭh'' ko ta	Sūh' ta ya	Hē' vă tăn iu
	(Hō tăm ĭ tăn' iu)		
10. Ŏ mĭs' sĭs	Ŏ mĭs' sĭs	Ŏ mĭs' ĭs	Ŏ mĭs' sis

The order in which these group divisions were camped followed the numbers given in the table. No. 1 was immediately south of the opening in the east or southeast side of the main camp-circle, the lodges of each group being placed close together. No. 2 was south and west of No. 1, and so on following around the circle to Omissis. Standing within the circle, not in the center but toward its south border and forty or fifty yards from the circle of lodges, were the two sacred lodges in which were kept the sacred medicines of the Cheyennes, the arrows, Ma hūts', in the easternmost, and the sacred hat, or bonnet, Issiwun, in the westernmost. Except for these two, which were usually marked with double crosses—signifying grasshoppers or dragonflies—there were no other lodges within the circle, save when on special occasions—as for a dance, a council, or some other important event—a large lodge might be put up in the center of the circle.

It may be conjectured that the fashion of camping in a circle is comparatively modern and was not adopted until the permanent houses, which the Cheyennes once occupied, had measurably been abandoned and the people had become nomads, following the buffalo. The practice may have been borrowed from some other tribe, for it was practiced by many of the

Plains people, for example, by the Arapahoes and Kiowas, who were early associates of the Cheyennes, but not by the Comanches, with whom also the Cheyennes were often in contact.

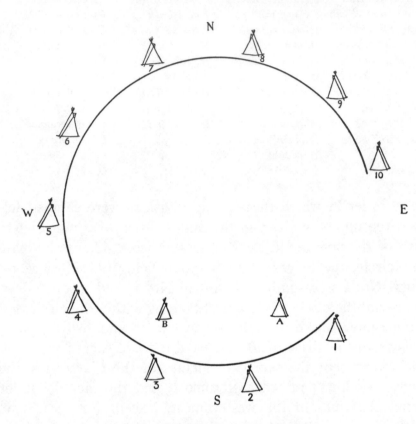

THE CHEYENNE CAMP CIRCLE

Numbers indicate positions of different tribal divisions. A, lodge of medicine arrows; B, lodge of the buffalo cap, issiwun.

The most aged men of the Cheyennes from about the year 1890 on for twenty-odd years have declared to me that in old times the different groups were supposed to be bodies of kindred, descendants of a common ancestor, but this was not thought to be true of the Suhtai. The further fact that some informants declare that some of the named divisions have split off from other groups implies that the formation of the groups is comparatively recent. The amount of testimony received from a number of old men as to the practice of exogamy in old times cannot be ignored, yet at the same time the evidence of a clan system is not conclusive.

In old times, these old men declare, the rule forbidding marriage within the tribal group was absolute, and not to be violated. Descent was matrilineal. A woman born into the group remained all her life a member of that group, and her children were members of it. When a man married a girl he went to live with her group, though always known by his own group name. His position in this group was what he himself made it. The famous Black Kettle, who was killed in the so-called battle of the Washita in 1868, was a Suhtai who married a girl of Wuhtapiu. He went to live with that group and became its chief. His children belonged to their mother's group, and not to his own. The reason now given for this rule is that there was always a possibility that a man might throw away his wife and take a new one, and that in such a case the wife and children must be cared for by the woman's group; that is to say, by her relations. When the woman's sons grew up and married, each went to live with his wife's group. Rarely, if the father was divorced from his wife and took a new one from another group, he might take with him to the group he was now to live with his eldest boy, if he was approaching manhood; but this boy was always spoken of as belonging to the group of his mother. A man might live in several groups during his life, a woman in but one.

Each tribal group or division had its own special tabus, ceremonies, and special medicines connected with the group ceremonies, but it is not now possible to learn much about these ancient practices, because the rigid observance of these customs passed out of use long ago. It is stated that when the tribe lived in the North they followed closely the customs that had been handed down to them, but with the migration, the breaking up into separated settlements, and the invasion of their old country by civilization, these old customs were neglected, forgotten, and lost. In fact, the ancient customs and beliefs as to relationships and groups have been so very greatly modified that it is now impossible to find among young people anyone who knows about these old matters. Such young people positively assert today that the tribal descent is in the male line, and it cannot be doubted that present-day investigation would lead people to that conclusion. The old men up to twenty or twenty-five years ago, however, were unanimous in saying that the children belonged to the mother's group.

In the effort to learn something definite about exogamy among the Cheyenne groups, I made—about 1902—detailed inquiry concerning more than fifty marriages of old people, with the result that in all cases, except where the Suhtai were concerned, the man and the woman had belonged to different groups. Their customs permitted the Suhtai to marry among themselves and it was even said that they sometimes married their own relatives. A case is given of a Suhtai man, Long Neck, who married his aunt. Among the Cheyennes, on the other hand, there still exists the strongest feeling against marriage between relatives, no matter how distant, and by many old men the clans or groups are still considered as bodies of kindred —descendants of a common ancestor. Many old men have declared to me that the members of a clan consider all of the clan their relations and it is certain that usually marriages took place between men and women who belonged to different groups. In old times if a young man wished to marry some girl in his own clan the old people, when they learned of it, asked him what he meant and whether he wished to marry his relative.

About the year 1900 a Northern Cheyenne came down to Oklahoma and persuaded a daughter of Hunter to elope with him. The young man took the girl up to Clinton, Oklahoma, where his aunt lived and stopped there in order to make the marriage formal by presenting horses and other gifts. William

Fletcher of Darlington, an educated Cheyenne and half-brother to Hunter, was sent to Clinton to represent the girl's family at the intended marriage. When Fletcher reached the place, however, and found out who the Northern Cheyenne was, he said: "I will have nothing to do with this marriage. This young man is kin to our family and is trying to marry one of his own relations. That cannot be, and I will have nothing to do with the matter."

One of the first things to be done in considering a marriage was to find out whether any relationship—no matter how distant—existed between the young man and the girl. If there was found to be any kinship whatever, the marriage was forbidden. The rules with regard to intermarriage or even courting among relatives were seldom infringed. Girls were closely watched as well as the young men who came to court them, and if one of these young men was related to the girl, both he and the girl were warned. Often young people did not know very much about these degrees of relationship and were likely to make mistakes. From hearing the talk of their mothers the girls were likely to be better informed than the boys. If a girl knew or learned of any relationship between herself and a suitor she always told him of it and warned him not to come again. If, through inadvertence or lack of knowledge of his relationship, a young man tried to court a girl who was related to him or even a member of the same division, the old women spoke to him and the young man, warned of the mistake, was much mortified.

It is said that the men of Ō ĭv' ĭ ma nah' were the first to marry within their own division, but that this did not begin until after the Sand Creek massacre. The cholera of 1849, which decimated some of the camps, may have had something to do with the breaking up of old customs.

1. *Ī vĭsts' tsĭ nĭh' pah*. This word is said to mean "closed gullet" or windpipe, or "closed aorta." The Northern Cheyennes say that the last name was given because on one occasion when a war party

was without a pipe they made one from the scorched or dried aorta of a buffalo. The explanation of the term "closed gullet" refers to the killing by a man of a medicine beaver, the eating of which caused all who partook of it to choke and thereafter made the flesh of the beaver, a beaver-skin, or anything pertaining to a beaver, tabu to these people and to their descendants.

The women of this group sit on the ground with their feet to the left and are called the left-foot sitters—*Na mŭhkt sĭ vā iu*. In all other groups the women sit with the feet to the right.

Ivĭsts = aorta; *nĭh' pāh* signifies stopping or closing a hole.

2. *Ŏ ĭv' ĭ mă năh'*. Scabby band; a trivial story is told about this group, whose horses one winter are said to have been afflicted with mange or scab.

3. *Hēv' ă tăn iu*. In one place Mr. Petter calls these people "pelt men" or "fur men," and in another place "rope men." The derivation has been given me as from *Hevă' o*, a hair rope, and *hē tăn*, man. This group was so called because they used ropes twisted of hair, while the other people for the most part used lines of rawhide. The old women of the present southern group made hair ropes by twisting buffalo forehead hair on a wooden hook. Some people say that the people of this group were more devoted to catching horses than others and were constantly making war journeys against the Kiowas and Comanches, and for these journeys were always making hair ropes to use on the captured horses. This seems to imply that the name was given since this group moved south, which probably is not true.

There are various trivial explanations of the name.

4. *Ĭssio mē' tăn iu*. Hill people or men on the ridge. Presumably given from some supposed preference of this group for camping on high ground. *Ĭsĭōm'*, hill; *hetan*, man.

5. *Wŭ' tă piu*. This is given as a Sioux word meaning eaters and is thus an equivalent of Omissis. It is said that one-half of these people had the name Wutapiu and the other half were called *Hōōhkts' i tan*, logmen—so called because it was their custom, when cold weather came on, to go into the thick timber and remain there all winter without moving about. While camped there—if the snow became deep—they chopped down large cottonwood trees in order to

provide twigs, bark, and browse with which to feed their horses. Camping places such as these, which show the stumps of trees felled when the snow was deep, are occasionally seen in the former range of the Cheyennes, but I do not know that the practice was confined to the Cheyennes; in fact, one has heard of it among the Sioux as well. The famous old Bark, Ugly Face—Abert—belonged to this group.

6. *Hōf' nō wa.* Poor people. I know of no explanation of this name.

7. *Ōhk tŏ ŭnna.* This name is explained as lower jaws protruding; that is to say, undershot. It is said also to carry the idea of the jaws moving, some say eating so eagerly that the lower jaw protrudes. It has also been explained to mean people drifted away.

A dance peculiar to this group, said to have been practiced by the young men before they started out to war, was known as the deer dance. It was held before a special lodge known as the deer lodge, which was not pinned together in front, but was open to the east. Some of the described practices suggest the Massaum ceremony, for lines of cottonwood branches extended for about thirty yards to the east from the front of the lodge.

The dancers carried each a shield and a lance and were painted yellow over the whole body, except one man, whose body was painted black, and who was known as the black deer. Each man held in his hand with the lance shaft the dried tail of a mule-deer. The dancers imitated the action of the deer, and the ceremony was for protection against wounds or death in war as well as against sickness. It is understood that the dance has not been practiced since about 1870 and its details are forgotten.

8. *Sūh' tai.* The meaning of this tribal name seems to have been forgotten. Some old men have said that it was from *Is sūht;* interpreted as ridge or hill. Other definitions imply a speech difficult to understand, or perhaps talk like the cry or grunt uttered by buffalo in the rutting season. Willis Rowland, however, declares that the word seems to contain the meaning of backward or behind, and Mr. Petter feels confident that it contains this idea and may very likely mean "people left behind."

9. *Māh sĭh' kŏ ta.* This term has been defined as lying on the side

with the knees drawn up. Mr. Petter gives it as reclining with one knee bent and the foot over it, and says that it is from the same root as the word cricket, *ma sĭs kot.*

This group was characterized by an unusual number of gray-haired children. It was finally absorbed by the soldier organization, Hotamitaniu, and is now seldom spoken of, though perfectly well remembered.

10. *Ŏ mĭs' sĭs.* Eaters. This, the largest group of the Cheyennes, never moved south in numbers. It now constitutes the northern section of the tribe, which in numbers almost equals the southern, and is made up almost wholly of Omissis and of Suhtai. The southern people used to say that the name was applied to the group because they were not scrupulous as to their food—which is only another way of saying that their food habits did not agree with those of the people who gave the name. They would eat anything. They are said to have preferred tainted meat, and a lodge owner who possessed some meat that had begun to spoil would invite friends to a feast as to something especially delicate. As lately as the middle of the last century it is said that buffalo humps were kept until they had begun to spoil and then were cooked.

Other men say that the name was applied because the men of this group were especially active and energetic, were successful hunters and usually had abundant food—plenty to eat.

As with many other group names this one was perhaps at first applied in derision, as a nickname, but has been so constantly used that the term has lost the significance it once had.

Besides the names of divisions or clans there are or were many other families, camps, and groups—people who remained together for a time and at length came to receive an association name or nickname which might later be used as well to designate their descendants.

Most of these names were no doubt originally applied in order to identify the various camps which in early days were scattered from the watershed of the Red River of the North as far west as the Rocky Mountains, and perhaps from the Yellowstone River south nearly to the Arkansas River. In primi-

WOMEN TRAVELING

WOMEN, WITH TRAVOIS, DIGGING ROOTS

tive times, and indeed up to the end of the Indian wars, the tribe during the greater part of the year was divided into small companies, for each of which the important work in life was self-support—the task of securing food sufficient to carry it on from day to day. These camps wandered about from place to place, sometimes coalescing with another camp, occasionally losing families or individuals, who went off to visit temporarily, or, perhaps, permanently to unite with other camps. Occasionally two of these camps met, remained together for many months, and then separated to go in different directions. The different camps were often reported on and discussed by their tribes fellows and the need early grew up of some means by which to identify these scattered camps. So they soon came to receive names, sometimes that of the chief of the camp, sometimes a nickname derived from some characteristic of the people or some characteristic of one of the people. Indians are notably quick to observe a peculiarity, and at once to seize on some salient characteristic of an individual, an animal, or a group of living creatures, and from this characteristic to apply some expressive name.

New camp names were growing up all the time, as the Rev. Mr. Petter has pointed out, and as I stated nearly thirty years ago. Many of those now existing have not had a long life. When the people were migratory, as in the old days, their camp groups were ever shifting and new names were constantly being applied to the groups that were forming.

Many of these names have their origin in most trivial happenings. Thus *Ăn skō' vĭn ĭs*—narrow nose bridge, Petter—were a family who seemed narrow between the eyes or had the eyes close together. In later times Broken Dish or Crow White, *Wōhk' pĭ ŭhk o*, who for a time lived in the North and later came south with Dull Knife, was their leader.

Mōhk stā' hē tăn iu, commonly called Ute people—literally, black men—is a name that has long been in the tribe. The ancestor of the group, *Mō ē' mā hăn'*, Elk Man, is said to have been dark in color, like the Ute. Most of his descendants are still dark and with very large noses. They are not thought to have had relationship with any Utes.

A family name *Mō ĭ' sĭ yu,* which I have referred to as a clan name, Mooney calls the equivalent of Monsoni and Dr. Petter follows him. A number of old women declare that this name is not that of a Cheyenne division. The word is Sioux—the name of a little group of Sioux who a long time ago joined the Cheyenne.

The name *Tă tŏ' ĭ măn āh'* is explained by a recent story that the leader of this division had killed people of his own tribe, and that thereafter his people avoided others of the tribe.

Many years ago orders had been given that no one should disturb the buffalo, and the soldiers had been directed to keep everyone in camp. They were waiting for the buffalo to get together in such numbers that, in the chase, everyone might have an equal chance to secure food. Buffalo Chief was in charge of the Dog Soldiers. A certain man had disobeyed the order not to hunt and had gone out secretly and killed buffalo and brought in the meat. The Dog Soldiers went to his lodge to destroy it as a punishment for his disobedience. While the soldiers were cutting up the lodge the owner came out and struck one of them. Buffalo Chief, the leader, seeing his young soldiers being struck, shot at the man and killed him. The wife ran out of the lodge with a butcher knife in her hand and he shot and killed her.

Buffalo Chief was now ordered to leave the camp. He gathered together all his relations and friends and they went off and for a long time camped by themselves, for now Buffalo Chief was an outlaw. At length, after they had been out away from the main camp for a long time, the people of Buffalo Chief's camp began to avoid the other people whom they met; were shy about speaking to them. Hence they were called Tatoimanah, the shy or backward band. This happened in the spring at the Black Hills near Nōv i vōos'.

Later Buffalo Chief again did something like this.

Buffalo Chief was well liked by many people and more and more families came to join his camp. At this time they were on the Platte at the mouth of Crow Creek. The main camp was below, where a little stream called Outer Edge Creek flows into the Platte.

Two of Buffalo Chief's men went down to the main camp. One of them was wearing a porcupine-quilled robe that he had borrowed from Buffalo Chief's son. The two men reached the main camp after night and found people there drinking some whiskey that they had got. A woman got drunk and her husband accused her of having been caught by the two young men from Buffalo Chief's camp, but nothing certain was known of it. Four men left the main camp to go to Buffalo Chief's camp to get satisfaction for this. These men were Bear Louse, Yellow Bull, Gray Tangle Hair, and Little Man, but Little Man did not reach the camp.

When they got to Buffalo Chief's camp, because of the robe that he owned, they accused Differently Colored, Buffalo Chief's son, of having committed the crime. The son denied that he had been away from camp, but the men from the main camp insisted that they were right, but said if he would give them certain horses that he owned they would forgive what he had done. When the three men had walked up to him and spoken to him he was out getting his horses. They told him what horses they wanted—a certain fast horse and a mare.

He said to them, "You are accusing me of something that I have not done," but they kept talking to him. He cut out of the bunch the horse that was fast and said to them, "You cannot have this one, but you can have any of the others." They insisted that they wanted this horse.

While they were disputing Buffalo Chief came out of his lodge and went to where the three men were talking to his son. When he got there he spoke to Bear Louse and said, "My son

99

has offered you any horse that you like out of the bunch, but that particular one I do not think he will give up."

Bear Louse said: "Ah, I have been looking for you ever since you took to killing people. I have been to war in my time and have beaten enemies over the head with my whip. I shall have this horse, which is the only one I want. I will knock you senseless too."

Buffalo Chief turned about and went into his lodge, took his gun by the muzzle and put it under his blanket so that it would not be seen that he had a gun, and came out again holding it so. He said to Bear Louse, "You had better take one of those horses down there; this one you cannot have."

Bear Louse said: "I will have this one; I will have him dead or alive. If he is not given to me I will shoot the horse."

Buffalo Chief said, "If you shoot the horse I shall shoot you."

Bear Louse shot at the horse and almost at the sound of his gun Buffalo Chief's gun sounded and Bear Louse fell over dead.

Differently Colored shot Yellow Bull and killed him. Gray Tangle Hair started to run and had crossed a ravine when Buffalo Chief shot at him and broke his leg.

Buffalo Chief had a peculiar way of handling his gun. After loading it he used to hit the stock on the ground. He never missed his aim.

Some other family and camp names are:

Na ko' ĭ mă nāh. The bear people, may have received the name from some important individual in the camp.

Wōhk' pō tsĭt—commonly called "white crafty" or "white cunning," and also sometimes spoken of as the White Wolf band. These people had the reputation of being more or less ill conditioned and disputatious, quarrelsome and hard to get along with. The name was considered a bad name because of this reputation. The founder of the family was *Wōhk po tsīt' sĭ ma hăn,* and the name was given him on account of his bad disposition. The family was once large.

Nō tā mĭn'—facing the north—may perhaps have had some relation to the Arapahoes or to the people who were commonly known as Gros Ventres of the prairie.

Hō nĭs' kŭ. Elk River long ago gave me this as a group name, but I have nothing about it except the name.

The readiness with which nicknames, applied to camps, bands, and sections of tribes, may grow up is indicated by a number of local names which have been given and become current among the Northern Cheyennes within comparatively few years. Thus, the Lower Tongue River Cheyennes are called Scabby Band, because, it is said, Badger, a principal man among them, had a skin disease. Those who live on Upper Tongue River are called the Backward or Shy Band, because they prefer to camp by themselves. The Lame Deer Indians are called Black Lodges, because they are on especially friendly terms with the band of Crows known as Black Lodges, while the Rosebud Cheyennes are called the Ree band, because among them there are several men who are Arikaras or have much Ree blood.

The last seventy-five years have wholly transformed the Cheyennes, and the diseases introduced by the whites and the wars that have been carried on and the changed conditions generally have destroyed great numbers of the tribe. It is said that the cholera of 1849 almost put an end to the group Masihkota, while perhaps half of the whole tribe died. Ohktounna were nearly exterminated and so were the Hofnowa. There are left still many of the Hevataniu, Suhtai, Omissis, and Oivimanah. It is said that there are many women of the Iviststsinihpa left alive, but few men. On the other hand, the conditions that have existed since 1890 or 1895 have so greatly reduced the death rate among the Cheyennes that they are now perhaps nearly as numerous as they were reported to be by Morse in the year 1822, and are likely to increase.

THE BOY AND THE GIRL

PEOPLE who know of the Indian only from books think of him solely as a warrior. As they have heard of him chiefly when he is at war, they do not realize that this phase of his life occupies but a small part of his existence, or that aside from this he has a communal and family life on which his well-being depends. He has a wife and little ones whom he loves as we do ours; parents and grandparents whom he respects for their experience and the wisdom derived from it; chiefs and rulers to whose words he listens and whose advice he follows, and spiritual directors, who tell him about the powers which rule the earth, the air, and the waters, and advise him in his relation to the forces of the unseen world. In other words, his is a complex life, not devoted solely to one pursuit, but full of varied and diverse interests. He must provide food for his family, must maintain his position in the camp, and must uphold the standing of the tribe in its relations to other peoples. All these duties call for the exercise of a discretion and self-restraint in his living which can be acquired only as a result of some system of education.

Even those who have had much to do with Indians hardly realize that their children are taught. They see the little boys constantly playing about the camp, engaged in sham battles, or swimming in the stream, or, in winter, sliding down hill on sleds made of buffalo-ribs, or throwing their javelin-like darts, or practicing with the bow and arrow, or stealthily hunting small birds or rabbits; and, contrasting this life of freedom with that of the white child, who spends much of his time in the schoolhouse, they assume that the Indian child grows up without instruction and without guidance. Yet no group of people could possibly live together in peace and harmony if each member of it followed his own inclinations without regard to the wishes and rights of his fellows. Like other people, the Indians have sufficient care for their own comfort to see to it that no member of the tribe shall unduly interfere with this, or infringe on the rights of others.

Among the Cheyennes the men were energetic, brave, and hardy; the women virtuous, devoted, and masterful. Though they were savages of the stone age, their code of sexual morality was that held by the most civilized peoples. Such fathers and such mothers were likely to produce and rear children like themselves: impatient of control or restraint, perhaps, and fierce and cruel in taking revenge for injuries, yet after all possessing many of the qualities which we wish to see in our children: courage, independence, perseverance—manliness. These qualities they inherited, but how were they brought out?

The Indian child was carefully trained, and from early childhood. Its training began before it walked, and continued through its child life. The training consisted almost wholly of advice and counsel, and the child was told to do, or warned to refrain from doing, certain things, not because they were right or wrong, but because the act or failure to act was for his advantage or disadvantage in after life. He was told that to pursue a certain course would benefit him, and for that reason was advised to follow it. His pride and ambition were appealed to, and worthy examples among living men in the tribe were pointed out for emulation. Of abstract principles of right and wrong, as we understand them, the Indian knew nothing. He had never been told of them. The instructor of the Indian child did not attempt to entice him to do right by presenting the hope of heaven, nor to frighten him from evil by the fear of hell; instead, he pointed out that the respect and approbation of one's fellow men were to be desired, while their condemnation and contempt were to be dreaded. The Indian lived in public. He was constantly under the eyes of the members of his tribe, and most of his doings were known to them. As he was eager for the approval of his fellows, and greedy of their praise, so public opinion promised the reward he hoped for and threatened the punishment he feared.

Indians never whip their children, nor punish them in any way. Sometimes a mother, irritated by the resistance of a yelling child, will give it an impatient shake by one arm as she drags it along, but I have never witnessed anything in the nature of the punishment of a child by a parent.

When a Cheyenne baby was born it was warmly wrapped up, and for a time carefully protected from the weather. During the first two or three months of its existence, if the weather was cold or stormy, the child was carried about in its mother's arms, and was not laced on a baby-board or cradle until it had become so hardy as to be able to endure some degree of exposure. Old people say that in earlier days, when the tribe lived in lodges, and moved about over the prairie, a large proportion of the children born in winter died. It can readily be understood that while living this nomadic life it might have been very difficult to protect new-born children from the cold.

As soon as the child had become strong and hardy enough, and the weather had grown milder, it was lashed on the cradle or baby-board. During a good part of the time it was carried about on its board, which, when the mother put it down, was sometimes hung up to a lodge-pole, or leaned against the side of the lodge in the camp. When the child was not on the board, and was not scrambling about on the ground, it was carried on its mother's back, her blanket or robe holding the little body close to hers, passing around her shoulders, and being held by her in front. The child's head was a little higher than the mother's; its hips lay between her shoulders, its heels showing through the blanket just above her loins. In such a position the child seemed perfectly comfortable and at home. It ate, if the mother passed food to it over her shoulder, or slept, its head rolling about on its neck, as its mother moved, like a toy Chinese mandarin.

The mothers played with their babies, and tried to keep them amused and quiet.

When the camp moved, the women carried the babies on their backs, or hung the boards on saddles or travois poles, while the little boys old enough to look out for themselves ran along on foot, or rode colts or horses, as the case might be. The little girls rode by twos or threes on top of the packs. Many children, however,—too young to be allowed to go without the guidance of some older person, yet too old and big to be carried by an overworked woman who was busy driving and minding half a dozen pack-ponies—were carried on a travois, confined in a cage made of willow twigs and shaped like a sweat-house. The flat bottom rested across the travois, which was hauled by some steady old packhorse. In old times, when many children were carried in travois hauled by dogs, runaways sometimes occurred, though not often. A dog, tempted by the sudden appearance of game, might start off in pursuit, and, tipping over the travois, leave the child howling on the prairie, to be recovered by the alarmed mother. Usually, however, the mother led the dog that hauled her baby.

When a little baby reached the age of from three to six months, it was time for its ears to be pierced. At the next Medicine Lodge, therefore, or at any great dance or gathering of the people, the mother took the child to the place of the meeting; and the father requested the old crier to call out and ask a certain named person to pierce the child's ears. The person invited to do this might actually pierce the ears, or might merely pierce them ceremonially—i.e., make the motions of piercing them. Before doing either, he counted a coup, telling of some important act performed in war. If the man merely performed the operation ceremonially, the ears might afterward be pierced in fact by anyone, without ceremony. As an acknowledgment of the service, the father presented the person with from one to three horses, and perhaps other good presents. If a man should have his child's ears pierced without this ceremony, it would create a scandal in the camp. People would say that he had no affection for his child.

In ancient times the person who actually pierced the child's ears made a long cut in the outer margin of the ear, from the top nearly to the lobe, and the strip on the outside was wound with beads or with brass wire.

A father who was very fond of his child, and could afford it, might have the child's ears pierced several times. He might give a horse each to two or three different men for the same service. In one reported case, a man gave eight horses for this purpose. Such liberality showed the man's affection for his child, and caused him to be talked about and praised.

Wealthy people sometimes had their child's ears pierced even before birth, making up an image on the occasion of some great dance, and having the ears ceremonially pierced. This was an old-time way.

Occasionally, among tribes on the buffalo plains, we find accounts of cases where a father himself has been obliged to care for and bring up an unweaned babe, without a woman's help. I have heard of such instances among the Cheyennes. Young Woman, who was born in 1830—three years before the stars fell—has told me that she was so reared. Her mother was an Arapaho, and her father half Cheyenne and half Arapaho.

When her father was a young man returning from the warpath, he learned that his wife had run off with another man. Instead of returning to the camp, he sent a friend to it to get his little baby, and when it was brought to him, he carried it from where they were camped, on the head of the Platte River, south to Bent's Fort, on the Arkansas. The baby was unweaned, and to support it he killed cows which had calves, and cutting out the udders gave them to the child to suck. In the same way he killed female deer and antelope, and let the child suck the udders. So he nourished her until he reached the Cheyenne camp, where a woman took charge of the child. Afterward she lived among the Northern Cheyennes. A like case was that of Arapaho Chief, a Northern Cheyenne.

At first children are called only by pet names. *Mŏk' sō ĭs,* meaning "pot belly," is a term of endearment for a little boy; *Mŏk' sĭ ĭs'* is a term for a little girl.

Such names were used only for very small children. When a child reached the age of five or six years, a more formal name was given it. A boy might be named after his father's brother, or after his grandfather. A good name was always chosen, though he might have also a nickname by which he was commonly called. A woman's daughter might not be named after the relations of the mother, but after some relative of the father. In fact, children were almost always named after their father's relatives.

Formal names were always given to children by the time they were six or seven years of age, and sometimes much earlier. Not long after a child was born, the father's brother-in-law or father might send for the baby, and when it was brought to him might take it in his arms and give it his name, and a horse. He would say, "I give him my name,"—Na vĭ' hĭsht nāt' ă mīt" "my name I give to him"—or the order might be reversed. Then he specified which one of his names he wished given.

If the uncle did not send for the child, the father was very likely to give the child the name of one of its uncles; or if it had no uncle, of its grandfather. A cousin, or some near relative, notified the man whose name had been given to the child, and he was expected to present to it a horse. The name having been given and the horse received, the same horse was given away when the child's ears were pierced.

In the case of a girl, the same thing happened. The father's sister very likely made a cradle for the baby, whom she herself wrapped up and put in the cradle, and then gave her a name and a pony. After a time the man gave his sister a horse in return for the cradle. If the sister did not offer to name the child, the mother might choose a sister-in-law's name, and she was expected to give a horse. The child might be named after a brother or a sister killed in battle. Then, of course, no horse was given. Names thus remained in families. Such a name the child retained until he had made a journey to war.

The infant's education began at an early age, its mother teaching it first to keep quiet, in order that it should not disturb the older people in the lodge. Crying babies were hushed, or, if they did not cease their noise, were taken out of the lodge and off into the brush, where their screams would not disturb anyone. If older people were talking, and a tiny child entered the lodge and began to talk to its mother, she held up her finger warningly, and it ceased to talk, or else whispered its wants to her. Thus the first lesson that the child learned was one of self-control—self-effacement in the presence of its elders. It remembered this all through life.

This lesson learned, it was not taught much more until old enough, if a boy, to have given him a bow and arrows, or if a girl, to have a doll, made of deerskin, which she took about with her everywhere. Perhaps her mother or aunt made for her a tiny board or cradle for the doll, and on this she commonly carried it about on her back, after the precise fashion in which the women carried their babies. She treated her doll as all children do theirs, dressing and undressing it, singing lullabies to it, lacing it on its board, and, as time passed, making for it various required articles of feminine clothing. Often as a doll she had one of the tiny puppies so common in Indian camps, taking it when its eyes were scarcely open, and keeping it until the dog had grown too active and too much disposed to wander to be longer companionable.

As soon as she was old enough to walk for considerable distances, the little girl followed her mother everywhere, trotting along behind her, or at her side, when she went for water or for wood. In all things she imitated her parent. Even when only three or four years of age, she might be seen marching proudly along, bowed forward under the apparent weight of a back-load of slender twigs, which she carried in exact imitation of her mother, who staggered under a heavy burden of stout sticks.

Boys learned to ride almost as soon as they learned to walk. From earliest babyhood infants were familiar with horses and their motions, and children two or three years of age often rode in front of or behind their mothers, clinging to them or to the horses' manes. They thus gained confidence, learned balance, and became riders, just as they learned to walk—by practice. They did not fear a horse, nor dread a fall, for they began to ride old gentle pack-ponies, which never made unexpected motions; and by the time they were five or six years of age, the boys were riding young colts bareback. Soon after this they began to go into the hills to herd the ponies. They early became expert in the use of the rope for catching horses.

Little girls, too, learned to ride at an early age, and while they did not have the practice that boys had, they became good horsewomen, and in case of need could ride hard and far.

In summer little girls as well as little boys spent much time in the water, and all were good swimmers. The courage of such children in the water is shown by an incident in the lives of three old women who in 1912 were still alive on the Tongue River Indian Reservation. When ten or twelve years of age, these children had been sent down to the stream to get some water. Their mothers were at work fleshing buffalo-hides and had so many to work on that the hides were beginning to get dry. The little girls were sent to get water to keep the hides damp until their mothers could flesh them. They went to the stream, and one of them proposed that before carrying up the water they should take a swim. They took off their clothes and ran out onto a fallen tree that projected over the water; and, when about to dive in, one of them noticed a hole in the bank deep under the water, and proposed that they should see where it led to. They swam under the water into the hole. It was dark and nothing could be seen; but the little girls felt something large and soft pass by them, going out of the hole as they were going in. They went on a few feet and saw a little light and, raising their heads, found themselves in a beaver's house. A little frightened by the creature that they had met in the water, which was of course a beaver, they did not like to go back and, seeing the opening at the top of the house through which light filtered, they readily broke a hole through the roof and crept out onto the bottom. Here they found themselves in the midst of a thick growth of wild roses and had a very difficult time, and were much scratched up in getting out of the bushes. This must have taken place perhaps between 1850 and 1860, and the women were Buffalo Wallow Woman, Omaha Woman, and the wife of Big Head, who was sister to White Bull.

Little companies of small boys and girls often went off camping. The little girls packed the dogs, and moved a little way from the camp and there put up their little lodges—made and sewed for them by their mothers—arranging them in a circle just as did the old people in the big camp. In all that they did they imitated their elders. The little boys who accompanied them were the men of the mimic camp.

In the children's play camps the little girls used tiny lodge-poles—often the tall weed-stalks that are used for windbreaks about the lodge—and the boys sometimes acted as horses and dragged the lodge-poles, or hauled travois with the little babies on them. To the sticks they rode as horses, as well as on the dogs, they sometimes fixed travois.

When the lodges were put up the boys used to stand in line, and the older girls asked them to choose their mothers. Each boy selected the girl who should be his mother, and they played together. The girls played in this way until they were pretty well grown, fourteen or fifteen years of age; but the boys gave it up when they were younger, for they strove to be men early, and usually soon after they had reached their twelfth year they began to try to hunt buffalo, killing calves as soon as they could ride well and were strong enough to bend the bow.

Sometimes two camps of children, one representing some hostile tribe, were established near each other. The boys of one camp would go on the war-path against those of the other, and they fought like seasoned men, taking captives and counting coups. They tied bunches of buffalo-hair to poles for scalps, and after the fight the successful party held dances of rejoicing. They carried lances made of willow branches, shields made of bent willow shoots with the leafy twigs hanging down like feathers, and little bows and arrows, the latter usually slender, straight weed-stalks, often with a prickly-pear thorn for a point. After the camp had been pitched, another party of boys might attack it, and while its men were fighting and charging the enemy, trying to drive them back, its women, if they thought the battle was going against them, would pull down the lodges, pack up their possessions, and begin to run away. In such a battle the men might often shoot each other, and when the wounded fell, men and women rushed out and dragged them back, so that the enemy should not touch them and count a coup. If the village was captured, all the food its people had was taken from them. This often consisted chiefly of roots gathered by the women, and tender grass-shoots, of which they often gathered a great deal.

The little boys when playing at going to war rode sticks for horses, and each one also led or dragged another stick, which represented another horse, the boy's war-horse. If an attack was threatened by a pretended war-party, those attacked changed horses, and leaving their common horses and their things together in one place, they rode out to meet the enemy and the battle began. The opposing forces charged and re-treated forward and backward, just as in a real battle. Each party knew or suspected where the others had left their things, and if one group drove back the other, it might capture its opponent's horses and other property and thus win a great victory.

In their pretended buffalo hunts also the boys rode sticks for horses, and lashed them with their quirts to make them run fast. Sometimes, when buffalo were close by and the real hunters of the big camp killed them near at hand, the little boys rode their stick horses out to the killing ground and returned to the play camp with loads of actual meat tied behind them on their horses. Some boys merely picked up pieces of the meat that had been thrown away, but often a good-natured hunter would give the lads pieces of meat to use in their camp.

If there were no buffalo about, perhaps some children went out from the camp, and returning by a roundabout way, pretended to be buffalo. Others in the camp, discovering them, prepared to go out to surround them. The children representing the buffalo went out on the prairie in a company; they were both boys and girls—bulls and cows. Some pretended to be eating grass, and some were lying down.

The boys who were to run buffalo had small bows and arrows. Those who represented the buffalo carried sticks three or four feet long, sharpened at one end. On this sharp end was impaled the flat leaf of a prickly-pear, which still bore its thorns. In the middle of the leaf, on either side, was rubbed a little spot of dirt. This leaf had two meanings: it represented the buffalo's horn or weapon of defense, but, besides this, the little spot of dirt represented the buffalo's heart. If an arrow pierced this, the buffalo fell down and died.

Some of the boy buffalo runners started out on the hunt far ahead of the others, so as to get beyond the pretended buffalo and cut off their flight. The others formed a wide crescent when making the charge. When the proper time came, the hunters rushed toward the herd, which in turn ran away. The larger boys, who represented the bulls, ran slowly behind the herd, and the hunters avoided them, because, if wounded, they might

TEETH'S GRANDMOTHER

turn to fight, and chase those who were pursuing them; and if they overtook the pursuers, might strike them with the prickly-pear leaves which they held on the sticks, and fill the hunters' skin with thorns. If this happened, it was told through the camp, "A bull has hooked and hurt" so-and-so. If the dirt-marked center of the prickly-pear leaf was hit, and the buffalo who carried it dropped to the ground dead, the hunters pretended to butcher it, and to carry the meat home.

With their dog travois, the little girls followed the hunters out to the killing ground.

Often some of the buffalo proved too fast for the hunters and ran a long way off, and then stood on the prairie and looked back. The hunters could not overtake them.

Perhaps a number of the boys might appear on the prairie not far from camp and pretend to be wild horses, and others started out from camp on their stick horses to chase and try to catch them, throwing ropes over those that they overtook.

The little girls often had trouble with their pack-dogs, just as did their mothers in real life. Many old and gentle dogs stayed about with them, but others, younger and more playful, were hard to catch when they wished to move camp, or might even run away and go back to the real camp.

Food must be had for the mimic camp, and the children went down to the creek to get fish. They thrust straight twigs in the mud of the bottom, across the stream in a half circle, the concavity being upstream. The sticks were so close together that the fish could not pass between them. In the middle of the stream, in what would be the center of the circle, if it were complete, a taller twig was thrust into the stream-bed, to the base of which a piece of meat was tied. Above the half-circle, on one bank, was fastened a flexible fence or gate of willow twigs closely strung together on sinew, and made like a mattress or a back-rest. It was long enough to reach from one bank to the other.

When all preparations had been made, the boys went a long

way up the stream, and entering it, formed a line across it, and came down, wading through the water, beating it with sticks, making a great noise, and so driving the fish before them. If the water was roily, the girls who remained below near the trap perhaps saw no fish, but if there were many there, they tugged at the meat and shook the willow twig which stood alone. Then the girls quickly entered the stream, and stretched the flexible fence or gate across it, making it impossible for the fish to pass up the stream. All now plunged into the water, and with their hands caught and threw out on the bank the fish that were confined between the half-circle of twigs and the fence above it. In this way they caught many fish, and these they cooked and ate.

The children did not stay out all night, but during the day they pretended that it was night, and went to bed. During the day they moved the camp often; even every hour or two.

These children imitated the regular family life, pretending to be man and wife, and the tiny babies—who were their brothers and sisters—served them for children. Little boys courted little girls; a boy sent to the girl's lodge sticks to represent horses, and if his offer was accepted received with her other sticks and gifts in return. Babies able to sit up were taken out into these camps, but not those that were too young. Sometimes a baby might get hungry and cry, and its little sister who was caring for it was obliged to carry it home to her mother, so that the baby might nurse.

Soon after the little boy was able to run about easily, a small bow and some arrows were made for him by his father, uncle, or elder brother, and he was encouraged to use them. When he went out of the lodge to play, his mother said to him, "Now, be careful; do nothing bad; do not strike anyone; do not shoot anyone with your arrow." He was likely to remember these oft-repeated injunctions.

After that, much of his time was spent in practice with the bow. He strove constantly to shoot more accurately at a mark, to send the shaft farther and farther, and to drop his arrow nearer and nearer to a given spot. As he grew more accustomed to the use of the bow, he hunted sparrows and other small birds among the sagebrush and in the thickets along the streams, with other little fellows of his own age; and as his strength and skill increased, began to make excursions on the prairie for rabbits, grouse, and even turkeys. Little boys eight or ten years of age killed numbers of small birds with their arrows, and sometimes even killed them on the wing.

Though he keenly enjoyed the pursuit, the Cheyenne boy did not hunt merely for pleasure. To him it was serious work. He was encouraged to hunt by his parents and relatives, and was told that he must try hard to be a good hunter, so that hereafter he might be able to furnish food for the lodge, and might help to support his mother and sisters. When successful, he was praised; and if he brought in a little bird, it was cooked and eaten as a matter of course, quite as seriously as any other food was treated. The first large bird, or the first rabbit, killed by the boy, he exhibited to the family with no little pride, in which all shared.

In their hunting, these tiny urchins displayed immense caution and patience, creeping stealthily about through the underbrush of the river bottom, or among the sagebrush on the prairie, striving to approach the woodpeckers climbing the trunk of a cottonwood tree, or the blackbirds swinging on the top of a bush, or the meadow larks stalking about in the grass. The care with which they twisted and wound in and out of cover when approaching the game, taking advantage of every inequality in the ground, of the brush, and of the clumps of rye grass, was precisely what they would have to practice when hunting later in life. At first, to be sure, they missed most of their shots, but they did not become discouraged, and now and then they killed a bird.

As a boy grew older and more skillful, he often took with him two or three little boys when he set out to kill small birds.

The bigger boy shot the birds with blunt arrows, and the little fellows gathered them up and carried them, by passing the heads under the gee-string, about the waist. Sometimes when the boys had enough birds, they chose a place for camping and built a fire. They picked and dressed the birds, and roasted them on the coals.

The older boys often set out in companies of four or five, and traveling across the prairie, a bow-shot apart, beat a considerable width of country. If game was detected, they strove to approach within shot before startling it, and often succeeded. Jackrabbits, however, were likely to bounce up under their feet, and to scurry away, pursued by a flight of arrows. If the animal escaped, the boys watched it, if possible, until it had stopped for the last time, taken its last look about, and settled down to hide. Then, having closely marked the spot, they very slowly and cautiously approached it in a half-circle, scanning the ground with the utmost care. If one discovered the rabbit squatting close, he indicated its position to the others, and they tried to surround and, if possible, to shoot it, before it started to run. They were often very successful in this hunting. Sometimes in the spring they succeeded in killing a kid antelope or two—a great prize.

While engaged in this hunting, the boys not only learned how to approach and secure game, but also unconsciously picked up a knowledge of many other things incidental to success in life. They came to understand the signs of the prairie, to know the habits of wild animals, learned how to observe, how to become trackers, where the different birds and animals were found, and how they acted under different conditions; and were training themselves to habits of endurance and patience.

As little boys grew larger they were often warned by their parents and uncles always to be quiet when older people were about, not to be noisy, not to play in the lodge, not to run in front of anyone. In the lodge they were not allowed to pound or knock on anything, and especially not to tap or hack with a knife any stick in the lodge, and above all not to tap on a stick in the fire. To do this might cause bad luck; a boy who did any of these things might even cut off his finger.

If by an unlucky chance a boy at play threw a stone or a piece of dirt or a mud ball against the lodge of a priest—a medicine man—it was necessary, to avert bad luck, that he should be purified by the medicine man, who unwrapped his sacred bundle, and with long ceremony and much passing of hands over the offender, and wiping him off with white sage-brush, prayed that his error might be pardoned. Unless this were done, the medicine would be broken, and many evil things might happen. Perhaps the lad might be struck by lightning.

From the beginning the boy was taught that his chief duty in life was to be brave, and to go to war and fight. He was treated always with great consideration, for it was remembered that he might not be long with his people, that in his first fight he might be killed; and, therefore, while he was with them they wished to treat him well—to make him comfortable and happy. For this reason, a boy was better treated than a girl. He had a good bed, often at the back of the lodge. For a lad to bring in a stick of wood or a bucket of water was considered unfitting. If he did a thing like this, it was talked of in the camp as something to be regretted, as more or less of a scandal.

When a boy was about twelve years of age, some old grand-father began to talk with him, and advise him as to how he should live. He was instructed in manly duties. He was told that when older people spoke to him, he must listen and must do as they told him. If anyone directed him to go after horses, he should start at once. He should do nothing bad in the camp, and should not quarrel with his fellows. He should get up early; should never let the sun find him in bed, but must be early out in the hills looking for the horses. These were his especial charge, and he must watch them, never lose them, and see that they had water always. He was told that when he grew older it was his duty to hunt and support his mother and sisters. A man must take good care of his arms and keep them in good order. He must never boast. To go about bragging of the brave things that he might intend to do was not manly. If he performed brave deeds, he himself should not speak of them; his comrades would do that. It was predicted that if he listened to the advice given him he would grow up to be a good man, and would amount to something. In this way their fathers, uncles, and grandfathers talked to the boys, and often wise old men harangued little groups who were playing about the camp.

A boy had usually reached his twelfth, thirteenth, or four-teenth year when he first went out to hunt buffalo. Before this he had been instructed in the theory of buffalo running, and had been told how and where to ride, and where to hit the buffalo if he was to be successful. If on his first chase a boy killed a calf, his father was greatly pleased, and, if a well-to-do man, he might present a good horse to some poor man, and in addition might give a feast and invite poor people to come and eat with him. Perhaps he might be still more generous, and at the end of the feast give to his guests presents of robes or blankets. As soon as the boy reached home and his success was known, the father called out from his lodge something like this: "My son has killed a little calf, and I give the best horse that I have to Blue Hawk." If he gave a feast, he explained again, saying: "My little boy has killed a calf. He is going to be a good man and a good hunter. We have had good luck." The man to whom the horse had been presented rode about the camp to show it to the people, and as he rode he sang a song, mentioning the name of the donor and telling why the horse had been given to him.

Bird Bear, whose boy name was Crow Bed, told me that as a child his father talked to him but little, while his grandfather gave him much advice. This was natural enough, since at that age the father was still engaged in war and hunting, which occupied most of his time, while the older man had passed the period of active life.

Crow Bed was quite young when he went on his first buffalo

chase, but he had a good horse, and was soon among the buf-falo and close up alongside of a little calf. He was excited and shot a good many arrows into it, but he kept shooting until the animal fell. After he had killed the calf he felt glad and proud. He dismounted and butchered the calf, and with much labor put it on his horse and took the whole animal home, not cutting the meat from the bones and leaving the skeleton on the ground, as a man would have done. When he reached his lodge, his people laughed at him a little for bringing it all home, but his father praised him and said that he had done well. "After a little while," he said, "you will get to killing larger ones, and pretty soon you will kill big buffalo."

His father then shouted out, calling a certain man named White Thunder to come to the lodge and see what his son had done; that he had brought meat into the camp. After White Thunder had come to the lodge, his father presented to White Thunder the horse the boy had ridden and the pack of meat that he had brought in. The incident was discussed all through the village, so that everyone knew of Crow Bed's success.

A year or two later, when a party was made up to go to war against the Snakes, his grandfather advised Crow Bed to go with it. Before they started out the old man said to him: "Now, when the party is about to make a charge on the enemy, do not be afraid. Do as the others do. When you fight, try to kill. When you meet the enemy, if you are brave and kill and count a coup, it will make a man of you, and the people will look on you as a man. Do not fear anything. It is not a disgrace to be killed in a fight."

When Crow Bed started, his father gave away the best horse that he had, because his son was starting on his first war-path. He cried out, asking any poor person in the village who needed a horse to come and see his son starting to war for the first time. He did the same thing when Crow Bed returned from the war-path, although on this first war journey the party had traveled for many days without finding enemies, and returned to the village without accomplishing anything.

My friend, Shell,—who died years ago, more than eighty years of age,—told me that his instruction came chiefly from his father, who gave much advice to him and to the other boys of the family. He remembered especially the father's warning to his children to be truthful and honest, never to lie. His father was a chief, and almost every night there were many people in his lodge, talking about different things, and the children listened to the conversation of their elders, and learned much. Shell was thirteen years of age the summer when he went on his first buffalo hunt. His father was a skillful arrow-maker, and the boy had plenty of arrows; and as he was riding a good horse, he killed three calves on this first chase. After the hunt was over, his father, who also had been running buffalo, came back and asked the boy if he had killed anything. Shell pointed out the three calves, and his father got off and cut up the meat. When they reached the camp, his father called out to a certain man to come and see what his son had done. When the man reached the lodge, his father gave him the horse Shell had ridden, and the pack of meat which it bore.

As Shell and his brothers grew older, his father used to teach them all good things, but especially that when they went to war they must be brave. That is why the Cheyennes used to fight so hard. They were taught it from childhood.

His father used to tell him never to associate with women, and, above all, never to run off with one. He would say: "Whenever you find a woman that you love, give horses and marry her. Then you will be married in the right way. Whenever a man runs off with a woman, both are talked about, and this is bad for both."

Older men gave much advice to their grandsons, sons, and nephews, and tried constantly to warn them against mistakes and to make life easier for them. A well-brought-up man was likely to advise his grown son that occasionally, when he killed a good fat buffalo, he should seek out some old man who possessed spiritual power and offer him the meat, in order to secure his friendliness and the benefit of his prayers. If the old man accepted the present the carcass was pulled around on its belly until the head faced the east. The old man slit the animal down its back, took out the right kidney, and handed it to the young man, who pointed it toward the east, south, west, and north, then up to the sky, and down to the ground, and placed it on a buffalo-chip. The old man was likely to say to the young man: "May you live to be as old as I am, and always have good luck in your hunting. May you and your family live long and always have abundance." As the old man went back to camp with the meat, he called aloud the name of the young man, so that all might know he had given him a buffalo. This was an ancient custom.

The training of the little girls was looked after even more carefully than that of the boys. Their mothers, aunts, and grandmothers constantly gave them good advice. They recommended them especially to stay at home, not to run about the camp, and this was so frequently impressed on them that it became a matter of course for them to remain near the lodge, or to go away from it only in company. Both mothers and fathers talked to their daughters, and quite as much to their sons, but in a different way. The mother said: "Daughter, when you grow up to be a young woman, if you see anyone whom you like, you must not be foolish and run off with him. You must marry decently. If you do so, you will become a good woman, and will be a help to your brothers and to your cousins." They warned girls not to be foolish, and the advice was repeated over and over again.

As a girl grew larger she was sent for water, and when still older she took a rope and went for wood, carrying it on her back. The old women early began to teach the girls how to cut moccasins, and how to apply quills and to make beadwork. As they grew older they learned how to cook, and to dress hides, but girls were not put regularly to dressing hides until they were old enough to marry.

Boys and girls alike had each some special friend of their own sex to whom they were devotedly attached, and each pair of friends talked over the advice received from parents.

Children seldom or never quarreled or fought among themselves, and though, as they grew older, continually engaging in contests of strength, such as wrestling and kicking matches, and games somewhat like football, they rarely lost their temper. Two boys might be seen swaying to and fro in a wrestling bout, each encouraged by the shouts of his partisans among the onlookers, and each doing his best. When finally one was thrown all the spectators raised a great shout of laughter, but he who had been overcome arose laughing too, for he realized that the others were not ridiculing him, but were showing their enjoyment of the contest they had witnessed. The Cheyenne boys are naturally good-natured and pleasant, and the importance of living on good terms with their fellows having been drilled into them from earliest childhood, they accepted defeat and success with equal cheerfulness. Among a group of white children there would be much more bickering.

Usually, but by no means always, the Cheyenne boy learned to kill buffalo before he made his first journey to war. Sometimes—as in the case of Bald Faced Bull, elsewhere mentioned —the little fellow's ambition for glory, and ignorance of what war meant, led him to join a war-party at a very tender age. Little boys who did this received much consideration from the older members of the party, and were carefully looked after. They were taken in charge by some older man, and were kept apart from the younger members, who would be likely to tease and embarrass them, and in all ways the journey was made easy for them. Yet when the moment came to fight, they were given every opportunity to distinguish themselves, which meant to fight and to be killed. Because on the occasion referred to Bald Faced Bull was riding a very fast horse, he was chosen as one of ten to charge the camp of the enemy, the most dangerous work in the fight. While such little boys did not often accomplish any great feat, yet sometimes they did so, and returned to the village covered with glory, to the unspeakable delight and pride of their families, and to be objects of respect and admiration to their less ambitious and energetic playfellows. Even when they did nothing especially noteworthy, they were undergoing a training, were learning to know themselves, and to be steady under all conditions, and were hardening themselves to the toils which were to be their most important occupation for the next twenty-five years.

If on such a journey the boy performed any especially creditable act—if by some chance he killed an enemy, or counted a coup—some one of his near relations, his mother or aunt or an uncle, gave away a horse on the return of the party, and presented him with a new name. If the mother gave the horse, she selected a name that her brother had borne; if the aunt, she chose her brother's name; if the uncle, his brother's name. The name was always a good name—that of some brave man. The name before being given was discussed in the home and chosen with deliberation. If the name given was that of a living man, that man took another name, perhaps that of his father or of an uncle.

A result of all this training was that the best of the Cheyenne youths had for their highest ambition the wish to be brave and to fight well; and hence they desired always to be going to war. If a few of them were traveling over the prairie in time of war, and people were seen, there was immediate rejoicing. "Ha!" one would say to his neighbor, "there are some people at last. Now we are going to have a good time. Now we will have fun. Hurry! hurry! Get ready to fight!" Meantime, any loads carried on the saddles, all extra clothing, and often the saddles themselves, were stripped from the horses and thrown on the ground, and the party, laughing and chattering in the highest possible spirits at the prospect of a fight, set out in hot haste to attack the strangers. If these proved to be friends, the disappointment of the young men was great. I recall a case in which a party of Cheyennes, scouting for the Government, charged a group of about their own number, which they presently discovered to be other scouts of their own people under command of the late Lieut. Edward W. Casey. They were much cast down.

A boy's education by advice and admonition usually ended with his first journey to war. When he had made that, he was supposed to have reached years of discretion and to have acquired by practical experience enough discretion to decide for himself what he ought to do, or to consult with older men and ask their advice. The first war journey was often long and hard and without any results, the boy returning to the village with nothing to show for his trip, but with a store of practical knowledge which would be useful to him all his life long.

Some of the young Cheyenne boys were practical jokers and, like many practical jokes, theirs were sometimes thoughtless and cruel. Little Hawk, born between 1840 and 1850, was a practical joker about whom many stories were told. Sometimes he hid by the trail along which the women passed in going for water; and when a woman passed, carrying a skin full of water, Little Hawk shot an arrow through it, and laughed delightedly at the sight of the water spurting in two straight streams from the holes where the arrow had gone in and come out. The water-skin was ruined beyond repair.

As late as the middle of the last century, the Mexicans often came north to the Cheyenne camp to trade; and brought with them some foods that the Cheyennes were very fond of. Once when the Mexicans had come to the camp, and almost the whole tribe had gone out to where the Mexicans were, to get a taste of the food they brought to trade, Little Hawk went around among the lodges, and from every lodge that had no occupant he took from the quivers all the arrows, carried them to his own lodge and hid them behind its lining. That night an alarm was given that Pawnees were about and had already taken a bunch of horses. It was ordered that all should arm themselves and scatter out on the edge of the camp to guard it. The men seized their bows; but when they took them, there were no arrows in the cases. It was a time of great confusion; but at length someone shouted out that Little Hawk must have done this and, rushing to his lodge, they found their arrows. Some of the men cried out: "Divide them up now and let us start out to meet the enemy. We can exchange arrows tomorrow."

On another occasion, one night the people heard a loud shout saying, "The Mexicans have come to trade; they are camped here just outside the circle." All the women jumped out of bed, got together the things that they had to trade, and rushed off in the direction of the voice. When they got outside the circle they could see no camp, and looked around, not knowing what to do. Then from behind them on the other side of the camp came the shout, "The Mexicans are camped here, and have plenty of things to trade." At once the women, thinking they had made a mistake, turned about and ran in that direction; but when they reached the border of the camp on that side, no Mexicans were to be found. Then the cry sounded from still another direction, saying: "This is where the Mexicans are; come this way"; and some of the women started, but presently someone shouted out, "Oh, it must be Little Hawk who is calling us about from one place to another." It proved to be Little Hawk, and there were no Mexicans.

About the middle of the last century the Cheyennes still, to a large extent, made their war journeys on foot; and were extremely tough and enduring. Such men lived until a few years ago; and an example of this came out in a story told of an incident that happened to She Bear when a young man.

She Bear possessed a sense of humor which made him quite ready to laugh at a joke even if it were against himself. He said that when he was a young man he heard of a dance that was to be held in two or three days at a neighboring camp, distant from his home about seventy-five miles, and set out to walk to that camp to attend the dance.

He had gone about half the distance, and was walking along singing to himself and practicing his dancing steps as he walked. Presently someone behind him said: "You are dancing well; the girls will look at you"; and turning about he saw close to him Spotted Wolf, who also was on his way to the dance and had been watching She Bear from a place of concealment. She Bear told this as a joke on himself; but the interesting part of the story seemed to me that a young man should start off to walk seventy-five miles in order to attend a social dance.

WOMAN AND HER PLACE

STATUS OF WOMEN

ON few subjects has there been such persistent misunderstanding as on the position of women among the Indians. Because she was energetic, always busy in the camp, often carried heavy burdens, attended to the household duties, made the clothing and the home, and prepared the family food, the woman has been pictured as the slave of her husband, a patient beast of burden whose toils were never done. The man, on the other hand, was said to be an idler who all day long sat in the shade of the lodge and smoked his pipe, while his industrious wives ministered to his comfort. Most of those who have written of Indian life seem to have comprehended nothing of the strenuous labors of the hunt, and of the war-path, and to have realized not at all that the woman was the man's partner, who performed her share of the duties of life, as he performed his, and who wielded an influence quite as important as his, and often even more powerful.

It is true that the women performed many laborious tasks—tasks that civilized man regards as toil—and that the work done by the men—hunting and going to war—are occupations that civilized man is disposed to regard as sport or recreation; but for this division of labor there were good reasons. The work of providing food and of defense against enemies was hard and dangerous; while fighting and the use of arms were no part of woman's work. As almost everywhere in the world, her share in the life of the community was the care of the household—the welfare of the family. The man's duty was to defend his wife and children, and the tribe at large, in case of an attack, and if the enemies were too strong to be defeated and driven away, at least to fight them off, to hold them in check, so that the women and children might escape by flight. To fight to advantage, to be in a position to repel enemies that might try to kill his people, a fighting man must be unhampered by a load, and must be light and active, so that he might get about quickly and have an equal chance with the attacking party, who presumably were prepared for war. Chiefly for this reason, the men, carrying only their arms, commonly went ahead, and the women, following behind, looked after the children, bore the burdens, or cared for the animals which transported the camp property. At an earlier day, before the white man had come, before the Indians had obtained horses, and when enemies were not so often encountered on the prairie, the whole marching camp—men, women, children, and dogs alike—carried loads, apportioned according to the strength of the bearer.

In the Cheyenne camp, as everywhere in the world, the man was the provider, the one who procured the food and most of the material for the needs of life, while the woman bore the children, cared for the home, and thus did her share of the most important work that the Indians knew—the promotion of the tribal welfare. The man and the woman were partners, sharing equally in the work of the family, and often in a deep and lasting affection which each bore toward the other—an affection which, beginning in youth with love and marriage, lasted often to the end of life. I have seen many examples of such attachment, seldom expressed in words, but shown in the daily conduct of life, where in all his occupations the man's favorite companion was the wife he had courted as a girl and by whose side he had made his struggle for success and now at last had grown old.

Among the Cheyennes, the women are the rulers of the camp. They act as a spur to the men, if they are slow in performing their duties. They are far more conservative than the men, and often hold them back from hasty, ill-advised action. If the

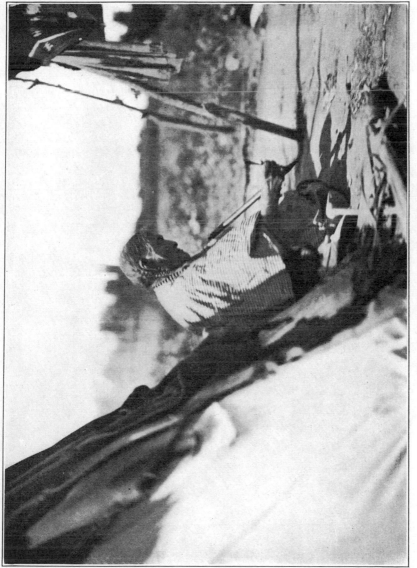

RED BEAD WOMAN, SMOKING

sentiment of the women of the camp clearly points to a certain course as desirable, the men are quite sure to act as the women wish.

In the severest winter weather, women did not do much at the dressing of robes, but on pleasant days in winter they often worked at that task. A winter camp was usually made at some point where there was abundant timber; and in some sheltered place among this timber the women cleared away the weeds and undergrowth from a considerable space, hung up robes or lodge-skins about it to serve as windbreaks, and building a big fire in the middle, worked about this at their tasks. Such a place was comfortable, almost like the inside of a lodge, except that it was open at the top.

Family rank, which existed among the Cheyennes as among other Indians, depended on the estimation in which the family was held by the best people. A good family was one that produced brave men and good sensible women, and that possessed more or less property. A brave and successful man has raised his family from low to very high rank; or a generation of inefficient men might cause a family to retrograde.

The passage of a girl from childhood to young womanhood was considered as hardly less important to the tribe than to her own family. She was now to become the mother of children and thus to contribute her part toward adding to the number of the tribe and so to its power and importance.

When a young girl reached the age of puberty and had her first menstrual period, she, of course, told her mother, who in turn informed the father. Such an important family event was not kept secret. It was the custom among well-to-do people for the father of the girl publicly to announce from the lodge door what had happened and as an evidence of his satisfaction to give away a horse.

The girl unbraided her hair and bathed, and afterward older women painted her whole body with red. Then, with a robe about her naked body, she sat near the fire, a coal was drawn from it and put before her, and sweet grass, juniper needles, and white sage were sprinkled on it. The girl bent forward over the coal and held her robe about it, so that the smoke rising from the incense was confined and passed about her and over her whole body. Then she and her grandmother left the home lodge, and went into another small one near by, where she remained for four days.

If there was no medicine, no sacred bundle, and no shield in her father's lodge, the girl might remain there; but if she did so, everything that possessed a sacred character—even the feathers that a man wore tied in his head—must be taken out.

At the end of the four days, her grandmother, taking a coal from the fire, and sprinkling on it sweet grass, juniper needles, and white sage, caused the girl, wrapped in a robe or sheet, to stand over the smoke, with feet on either side of the coal, purifying herself. This was always done by young unmarried women.

For four days a woman in this condition might not eat boiled meat. Her meat must be roasted over coals. If the camp moved she might not ride a horse, but was obliged to ride a mare.

Young men might not eat from the dish nor drink from the pot used by her; one who did so would expect to be wounded in his next fight. She might not touch a shield or any other war implement, nor any sacred bundle or object. A married woman during this time did not sleep at home, but went out and slept in one of the menstrual lodges. Men believed that if they lay beside their wives at this time they were likely to be wounded in their next battle. Women in this condition were careful to avoid entering a lodge where there was a medicine bundle or bag. For four days women did not walk about much. They spent almost all their time in the small lodge.

The owner of a shield was required to use special care to avoid menstruating women. He might not go into a lodge where one was nor even into a lodge where one had been, until a ceremony of purification had been performed. If the woman thoughtlessly visited the lodge of a neighbor, no shield owner might enter it until sweet grass and juniper leaves had been burned in the lodge, the pins removed and the lodge covering thrown back, as if the lodge were about to be taken down. When this had been done, the covering might be thrown forward again, and pinned together. The lodge having been thus purified, the shield owner might enter it.

The Cheyenne young women and young girls always wore the protective rope, and most of them still do so. This is a small rope or line which passes about the waist, is knotted in front, passes down and backward between the thighs, and each branch is wound around the thigh down nearly to the knee. The wearing of this rope is somewhat confining, yet those who wear it can walk freely. It is worn always at night and during the day when women go abroad.

It is a complete protection to the woman wearing it and is assumed by girls as soon as the period of puberty is reached. All men, young and old, respect this rope, and anyone violating it would certainly be killed by the male relations of the girl. I have heard of one case where a middle-aged man attempted to disregard this protection. The girl and her mother were the only two of the family left, all their male relatives having died. Not long after the attempt was made, the mother and daughter, arming themselves with heavy stones, waylaid the man, took him by surprise, gave him a frightful pounding, and left him for dead. He recovered after a long siege, during which he received sympathy from no one.

In the Cheyenne camp, love and courtship and marriage had their place, as they have the world over.

In modern times the young Cheyenne lover did his courting in the old-fashioned Sioux manner. When he became fond of a girl, he went near to the lodge in which she lived, and, wrapped in his blanket or his robe, which was over his head and hid his features, he stood there, waiting for her to come out. When she passed, on her way to get wood or water, or on her return, he stepped up beside her, and threw his arms and his blanket around her, quite covering her person with the blanket. Then he held her fast and began to talk with her. If she did not like this, she broke away from him, and he went away, much mortified; but if she listened to him, he might talk to her for an hour or two—perhaps much longer. If she did not come out of the lodge, he might wait four or five hours, and then go off, to return and try once more.

A girl whose beauty or whose pleasing manners made her popular might have a number of suitors. Often, when a girl had been off with some of her fellows to get wood, or gather roots, or play football, she might find on her return to the lodge several young men standing near it, waiting to talk with her and court her. The young men did this in turn, the first to arrive having the first opportunity. If two or three young men were waiting for her, the first to reach her took her in his arms and talked, and the others stood at intervals toward the lodge door, each awaiting his turn as she came on. The man nearest the door was usually he who talked the longest with her. If only one young man was waiting, he and the girl might sit down by the lodge. Very likely the girl's younger sisters, as well as the young men, were watching for her return, and when the lover threw his arms around the girl to hold her, her young sisters might run up and take the rings off his fingers or the bracelets from his wrists, or might even twitch off one or more of his silver hair ornaments. Whatever they did, he paid no attention to them. All this is borrowed from the Sioux within the last century.

In old times, however, courting was not done in this way. Then, no boy would ever have thought of throwing his arms around a girl. He waited for her, as she was going for wood or water, and as she passed him, plucked at her robe to attract her attention, and stop her. Usually she stopped to converse, but if she did not stop, the young man felt that he had been badly treated and went away, mortified at the rebuff. Sometimes young men did not dare to go as far as to pull at the girl's robe. They stood at a little distance, and whistled or called to her, to endeavor to get her to look at them, in the hope that she would smile, or in some way encourage them to be a little bolder.

When meeting girls in front of the lodge and courting them, young men did not usually talk to the girls of love, but conversed on general topics, giving the news and discussing the affairs of the camp. A young man who wished to ask a girl to marry him did not often put the question himself, but requested some friend to meet the girl and ask her if she would marry him. This is of more modern times. In earlier days some aged friend or relation was sent to convey this message.

In olden times the young people used to wear rings; at first, made by themselves, of horn, and later of metal. Often two young people would plight their troth by an exchange of rings. If a young man wished a girl to marry him and spoke to her about it, she might say to him: "Are you telling the truth? If you are, take off my ring," and she held out her hand. He took the ring and put it on his finger. If he asked her if she was telling the truth, she did the same thing. In this way they promised to marry each other, although some time might elapse before the marriage took place. Sometimes it might not take place at all, but if the girl did not marry the man to whom she was pledged, but married another, the man whose ring she had taken might send someone to ask her that his ring be returned to him, and in such case it was sent back. On the other hand, if the man married another girl—not the one to whom he had given his ring—she who had received the ring might throw it away, signifying that at the same time she threw away both ring and man.

Sometimes, when the young people were talking outside the lodge, a boy might slip the wristlet off a girl's arm and take it home with him. If the girl was willing that he should keep it, she said nothing; but she might go in and say to her mother, "So-and-so took my wristlet and carried it away, and I do not want him." In such a case the family sent a messenger for the wristlet, and the young man gave it up.

A girl was not likely to become engaged to a young man who had not been to war, because of the feeling that one who had not been to war was not yet a man, that is, grown up.

The flute was sometimes played by young men merely for the pleasure of making sweet sounds. Others played it in order to help them in their courtship. Some flutes had a special power to influence girls. A young man might go to a medicine man and ask him to exercise his power on a flute, so that the girl he wanted would come out of the lodge when she heard it. The young man began to play the flute when he was at a distance from the lodge, but gradually approached it, and when he had come near to the lodge he found the girl outside waiting for him.

If a young man fell in love with a girl who did not care for him, he might fill a pipe and take it to a medicine-man who had power in affairs of love, ask him for help, and tell him his troubles. Perhaps the medicine man gave him some spruce gum, used for chewing, and told him that if he could get the girl to chew it her thoughts would constantly be of him. The young man might himself offer the gum to the girl, or might persuade some woman friend, married or unmarried, to induce the girl to take it. If the girl chewed it, her thoughts were certain to turn to the young man, and she thought of him constantly.

The white-tailed deer[1] are powerful in love affairs, and are to be asked for help. Those who have these deer for their helpers wear on the shoulder belt the tail of a deer, with some medicine tied to it. Such ornaments were made for those who have love troubles. Those who understood the deer and its ways taught the young man what to do. In approaching her he should

[1] Timber deer waving—*mā tā′ ē wă sĭ ŏm stă sĭn′ ni.*

always walk up to the girl on the windward side, so that she might get the scent of the tail and of the medicine.

The following story bears on these beliefs:

There was a young man, afterward named Black Wolf, who loved a girl in the next camp, and wished to go to see her. It was some distance away, and two days and one night were required to reach it. The young man asked Elk River's wife to give him some food so that he might stop on his journey and eat.

As he was traveling he came to a ridge, from which he saw a stream running in the direction he wished to go. He went down into the valley, toward the stream, and as he approached it he saw some lodges in a thick growth of willows, and up the creek a large lodge standing near the bank. He determined to go to this lodge, but went down to the stream to follow it up on the ice, for it was winter. As he went along, he said to himself, "The camp is not so far off as I had thought; here it is now."

When he had come near to the lodge he stopped to look at it and to see whose it was. There was a light within, and he saw standing near the lodge young men playing on the flute, as if courting. In the lodge he could hear people playing the finger-bone game. He determined to enter and ask the people there where he should go to find his relatives in the camp. He peeped in through the door and saw within a number of beautiful girls and fine-looking young men, some playing the finger-bone game and some the seed game. Some of the girls had on striped Navaho blankets, and some painted robes—all very pretty. The young men, too, were finely dressed. The young people outside stood about, wearing their robes hair-side out. When he saw all these girls, he felt bashful, and did not go in. Presently he went around to the back of the lodge to think what he should do. There he stopped and considered, and taking courage, started back to the door, intending to enter; but as he was walking he turned his head, and for a moment looked away from the lodge, and when he looked back, the lodge was not there. Instead of all these beautiful girls and men, there were deer, going off through the timber. He wondered to himself what had happened, and went down through the timber and continued on his way, often looking back and fearing lest something bad might come to him before he could get away.

All night he went on, and near morning stopped, and built a big fire and rested there nearly all day. He pondered so much on what he had seen that he forgot to eat until just before he started on. Night began to fall before he had gone far, and just before dark he saw smokes and heard dogs barking. He knew he must be near the camp and stopped to rest.

That night he went down into the camp, and walked about, looking for some of his people with whom he might stop. As he passed each lodge he stood still listening for a voice that he knew, and at last he found the right lodge and went in. He did not stay there long, but said to his relations, "I have come a long way to see my sweetheart," and went out again. He went about through the camp looking for the girl's lodge, but when he found it, he saw a young man there courting her, and other young men waiting. He stepped back out of sight to wait until some of them had gone away.

When all had gone, he stepped up, and the girl looked at him, and knew him, and said, "Ah, it is you!" and she hugged him. "How did you get here?" she asked. "Did you come out of the sky, or did you creep up out of the earth?"

The young man said, "I came through today"—which was not true. "I thought about you the other evening, and started off to find you. I do not suppose that you have thought much about me."

"Yes," said the girl, "I have thought of you many times. Every time I see the ring you gave me I feel lonely, but I cannot get to where you are; it is too far to go." They kissed each other.

The young man had gone to the camp to give back the girl's ring and to take his own from her. He did this because he was going to war. He did not wish to be killed with the girl's ring on his finger.

Before he had left his own camp an old man had cried through the village that the camp was to be moved to a certain place. The young man waited in the girl's camp so that his own camp might be moved before he returned to it.

After he had been in this camp four days and four nights, he said to the relative with whom he was stopping, "Give me some food for my journey; I think that by this time the camp is moved, and I shall go back there." They gave him some pounded meat and tallow. He wanted to see his girl again before he started, and that night he went to her lodge and she came out to meet him. He said: "I have come to see you once more. Tonight I am going home."

"Why are you going home?" asked the girl. "May I go home with you?"

"No," said he, "I cannot take you now. I am going to war as soon as I reach home. When I return from war I will take you to my camp." The girl cried.

The young man left her and started. He traveled until he reached camp. After two days' rest he set out on his journey to war, and before he returned he had counted a coup. After his return they had a great war dance, and danced all night. Elk River gave away a horse, and changed the young man's name to Black Wolf. He was the father of that Black Wolf who was Brave Wolf's son-in-law.

From the deer Black Wolf received the power to make any girl fall in love with him. He could put his medicine on a looking-glass, and flash it on the girl's eyes, and she would fall in love with him. He was a great man to make flutes for lovers, and wore a white-tailed deer's tail on a belt which passed over his shoulder. Men who were unfortunate in love used to go to him to get help. He was very skillful in playing the finger bone game and the seed game, but he hardly ever gambled in that way.

MARRIAGE

A Cheyenne boy was expected to court a girl from one to five years. After he felt sure of her consent, he applied to her parents for theirs, sending either an old man—some friend or relation—or perhaps an old woman—his mother—to ask the girl in marriage. With the messenger he sent the number of horses that he could give. The messenger tied the horses in front of the father's lodge, and then went in and delivered the message, saying, "Such a young man [naming him] wishes your daughter [naming her] for his wife." The messenger did not wait for an answer, but at once went away.

Sometimes the father decided for himself whether or not he

would consent to the marriage, but at other times he sent for his relatives to talk the matter over and to ask their advice before giving an answer. If this was unfavorable, the horses which the young man had sent were turned loose and driven back to his father's lodge; but if the marriage was acceptable, the girl's father sent her, and with her a number of horses, often greater than that sent by the young man, to the lodge of the young man's father.

The horses sent by the young man stood in front of the lodge of the prospective father-in-law until the question of the advisability of the marriage had been decided. Sometimes they stood there all day. Often not horses alone were sent, but any other presents that the suitor thought might be acceptable. Thus, if the girl had a young brother who was fond of going to war, the suitor might send a war-bonnet, or even his whole war outfit, bow, arrows, quiver, and his war clothes; or even a gun or a six-shooter.

The horses might not stand before the lodge of the girl's father more than one night; that is, twenty-four hours. They must be accepted or sent back within that time. Thus, there was no long engagement after the boy asked for the girl. The matter was soon decided, and the marriage often took place within twenty-four or forty-eight hours.

A young man who was courting a girl would often try to persuade her to run off with him and be married at once. She would not directly refuse, but would put him off, saying, "No, I cannot do it today; let us wait until some better opportunity occurs." If she had been given to a brother or a cousin to dispose of in marriage, she would be quite sure to reply to such a request, "No, I think too much of my brother—or cousin—to do that."

A girl might receive attention from ten or twelve young men; to be courted by five was very common. Sometimes an elopement actually took place, but in old times not often; usually a girl cared too much for her reputation to do a thing of that kind. Marriage without the consent of the parents and the conventional exchanging of gifts was thus very unusual, and when one took place, the father or brother might follow the couple and bring back the girl. More than once men have been killed on this account.

Sometimes it might happen that horses were sent, and the girl's hand was asked in marriage at a time when her brother was absent from the camp. He had a most important voice as to whether the marriage should or should not take place, and if he were absent, the horses might be returned to the sender, and the young man asked to send them again later. Usually, however, the suitor knew that the girl's brother was absent, and did not send to ask for her at such an inopportune time. He chose the most favorable occasion for getting a speedy and satisfactory answer.

In some cases parents gave a daughter over to a particular brother or cousin who was said to "own" the girl, that is, to have the charge or control of her disposal in marriage. When an offer of marriage was made for the girl in the absence of this young man, word was sent back that the person who had charge of the girl was absent. She could not be disposed of without his consent.

The young man who fell in love with a girl was likely to do everything he could to secure the favor of the one who controlled her marriage. If a suitor and the girl's brother were together on the war-path, the suitor might roast meat and bring it to the brother, or in various ways might try to make things easy for him. After a time he sent a friend to tell the brother that he loved his sister and wished to make her his wife.

The brother returned no answer, but when he reached home he told his mother of the kind things the young man had done for him and why he did them. The mother told this to the girl. If she was willing to accept the young man, she made no comment, but if unwilling, she said, "No, I do not wish to marry that young man"; and that ended the matter.

When the brother—or cousin—in charge of the girl made up his mind that the marriage might take place, he was likely to call into his lodge his brothers or cousins, or both, and tell them what was in contemplation. The matter was discussed. Some of those present might feel doubtful as to what should be done and might ask to have other relatives sent for to express their opinion. If the decision was favorable, the news was conveyed to the suitor, who called together his friends and told them that he was about to send presents to a certain lodge; that is, to the lodge of the brother or cousin who had charge of the young woman. His relatives and close friends contributed what they could afford. The horses were loaded, sent to the brother's lodge, and tied there.

Then the brother or cousin again sent for the friends and relatives with whom he had consulted about the marriage, and said to them, "There are the horses and other things." One by one they went out, and each took what he wished, it being understood that he was to return as much as he took. One perhaps led away a horse with its load. Another might say, "I do not think I can afford all this," and took from the pack a number of articles which he left on the ground. So all the presents were disposed of. A horse or two was always left for the young man who had control of the girl. Each man who took anything away would bring back something of about the same value— often of greater value—to be sent with the girl as a wedding gift. Property equal to or more than had been sent to the brother's lodge usually went with the girl. The girl did not set out for her new home on that day. She might go the next day or the day after that, but, at all events, within three or four days, and the time of her going was known.

Sometimes a girl who was fond of a man might learn that some other richer suitor was about to propose for her, and to send horses to her father. If she discovered this, she might anticipate the matter by running off with the man she loved. Perhaps then her parents might pretend anger with her, or really feel it, and when they learned of her act might send word to her not to return to their lodge, or might refuse to receive her if she came. In that case she went to the lodge of some near relative, an uncle, aunt, or favorite cousin, and was married from there. After a little while her parents again became friendly, and the old affectionate intercourse was renewed.

If a man whom she did not love sent horses for the girl, and she loved someone else, her parents would often try to make her marry the man who had offered himself; they talked to her, persuading and commanding her, and might induce her to accept the man against her will. They did not, however, beat or abuse her. In a case of this kind, the girl in her despair might go out and hang herself. Not a few cases of this kind have happened; for many girls were so obedient and so careful of appearances that they would not consider a suggestion to elope with their lover. Because her mother scolded her for meeting a young man of whom the mother did not approve, the sister of three women well known to me knotted a rope about a sage-brush root, on top of a high cutbank, put the noose about her neck, and swung herself over the bank. In very recent years one or two girls have hung or shot themselves for such reasons. At present, however, young people usually solve the problem by eloping; but in old times they did not do this, for an elopement was disgraceful, and was regarded as no marriage. But if, after it had taken place, the boy sent the customary gifts, this made the marriage valid, and the disgrace was wiped out.

Sometimes it might be understood beforehand with the girl's parents that she should run off with the young man. This was informal and unusual, but where a girl loved one man, and her brothers and cousins favored another, while the parents sympathized with the girl, they might encourage her to marry the man of her choice, merely to avoid trouble in the family. In such a case the girl might go off with the young man to his father's lodge.

The next morning the young man's parents were likely to

dress the girl finely, put her on a horse, and send her, with other horses and many good presents, back to her father's lodge. When she reached her former home, her father and mother sent for her brothers, cousins, and all her kinsfolk. They came to the lodge, and the men divided the horses among them, while the other presents, dresses, blankets, and so on, were distributed among the women relatives. Then the girl's mother cooked food for a feast, and her father gave away horses to anyone whom he might select, to show that he was pleased with the match. Late in the day, when they were ready to return to the lodge of the young man's father, the girl's male relations would bring horses to take back with her, and the women would bring presents of all sorts, sometimes even lodges. Besides the horses which they brought, young men used to bring many arrows. All these things they took back to the lodge of the young man's father, and they were divided among his kinsfolk.

During the four, five, or six years over which in old times a young man's courtship extended, he seldom or never made direct presents to the girl, but often made gifts to her father. If he returned successful from a war trip, he might drive four, five, six, or eight horses to her father's lodge, and leave them there. While a girl's lover—who was regularly courting her— was absent on a war journey, she might ornament a pair of moccasins, and perhaps a pair of leggings and a robe, with quills, and when he returned might present them to him, with a horse. This was an evidence of affection and appreciation. She, however, very seldom received a gift from him, unless perhaps a brass ring, or some trifling, inexpensive trinket. If he wished to make a present to her, and so to testify to his affection for her, he made it to her father. The marriage ceremony began when the young man sent his mother, or some other person, to the lodge with horses, to ask for the girl's hand.

To send as marriage gifts for a girl horses just taken from the enemy was the highest compliment that could be paid to the girl and to her family. Sometimes a young man very much devoted to a girl and eager to make a good impression on her family, went on the war-path, took horses and sent them as a present for the girl. A striking example of this took place—probably about the middle of the last century—when Beaver Claws, wishing to marry Elk River's daughter, went off on the war-path, found a camp, from which he took seventy horses, brought them all safely to the Cheyenne camp, and drove them home to Elk River's lodge, where he left them. When he reached his own home, he told his relatives what he had done; that he wished to marry Elk River's daughter, and that those horses about Elk River's lodge were all his, and had been left there by him. The marriage was arranged, in accordance with his hopes. A gift so large as the one made by Beaver Claws was unprecedented, and the memory of the occurrence has lasted to this day.

Beaver Claws died in the autumn of 1905, an old man, said to have been eighty-seven years. He was a half-brother of the well-known chief, Two Moon, who, however, was much younger, having been born about 1847. Beaver Claw's father was an Arapaho, while Two Moon's father was an Arikara.

After it had been determined to return a favorable answer, the horses presented by the young man were at once given to the near and dear relatives of the girl. One might go to a favorite brother, another to an uncle who was very fond of her, perhaps another to a favorite first cousin. Each of these relatives was likely then to catch his best horse and send it to her father's lodge, to go with the horses that were to be sent to the young man. Besides the horses, they usually sent other good presents. It was generally known beforehand that the marriage was likely to take place, and some preparations for it had been made.

The girl was now put on one of the best horses, which was led by a woman not related to her, and her mother followed behind, leading a number of the horses, all of which wore ropes or bridles. The other horses were all led by women. Before they reached the lodge of the young man's father, some of his relatives came out, carrying a fine blanket, which was spread on the ground; the girl was lifted from the horse and set in the middle of the blanket, and the young men, taking it by the corners and edges, carried her into the lodge. Sometimes, instead of carrying her in the blanket, the horse which she rode was led close to the lodge door; the women ran out from the lodge; the girl dismounted, put her arms about her mother-in-law's neck, from behind; other women took hold of her ankles, and lifted her feet from the ground, and she was thus carried into the lodge without stepping across the threshold. This was all done in silence.

When the girl set out she was dressed in fine new clothing, but after she had been taken into her mother-in-law's lodge, the sisters or cousins of her husband took her to the back of the lodge, removed the clothing that she wore, and dressed her in new clothing they had made, combing and rebraiding her hair, painting her face, and hanging about her various ornaments as gifts.

The husband's mother had of course prepared food, and when the young people had seated themselves side by side, she offered it to them. That prepared for the girl was cut into small pieces by the mother-in-law, so that the girl need make no effort in eating.

After the marriage had taken place, the girl's mother began to make up her wedding outfit, and in this work the mother-in-law also took part. The girl's mother usually provided the lodge and most of its furniture, such as beds, back-rests, cooking and eating utensils. Many of the other things, however, were furnished by the uncles, aunts, and other relatives of both the young people. When all these things had been prepared and were ready, the mother of the girl would pitch the lodge— usually somewhere near her own—and would furnish it with all the articles that had been contributed; and then would go

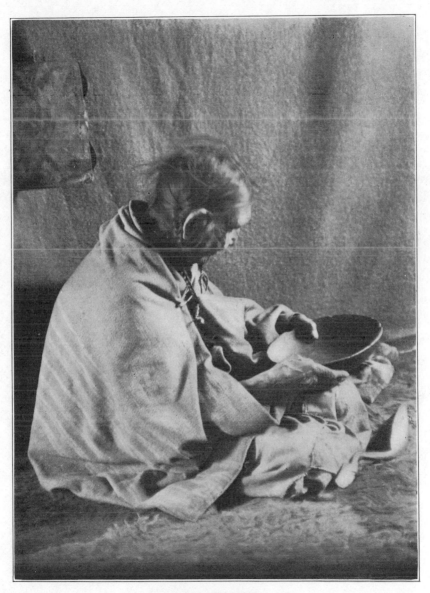

WOOL WOMAN
BOWL AND HORN SPOON

to her daughter and say: "Daughter, there is your lodge; it is your home; go and live in it."

Sometimes the lodge was made in advance, and the day before the couple were married was pitched in the circle, near the home of the father of the young man or woman. If near the lodge of the wife's father, it was set a little back of that lodge, in order that the young man might not see his mother-in-law too often.

After a girl had been married and had gone to her husband's lodge, she might still make use of the protective string for a period of from ten to fifteen days. The husband would respect the string for that length of time, but usually not longer. The Cheyennes say that this custom had the advantage of enabling the newly married couple to get used to each other, to sleeping together. Men tell me that they used to lie awake all night, talking to their newly married wives.

After marriage the young man did his best to support his wife by hunting. All their relatives made them presents, and the young couple usually started in life with a good outfit; but all the presents were made after the marriage.

The connection between a young married couple and their parents was closer with the girl's parents than with the boy's. If the boy was a good hunter, he strove to supply meat for his father-in-law's lodge; but he seldom or never visited it and of course he never spoke to, or knowingly went near, his mother-in-law. This old custom is now dying out. There are today mothers who live with their daughters.

Since a newly married young man was expected to bring in plenty of meat, he often took two or three extra packhorses to the hunting ground. If he failed himself to kill enough meat, his friends made it a point of honor to see that his horses were loaded. Sometimes when he returned from the hunt, he stopped a hundred or a hundred and fifty yards from his own lodge, and his wife and sister, if he had any, or some of his wife's friends, led the horses to his mother-in-law's lodge, and she took care of the meat. A part of it was cooked and a feast given to his friends, his wife asking some old man to call out the names of the husband's friends, inviting them to the feast. This old man generally sat inside the lodge door.

The owner's wife brought in the food to her lodge from his mother-in-law's lodge and it was cut up before being brought in. This was an act of courtesy between mother-in-law and son-in-law, and creditable to both.

When all the guests had arrived, the owner of the lodge said, "Everything is here; you may eat." Then the old man directed several of the young men to serve the food. He said, "First put out some for yourselves," for in the helping the dish was supposed to be emptied. Generally a very large portion was handed to the old man first; then, turning to the back of the lodge where the owner sat, the server pulled from the pot and placed on his hand five small pieces of meat and invited the owner of the lodge to step forward. He did so, holding his hands, palms up, stretched out in front of him. The five pieces of meat were put on his right hand at the four compass points and in the center of the palm; then he turned his right hand over on the left palm, leaving the meat on his left hand and made the usual offering to the four directions—*Nĭv stăn ĭ vō'*. This was the sacrifice offered and the blessing asked at an ordinary feast. After this was done the people ate.

Should there be more food than could be eaten, that remaining was given to the old man to take home to his wife and family. He strung the meat on a sharp stick and took home any fluid food in a bucket lent by the owner. His wife afterward returned the bucket.

If visitors came to a village, the old custom was for them to occupy the lodge of some newly married couple, who would give them possession and sleep elsewhere. This was an honor to the visitor.

Among people of good family, indirect courtesies often passed between a wife's mother and her son-in-law. It was not uncommon for a woman to make a lodge for her son-in-law, ornamenting it with quilled, painted, or beaded linings, pillows, bed-covering, and other furniture. Often a newly married woman had little to do, her mother looking after everything, even to making moccasins for the son-in-law.

Since a man was not permitted to speak to nor even to look at his mother-in-law, it was usual for her to ride up behind the lodge and slip into it at a time when she knew he was abroad. Nevertheless, a young man sometimes presented—but always through another—a horse to his mother-in-law. This was a creditable thing for him to do, and was an honor to the woman. It happened only among well-to-do people.

A woman might face her son-in-law if she chose formally to present him an ornamented robe. She selected for garnishing a good robe, but one on which the hair was not heavy, for the quills were more easily put on such a robe and the work looked better. The woman spread out the dressed robe, and on the flesh side marked the patterns where the quills were to go. After these had all been put on, she sewed on the final ornaments, which were usually little bits of red cloth. Then she cooked food for a feast, and sent for her son-in-law to come to her lodge, where were gathered all the members of the quilling society. Except these members, no one save the young man might enter. His new robe was spread at the back of the lodge, so that he should sit down on it, and in front of the lodge a horse was tied for him to ride away on; this also was a gift from his mother-in-law. When he entered the lodge door he turned to his right, walked around to the back, and sat down on the robe, which he drew up over his shoulders. Then his mother-in-law took a coal from the fire, and put it down before him, and sprinkled on it some sweet grass; and the young man, with the robe over his shoulder, bent forward over the coal, and let the smoke arise within the robe and cover his body. This was to give him a good heart—to make him feel happy. After this had been done, the young man rose and went out. He did not eat—the food was eaten by the members of the quilling society, or was taken by them to their lodges, where anyone might eat it.

After an exchange of gifts such as described, the mother-in-law tabu ceased to be in force.

When a child was to be born, a woman relative of the father usually made a cradle for it, though some woman not a relative might make one. When the cradle was brought to the lodge and presented, the father perhaps gave a horse to each one who brought a cradle. The mother of the girl to be confined asked certain women to assist at its birth. They—or even a male doctor called in for the purpose—gave the girl medicine from time to time, so that she might have an easy delivery. The medicine given was the root of *Balsamorrhiza sagittata,* called by the Cheyennes *hĭ tū' nē ĭss ē' ē yo,* or bark medicine.

When the birth was about to take place, they had a bowl ready in which to wash the child, and a knife—in old times of flint, and later an arrowpoint—was at hand to sever the umbilical cord, which was wrapped once about the finger and cut off short. The child was wrapped in a sheet or cloth, the inner surfaces of the legs being first dusted with powder from the prairie puffball, so that the tender skin should not chafe, and the navel was dried with the same dust.

The child was then put in its cradle. At first it was not allowed to nurse from its mother, but some other woman who had a young child nursed it. The medicine women for four days freed the mother's breasts from the early mammary secretion. During this time the mother was given doses of *mōt sī'-ĭ yūn,* the milk medicine (*Actæa arguta*), to induce a free flow of milk. Four days after birth the child might nurse from its mother.

At any time after the child had become strong, the father, as already stated, might lead out his best horse, and giving it away with other presents (and perhaps even his war-bonnet), might have his child's ears pierced—not actually, but formally.

It was long the custom that a woman should not have a second child until her first was about ten years of age. When that period was reached, the man was likely to go with his wife and child to some large dance or public gathering, and there, giving away at the same time a good horse to some friend or even to some poor person, to announce publicly that now this child was going to have a little brother or sister. To be able to make such an announcement was a great credit to the parents. The people talked about it and praised the parents' self-control.

Families were sometimes large. Shell's father had ten children, eight by one wife. Shell had eleven children, but was married several times. An old man named Half Bear had four wives and more than thirty children. Twins were not uncommon.

Young mothers sang to their babies to put them to sleep, and had many stories which they told to children a little older, with the same purpose. While such stories were being related the little child did not speak, and very likely had fallen asleep before two or three of them had been told. The tales were usually about small animals—about the mice, the little ground squirrels, or the chipmunks.

One or two examples will show their character.

This is what a little skunk says:

After the sun goes down I wander from place to place, looking for something to eat. If I find a trail, I follow it, and follow it, looking for something to eat; and I never stop until daylight. When daylight begins to come I look about for a place to lie down. I stop looking for food and lie down for the day. All day long I lie there with my little slim feet and my little long face.

This happened to an old frog:

A frog lived near the stream. She had many children. A snake came swimming down the stream and swam into the frog's house.

The frog was very much frightened, but she said: "Here is my brother come to see us. Brother, here are all your nephews and nieces. They are all named after you." Meantime the snake was looking about, waiting to get a chance to catch one of the children. "I am very glad to see them," said the snake.

The old frog whispered to her children to run. She said to the snake, "I will go out and get a little wood to make a fire." To the children she said, "Run away now; we are in a bad place; we are in danger."

The little frogs all hopped into the stream and swam away and were saved.

An old woman who told such stories might give one or more of them to one of the children in the lodge, after she had told it to the child so often that it knew it by heart and could repeat it. Little girls sometimes told these stories to their parents, and if they made mistakes might be corrected by them until they were letter-perfect in the tales.

A marriage custom among the Cheyennes that was very strong was this: If a young man killed in battle had sisters or female cousins, and a friend took special care of his body, one of these sisters or cousins was likely to be given the friend for a wife, to show the family's appreciation of what he had done. The family of one so killed were grateful to a man who cared for his body, took his own blanket to wrap about it and carried the body to a proper place for leaving it. It was difficult or impossible formally to bury one who had been killed at a distance from home, and the most that could be done would be to put the body in a suitable place. If the wolves devoured the dead man, that was not regarded as a misfortune. If a young man died from sickness and some young friend made a special ceremony of mourning for him, he also was likely to have a wife given him in acknowledgment of this. Marriages of this sort often took place.

In 1865, on Tongue River, there died a very old man named

Bull Could Not Rise Up. Long before that a small war-party of Cheyennes had gone off to take horses, and far over near the Missouri River a young man belonging to the Ivistsinihpah had been killed by the Crows. Bull Could Not Rise Up was with the war-party, and the young man who was killed was his close friend.

About one year afterward, Bull Could Not Rise Up got a sack made of old lodge-skins and one night went off alone. No one except his family knew that he had gone. All alone he made the journey to the place where his friend had been killed, to bring the young man's bones back to the village. This was a dangerous trip for a man alone and on foot, for in those days grizzly bears were abundant and were the thing most to be feared on the prairie. He was of course safe from the enemy, for he could hide and his tracks could not be followed. The sack was to hold the bones of his friend. He found the place where his friend lay, and gathering up the bones put them in the sack and set out on his return. When he drew near to the village, he left the sack of bones on a near-by hill, and went to his lodge, and after a time told what he had done. When the people learned that he who had been killed had now been brought back, they all ran to this hill, everyone mourning and wailing for the one that had died.

All the people in the village felt that Bull Could Not Rise Up had done a great thing in going after the bones of the dead man; and the same day the young man's family put up for him a fine lodge, and three wives—sisters and cousins of the young man—were given to him.

Bull Could Not Rise Up did not believe in ghosts. On one occasion while he was with a war-party a ghost came to the camp. All the men were frightened and ran out of the camp and hid from this ghost, but Bull Could Not Rise Up paid no attention to it, but went on eating his food, and after a time the ghost went away without harming anyone.

An odd custom referring to the old law as to early rising,

and indirectly to marriage, was related to me by Picking Bones Woman.

In those days—the early part of the nineteenth century—it was the custom, when a young man was first married, for many of his closest friends to visit him and, going to his lodge in the evening, to stop and sleep there. This old practice was still in vogue as recently as 1850.

The day after her marriage, when Picking Bones Woman arose in the morning, all the men who had come to visit her husband were still asleep. When she went out of the lodge, her uncle asked her if the young men were up and had eaten. She told him that they were not up; that all were still asleep. Her uncle said, "Do not wake them; let them alone," and went away to another part of the camp to find some man who had counted many coups.

This man, carrying in his hand a long, thick stick, came to the lodge just after the sun had risen. Outside the lodge door he counted a coup in a loud voice, to awaken all the young men within. They knew what was coming, and putting their robes about their heads, ran out of the lodge as fast as they could go; and as each ran out the man with the stick struck him a hard blow, and counted a coup. It was an old custom that if these visitors did not get up in the morning when they were called and told that their food was ready, they should be called in this way, and that the brave who called them, and carried the stick, should drive them down to the river and into the water.

The young men ran toward the river, and the brave after them, all running as hard as they could go. The young men dropped their blankets and robes, and as they ran tried to pull off their moccasins and leggings, racing fast, and with their breechclouts flying out behind them. They ran into the stream, and plunged into the deep water, and rose again, shaking their heads. Some had not had time to take off their moccasins or leggings, but got their clothing wet.

On another occasion, Gentle Horse was in the lodge with a newly married pair, and rushed out, holding his robe tight about him to protect himself from the blows. He ran down to the river, with the brave close behind him, and plunged into the water, robe and all.

Sometimes, if a large stream was not near, the man would chase the young men out on the prairie, following them and beating them until he grew tired of the sport. Those he was following were not permitted to resist.

The Cheyennes did not take many wives. The largest number I have heard of for one man was five. These were sisters who were married to Crooked Neck. When he was made a chief, he gave three of his wives away, but lived always with the other two. Younger sisters were the potential wives of an older sister's husband, but were not always married to him. Men seldom married a second wife who was not related to the first. When they did so, there was usually trouble, and the first wife was likely to leave her husband.

If a man found it impossible to live peaceably with his wife, he might divorce her in public fashion, notifying everyone that he abandoned all rights in her that he might possess. This action was usually taken in the dance lodge at some dance or gathering of his own soldier society, and according to a certain prescribed form. Before he acted the man notified his soldier band of what he purposed to do. At a set time in the dance, therefore, the singers began a particular song, and the man, holding a stick in his hand, danced by himself and presently danced up to the drum; struck the drum with the stick; threw the stick up in the air, or perhaps toward a group of men in the lodge, and, as he threw it, shouted: "There goes my wife; I throw her away! Whoever gets that stick may have her!" Sometimes to this was added, "A horse goes with the stick!" If this last was said, the person who secured the stick received the horse—but not the wife.

If the man threw the stick across the dance lodge at a group of men, each one of them was likely to dodge, or jump to one side, to avoid being hit. If one of them was hit, or was narrowly missed by the stick, other men were likely to joke him, and to say: "Ha! you want that woman, do you? I thought I saw you reach for that stick!"

By this act the man renounced all rights to the woman thrown away, and if anyone married her, the husband might not claim any gift or payment.

To be treated publicly in this way was a disgrace to a woman. In any dispute or quarrel that the woman might be engaged in later, the matter was likely to be brought up, and her opponent might say, "Well, I never was thrown out of the dance by the drum." If by chance a man married a woman who had been thus disgraced, and if they ever wrangled, he was likely to remind her of it. It was not forgotten.

This ceremony occurred but seldom, yet it is still well recognized. Perhaps the last case on the Tongue River Indian Reservation occurred in 1899.

A woman was in no sense the property of the man she married. If a man grew tired of his wife, or for any other reason divorced her, except by the drum, anyone else who married her must settle with the husband, often by paying him what he had given for the woman. If a woman ran off with another man, the latter must pay the injured husband. This usually settled the matter amicably; but sometimes the husband was angry, and might kill the man, or the woman, or both. Or, if the matter was not satisfactorily settled, he might kill horses belonging to his successor, or might injure him in some other way.

If a man stole another's wife, that is to say, either eloped with her or took her after her husband had thrown her away, he was likely to take an early opportunity of sending to the husband an old man carrying a filled pipe. The old man was authorized to talk to the injured husband and to offer him the pipe, telling him to ask for what he wished. If the husband smoked, the matter was settled amicably. The husband might ask for, and would receive, what he regarded as a suitable payment. In a case which occurred in 1877, Roan Bear eloped with another man's wife. Later, when the pipe was sent to the husband, he smoked, and sent back word that he wanted a dog to eat—a woolly dog. This was the valuation he placed on the woman.

If, however, a chief's wife ran away with a man, no one might come to offer him the pipe. His dignity would not permit him to take revenge on the woman, and to receive payment for such an injury would be disgraceful. When the chief decided to overlook the offense, he summoned his soldiers to his lodge, formally filled his own pipe, and smoked there with them. The purpose of this formal act was well understood. The similar conduct of the owner of a scalp shirt is explained elsewhere.

Young girls, as they were growing up, often had a number of horses given them by fathers, brothers, and near relatives. When the girl was married, the horses she possessed remained hers, and were entirely free of any control by her husband. The increase also was hers. Such property she was free to sell or to give away, or to bequeath by will, as she might choose. She might, of course, give one or two or more horses to her husband, and often did so; but those she retained were her own. There have been, and are, women in the tribe as wealthy, or nearly so, as any men.

The Cheyenne young man was not permitted to speak to his adult sister. While the little children of a family played together until they approached manhood and womanhood, still, young men might not speak to their sisters after the latter had grown up—when they were about fifteen years old. Until very recently this law has been rigidly observed. If a man went to the lodge of his brother-in-law to speak to him, or to get some article, and found him absent, he did not address the wife—his own sister—on the matter, but spoke to a child about it. Thus, he might ask a little child—even a new-born babe—in the mother's hearing, for the article which he required; or might give it a message for his brother-in-law. If he came to borrow something, very likely the wife presently took the article and put it down somewhere in his sight, and after a time the man took it and went away. The message left with the child in the wife's hearing was always delivered. The practice continued to old age.

The women of the Cheyennes are famous among all western tribes for their chastity. In old times it was most unusual for a girl to be seduced, and she who had yielded was disgraced forever. The matter at once became known, and she was taunted with it wherever she went. It was never forgotten. No young man would marry her. This seems the more remarkable, since the Arapahoes, with whom the Cheyennes have been so long and so closely associated, are notorious for the looseness of their women.

On the other hand, since the marriage tie among the Cheyennes, as with other Indians, is not a strong one, and a man might divorce his wife, either for cause or at his own caprice, there were occasional slips on the part of the married woman, who might divorce her husband by running off with another man.

Among the Cheyennes, as already said, the women have great influence. They discuss matters freely with their husbands, argue over points, persuade, cajole, and usually have their own way about tribal matters. They are, in fact, the final authority in the camp. There are traditions of women chiefs, and of women who have possessed remarkable mysterious powers or have shown great wisdom in council. If in later days the women did not take part in councils, they nevertheless exercised on the men of their families an influence that can hardly be overestimated, and in the councils so frequently held, where only men spoke, this influence of the women was always felt.

In old times women sometimes went to war, not necessarily to fight and take horses, but as helpers; yet many accounts are given of cases in which they have fought, and have struck their enemies. Sometimes women charged and counted coup on the killed. In later days, however, it was unusual for women to go to war; and in modern times they have not taken part in councils. Yet, sixty years ago women went to war, and even in the latest hostilities women occasionally accompanied the men.

Buffalo Hump said to me: "A brave woman down in the south rode with her brother into battle. Her brother's horse was killed, and she stayed in that place and fought where her brother fell. They were at close quarters, and the woman fought the enemy off until a young man came up and took her brother on his horse and got him away."

Another woman was prominent in Crook's fight on the Rosebud. This was the sister of Chief Comes In Sight, who in the early part of this century was still living in Oklahoma. I have already given an account of this battle, and of the achievement of Buffalo Calf Road Woman (*Mūts ĭ mī' ŭ nă*).[2] How highly the Cheyennes thought of her is shown by the fact that they gave to this fight the name "Where The Girl Saved Her Brother."

RELATIONSHIP TERMS

A woman's children called their mother's sister, mother, and her brother, uncle. They called their father's brother, father, and the father's sister, aunt.

Some relationship terms are these:

Father, also father's brother (my), nē' hyō.
Mother, also mother's sister (my), nāh' koă.

[2] The Fighting Cheyennes, p. 323.

Father's sister (or father's brother's wife) = aunt (my), nā hăn (ē hyai', your aunt).

Mother's brother = uncle (my), nă khăn (hĭsh ĭsh', that person's uncle).

The personal possessive pronoun is always present in these terms.

Brother, also male cousin, nāh nĭh', my elder brother; sēe' wăs' sĭn-mĭt, younger brother; tsī' hĭ nī hĭt, elder brother.

Sister, also female cousin (man speaking), nāh' kāh ĭm.

Brother-in-law (my) (used by men), nĭt' ōhph.

Sister-in-law (my) (used by men), nĭt' ăm (if used by women means brother-in-law).

Son, nāha'.

Grandfather (my), nām shĭm'.

Grandmother, also mother-in-law (my), nĭsh' kĭ.

Grandchild (my), nĭsh' a.

Son-in-law (the same).

A father's brother, being father, the previous generation, that is, the great-uncle, is called grandfather. The father's sister, being aunt, her mother would be also aunt.

A sister's children (nephews) (male), nā tsĭn' ōs ta.

A sister's children (female), hē' hyā mĭn'.

A brother's children (same as one's own) (my), nā nĭs' ō nē.

WOMEN'S SOCIETIES

AS the Cheyenne men had their soldier and other societies
or associations, so among the women socicties existed
which they felt were quite as important as those of
the men. Yet, because the association of a man with men becomes closer and more intimate than any he can have with
women, less is to be learned of the women's societies than of
those of the men. Nevertheless, some detail has been given me
of the ceremonial of one or two of these. There are probably
others of which I know nothing.

Some Cheyennes declare that women who have been to war
constitute a society, but what ceremony there may be connected with it, I do not know. It may be that instead of con-
stituting a society, they constituted a class. It is said that
women who have quilled thirty robes are in a group by themselves, as are also those who have made a lodge alone; that is
to say, without the assistance of any of their fellows. This
would mean the tanning and softening of the hides, their fitting
and sewing, and the making of the lodge-poles.

Women who had performed these operations were few in
number. They were highly respected for their extraordinary
achievements.

Of the women's associations referred to the most important
one was that devoted to the ceremonial decoration, by sewing
on quills, of robes, lodge coverings, and other things made of
skins of animals. This work women considered of high importance, and, when properly performed, quite as creditable as
were bravery and success in war among the men. The guild of

quillers included the best women in the camp. Its ceremony and ritual have been handed down from mythic times.

When a young woman greatly desired some good fortune— as the success of a brother or husband going to war, or the restoration to health of a sick brother or a child, she might vow that if this good fortune came to her, she would embellish a robe with quills for some priest, doctor, or warrior.

Such a piece of work must be done in prescribed ceremonial fashion, and the girl must be taught to perform it by some member of the quilling society who had previously done the same thing. The making and offering of such a robe in the prescribed way secured the maker admission to the society of women who had done similar things. Thereafter she might attend their feasts, and, having herself been taught, might teach others.

The name of this society is *Mē ē nō' ĭst st*,[1] which means quillers—those who apply quills to leather. They had a special crier, an old man, who called out through the camp what they were about to do.

The girl or woman who had pledged herself to ornament the robe went to some old woman who belonged to the society, and, after making her a present, told her what she wished to do, and asked her assistance. The old woman directed the candidate to hold her hands out in front of her, palms up and edges together. The old woman bit off a piece of a certain root, chewed it fine, and spat on the hands ceremonially, and the candidate made the ceremonial motions, passing her right hand over the outside of her right leg, from ankle to hip, her left hand over her right arm from wrist to shoulder, her left hand over her left leg from ankle to hip, and her right hand over the left arm from wrist to shoulder. Then the hands were placed on the head, and passed backward from the forehead.

The candidate now inquired of this old woman—usually some near relative, if the girl had one who belonged to the

---

[1] *Ēmē ē nī"*, she sews on quills.

LITTLE CREEK WOMAN
WORKING ON A MOCCASIN

society—as to the forms and ceremonies to be observed in inviting people to the feast, and in cooking the food. After she had been instructed as to these things, she asked the crier to go out and announce the feast. All those invited belonged to the society of quillers, all of whom must have ornamented lodge linings, back-rests, robes, possible sacks, stars for lodges, or baby cradles, in this ceremonial manner. Sometimes only one section of the society might be asked—only those who had quilled robes, or who had ornamented baby cradles or stars.

Among the Northern Cheyenne women there seem to be divisions or grades of the quilling society not recognized in the South. These divisions from lower to higher begin with: (1) moccasins; (2) baby cradles; (3) stars for ornamenting lodges; (4) buffalo-robes; (5) lodge linings, back-rests, and possible sacks. A woman in any of these grades might call a meeting in her own class, but all who belonged to any of the divisions higher than that class were privileged to attend.

When the guests were expected, the giver of the feast sat at the back of the lodge, and next to her on her right was the old woman who was instructing her. After the members had arrived, but before the ceremonies began, the old crier was perhaps told to call out, asking some poor person to come and see the candidate—whose name was mentioned—quill the first robe she had ever ornamented. The invited poor person came, and for coming received a good present—usually a horse.

The man or woman who had received the gift left the lodge after the ceremonies were over—before the food was served—and (if a man) mounting the horse rode about the camp, singing a song in which he told that the candidate, whom he named, had presented him a horse on the occasion of the ornamenting of her first robe.

When the old women first assembled they described the work that they had done, telling of the robes and other things that they had ornamented. This recital was formal in character, and among women closely paralleled the counting of coups by men.

If possible, a woman's statement was verified by a witness, or if not by a witness, by affirmation over the arrow or the pipe.

The instructress then exhorted the candidate, and offered a prayer, asking for her throughout her life good fortune, health, abundance, and success of all kinds; that her children, if she should have any, might do well and have plenty.

To this feast, from two to four men—good warriors—had been asked, and at the end of the old woman's speech, one of these rose to his feet and counted several coups—perhaps all he had ever made. After he had finished the narration, he reached forward and touched the edge of the kettle with the edge of his hand. The kettle, on this as on many other occasions, was regarded as standing for an enemy.

After the warrior had counted his coups, the instructress took from the kettle a piece of meat, and tore from it five small pieces which she put in her right palm. Then the old woman— the one either at the right or the left of the door, as might be indicated—rose and went over to the back of the lodge. She stretched out her right hand to the instructress, and received in it in ceremonial order the five little pieces of meat, which she then transferred to her left palm; she turned, went to the door, and passed out as she had come in. That is to say, if she had come in from the north, she went out toward the north. In other words, she did not pass in front of—did not cross—the doorway; no one might do that. She then walked around the lodge until she came to the star or ornament which was toward the east, when she took a piece of meat in her right hand, lifted it to the east, and holding it there for a moment, made a prayer, slowly lowered it to the earth, and placed it lightly on the ground. She passed on around the lodge to the south, and did the same, and so on, opposite the other stars on the lodge, each of which faced a cardinal point. When the fourth piece of meat had been put down, she did not keep on around to the lodge door and enter, but turned about and went back all around the lodge, and went in as she had come out. Then she went to the fire, held the fifth piece of meat to the sky, and after a prayer placed it at the edge of the fireplace. If there were several kettles, five pieces of food were taken from each kettle, and each set of offerings was treated in the same way.

While all this was going on, the instructress was exhorting the girl, telling her to note well what was being done, and to remember everything, so that hereafter, when she should be called to instruct at a feast of this sort, she might perform her part well.

Now the giver of the feast served the food. Each woman had brought her own dish, usually a large one, which was to be nearly or quite filled. Of this food she ate a portion, and took the remainder home with her. Soon after they had eaten, the feasters dispersed to their homes.

Later, the candidate asked some old woman to come to her lodge and, with white clay and a stick, to draw on the robe the pattern for the intended ornamentation. For this service she presented the old woman with a pair of moccasins, or some article of clothing, and gave her something to eat.

The lodge in which the feast was held was not necessarily owned by the candidate; it might be borrowed for the occasion. Usually it was one of those ornamented with four circular pieces of deerskin or buffalo-cow skin, decorated with vari-colored quills in concentric circles, sewed on the lodge covering halfway between the ground and the smoke-hole. These represent the four points of the compass. The two which looked toward the south and east were on either side of the door and were higher than its top. The ones toward the north and west were opposite these, on either side of the back.

The quilling society is considered very old, and the knowledge of the use of quills in the ornamentation of robes and dresses is said to have been brought to the tribe by the hero of a widely distributed story among Plains tribes which I have called The Buffalo Wife. The traditional account of the ceremony, given elsewhere in this work, rests on the authority of

Picking Bones Woman, who herself had quilled thirty robes, a very remarkable achievement. She has long been dead.

The smoother was made from the shoulder blade of a buffalo, and was about a foot long and three-quarters of an inch wide. It was used to smooth and flatten out the quills as they were being put on the robe. The operation of quilling a robe was something sacred, and the women working at it usually sat at the back of the lodge, as far as possible from the door. No one was permitted to pass in front of them. The woman who was quilling a robe did not take the robe out of the sack in which it was kept. Instead, she pulled from the sack only a portion of the robe she was working on, and thus did not soil the robe. Having in the sack all the articles she needed, she could continue her work without delays. A man might not rest his head against one of these robes which was being worked on; if he should do so, a bull might kill him. While working on the robes, the women covered their hands with white clay, or sometimes with burned gypsum, so as to keep their hands from soiling a robe.

The Southern Cheyennes no longer work in quills, because they have none, since there are no porcupines in the country which they now inhabit. Besides quills and grass, they formerly made use of the long, slender, black roots of a plant which grows along the streams in the valley of the Canadian. These they dye, and still put on canvas or cloth, somewhat as they used to put on quills. Twisted cornhusks, sometimes dyed, have recently been used in ornamentation as tassels. The sinew used in sewing on quills was very fine, and the sewing was wholly under the quills, so that it did not show.

All this quilling of robes was woman's work. Except in cases where an instructor was required, men were not permitted to enter the lodge where the ceremony was going on. For the women it was in a way almost as serious as the occupation of making shields for the men. Though men might not enter a lodge where women were putting on these things, there were some exceptions, thus: When women were in the lodge, ornamenting the linings, sewing stars, or putting on the final ornaments (*hǐ nǐm' nǐva nǐsts'*, singular), a very brave man who had counted many coups might go up to the lodge door, strike the lodge, and counting a coup might enter and take a pot of the food standing by the fire, and carry it away with him. This was done partly as a joke on the women, but they did not object to it, for it showed a respect for their ancient custom.

When the men contemplated doing this, they were likely to get together in a lodge and select someone who, when on the war-path, had first discovered the enemy, to go ahead as a scout to see what the women had to eat. He went to the lodge where they were at work and looked in, and then returned to report. As soon as the women saw him, they knew his purpose, and prepared for the visit of the one who would come after him by filling one or two kettles with food and placing them near the door, so that the visitor might take them. The scout having reported, they chose the bravest man, who acted as stated. He usually took with him a man to help carry the food away. When he entered the lodge, the women were ready for him, and said, "There it is," and he took the two nearest kettles and went away. On one occasion when I was in the camp when a lodge was being decorated, this action was proposed, but the man selected to go as scout refused to "bother the women."

Among the Southern Cheyennes a woman who had quilled thirty robes was supposed by that action to have secured for herself good fortune throughout her life, and was expected to live to old age. The woman who gave me this account explained that it was because she had done this that she was old, and that a number of her companions sitting about were also old. Among the Northern section a woman who has ornamented a lodge— put stars on lodge covering, decorated door, lining, and backrests, and a robe for the owner—had done the most important work that a member of the quilling society can do. At all meetings of these quillers, before the food was served it was usual for one old woman after another to get up and tell of the robes she had quilled, just as a warrior would recount his brave deeds.

When a woman who was quilling a robe made a mistake in her work and put on a line of quills in the wrong place, as sometimes happened, the mistake could be corrected only by the performance of a certain ceremony. She must call in some brave man, who counted a coup over the robe, reciting what he had done, where he had done it, and winding up with the statement, "And when I scalped him, I did it in this way." As he said this he passed the blade of a knife under the defective work, cutting the threads and so removing the work. In performing this operation he did not use his own knife, but one kept for this use by the quilling society.

When sewing stars on the lodge, if a woman made a mistake, four brave men were sent for, each of whom had counted a coup. If a star was put on in the wrong place, it was taken off; a man came up to the place, took the awl, counted his coup, returned the awl to the woman, and she sewed the star on again. The coup was to be counted only for those stars where a mistake had been made.

A man might not touch the decorations for a new lodge until they had been sewed on.

In sewing the stars on a lodge, a large one at the back below the smoke-hole—representing the sun—was sewed on first; next the one facing south; then the one to the west; then the one to the north, and last the one to the east. When the buffalo-tails were attached to the stars—which in the case of those facing the four directions was not done until the lodge had been raised—the woman who was making the lodge came out of the door, carrying the buffalo-tails, followed by the instructors, and turned to the south. When they reached the south star, the instructors and the lodge woman raised the lodge covering, passed under it directly across the lodge, and raising the covering on the other side, came out under the north star. Then they walked around to the east star, raised the lodge covering, and passing under it crossed the lodge and came out under the west star. Then they passed around from west to north, east, and south, and attached the first tail at the south star, and then passed around, attaching a tail at the west, north, and east star, successively. In pinning down this lodge, the first pin to hold down the covering was driven under the south star. Before being passed into the loop, it was moved forward and back toward the loop four times; then it was driven into the ground with four blows. The other pins were driven without this ceremony. The four pins first driven were those under the four stars in the usual order. Afterward the whole covering was pinned down without ceremony.

After the lodge was finished and set up, the women cooked food, brought it into the lodge, and set it in the center. Then the crier called up the people, and they stood off at a little distance from the front of the lodge. A man who had counted coup on an enemy in a lodge, walked up to the door, struck the lodge, and counted that coup. If he had taken an enemy's horse, he told of it. No one could go in until this man had counted a coup, and had himself entered. He was the first to go in.

For the ornamentation of clothing, robes, and lodges, porcupine quills, dyed in various colors, were most often used. A certain reed (?*Equisetum*) was also employed, as well as the slender black root and a black grass. A few years ago beautiful reed and quillwork was often seen on robes, moccasins, and tobacco pouches. The quills and reeds were then always fastened to the leather with sinew thread. Later, as white men's manufactures became more familiar articles of trade, hawk-bells and red cloth were used to ornament women's dresses, then shells of different kinds, and finally imitation shells of porcelain.

The quillwork and beadwork on the war shirts often consisted of concentric circles—or sometimes a many-pointed star

—representing the sun. The patterns on the upper side of a moccasin were often symbolic or pictographic. The design might represent lodges, or rivers, or people going to war. A common checkerboard pattern refers to the lining of the third stomach of a buffalo. This looks like a series of little uncovered boxes—somewhat like a honeycomb, in fact.

Although the tendency among observers is to see a meaning in every Indian design, many of these designs are not always symbolic. Often a woman makes a bead or quillwork design merely because she thinks it pretty, to satisfy her own idea of beauty. If asked what the design means, she may try to explain it, if she feels an explanation is expected, or she may say that she did it merely because it pleased her fancy.

Yet, as Mr. Petter has well pointed out, the decorative art of the Cheyennes in former days was in charge of certain women's societies, which were conducted with definite ceremonies and to which an initiation was required. These women were called the selected ones, *Mŏn in ĭ' heo*, and to them was referred a great deal of the decorative work by the use of quills, feathers, fine roots, cornstalks, and paintings, which the Cheyennes used. The women of this society were usually elderly and were those who understood the meanings of the different designs. Most women still follow the old designs in their beadwork, but they are not held by the old traditions, and are introducing changes according to their fancy. The selected ones "had strict rules in their designs and they kept secret the meaning and arrangement of the colors, as well as the relation of the designs to each other. The designs were always symbolic and talismanic, representing concrete organic objects, whereas the colors were more emblematic of the abstract in creatures and creation, *e.g.*, white for active life, very light blue for quietness, peace, serenity (from the cloudless sky); green for growing life; red for warmth, food, blood, home (from blood); amber yellow, ripeness, perfection, beauty (from the sunsets); black for cessation of enmity, hostilities (from a dead glow being no more hot). The meaning of the colors ramifies as they are combined, or, according as they are lighter or darker shade."[2]

[2] Petter, English-Cheyenne Dictionary, p. 97.

INDUSTRIES

THE industries of the Cheyennes were few and simple. Their clothing was made of the skins of wild animals, dressed soft, sewed with sinew, often highly ornamented with the quills of the porcupine, and trimmed with fur or feathers, or with the hair of enemies. Their dwellings, in historic times, were also made of the skins of large animals and were warm, comfortable, light, and easily transported. Their cutting tools, and also their hammers, were usually of stone, while other implements were fashioned of wood, bone, or horn. Some of their knives were of bone. Their dishes were of wood, horn, or clay; and their pots for cooking, of fired clay, were strong and durable. In old times the paunch or hide of the buffalo often served as a kettle for boiling or stewing. Cups and buckets were made from the lining of the buffalo's paunch, stiffened above by a circular wooden ring sewed to the membrane with sinew, the holes being plugged with tallow.

Among the Indians there was practical community in the matter of food. A man who was hungry need never suffer. If he entered the lodge of some neighbor or acquaintance—unless it was a time of actual starvation—food was at once set before him. In the same way, as happens often among groups of simple civilized men, there was community of labor in some matters and a general spirit of helpfulness, which made easy for members of the tribe certain tasks which, without the aid of friends and neighbors, could not readily have been accomplished. Examples of this were seen in the way in which women of the camp often came together for the purpose of helping one another to make new lodges; and among men in the organized fashion in which certain hunting operations were performed. This spirit of kindliness to one's neighbor, and this willingness to be of assistance to one another, were characteristic of all Indians, who, within the tribe, were a friendly, good-natured people. Although they had not formed habits of continued labor, they were always willing to take hold to help, even though this willingness did not result in any very long-continued effort.

With the coming of the white man, metal took the place of stone among the Cheyennes. After a time they ceased to make pottery; their ancient dishes were discarded for those of civilization, and the bowl made from the shell of the turtle, or from a knot knocked from a box-elder or other tree, began to take on a sacred character and came to be used only for the mixing of medicine by a doctor, or for the special dish from which he ate or drank. Until very recently, among the older Cheyennes, there were still some who would not eat or drink from the metal dishes made by white men.

As brass kettles and tin cups took the place of earthenware pots and the cups made of buffalo paunch, so the gun and its powder and ball in time supplanted the bow and its arrow; and at last the soft, warm, and comfortable skin clothing gave place to the cast-off uniforms of United States soldiers. But this relation is of an earlier day, when the bow was the usual weapon used in hunting and in war, though even then its stone or bone point had passed out of use, and the sheet-iron arrowpoint, filed to a sharp edge and then whetted on a smooth river pebble, gave to this weapon a range and a penetration which it could not have had in the olden time.

In the life of the Cheyenne camp, woman was an equal partner with man, and the division of duties which existed between the sexes appeared in their industries. The men usually made men's utensils and weapons, and many of the ceremonial implements, while the women provided the articles used in the household, as well as the dwelling, the family clothing, and the cooking utensils.

The Cheyennes knew nothing of the art of weaving, though certain simple attempts in this direction were seen, as in the snowshoes, made by crossing strands of rawhide over a hoop, or the similarly interlaced rawhide used in the wheel with which they played a favorite game. They braided or twisted ropes of sinew for use in softening the hides which they dressed; these were either plaited in four strands or were tightly twisted in two. They made ropes of the hair of the buffalo's head, twisting long strands on a hook, afterward twisting them tightly together.

ARMS

In modern times, that is to say, after the Cheyennes had left the Missouri River and moved out onto the plains and had begun to give less attention to agriculture and to devote themselves more and more to the pursuit of the buffalo, this animal furnished a very large proportion of the articles that they possessed, except such tools as were made of stone, or of stone and wood. To enumerate the articles manufactured from the products of the buffalo would be to give almost a catalog of their implements.

The Bow. Of the primitive utensils of the Cheyenne, perhaps the most important was the bow, on which he depended largely for subsistence, and almost altogether for defense. Yet it would seem that it is not very long since the Cheyennes began to use bows and arrows in war, and that it is still more recently that they learned how to feather the arrow. The Cheyennes say that the first people with whom they fought on their journey toward the plains were the Assiniboines, whom they met after that tribe had obtained guns. Some of the Cheyennes were killed and the others ran away. The Assiniboines tell the same story, and say that in this first great fight with the Cheyennes the latter were armed only with sharpened sticks and did not seem to know what guns were. In their fighting they ran up close to the Assiniboines, who easily killed many of them.

From the traditions told by old people today, we may picture the development of the arrow from a mere unfeathered dart to an implement which had the accuracy and considerably more than the range of the best old-fashioned revolving pistol. It is obvious that the tradition of the Indians cannot go back to the origin of the bow, but at least we have some accounts of its manufacture and improvement.

Some of the earliest stories of the Cheyennes refer to a time when they ensnared the animals which formed a part of their subsistence, and then beat them to death with clubs. They say that at that time they had no bows, but their weapons were chiefly clubs, or stones tied to the end of sticks. With these they killed animals after they had been snared or had been driven into some situation from which they could not escape.

Nevertheless, the Cheyennes developed a very excellent bow which they used with great skill. The modern bows made by the Cheyennes were short—three and one-half to four and one-half feet was the usual length. They were made of wood, or of the horns of animals—the elk, the buffalo, or the mountain sheep. A certain juniper tree (*Juniperus scopulorum*, Sarg.) was regarded as furnishing the best bow wood used in later times.[1] Usually a small upright tree was chosen, or a stick was split from a larger tree if the grain of the piece was straight. The heart wood was not used. This juniper wood was used for their bows by many of the Missouri River Indians, including Assiniboines, Arikaras, Mandans, and Hidatsas. After they had reached the country where it grew, Osage orange (*bois d'arc*) was used to some extent, more especially in the southern country, where juniper was not always to be had. It furnished a good bow wood. Cherry was not good, for "it did not have

[1] From the twigs of this tree the early whites of the Missouri River distilled an oil which, mixed with grease, made a good salve.

the right spring." In later times, when hickory became accessible, this was a highly esteemed bow wood.

Bows of elk-horn were made in two ways. In one, the maker filed flat, and glued together, a number of straight pieces of the horn, and then wrapped them with sinew. Another method was to take a whole long, more or less crooked, antler and treat it in one piece. If such a bow was to be made, an antler as nearly straight as possible was chosen, and was then whittled, scraped, and rubbed until fairly thin. It was soaked in water, and little by little more of it was taken off until it had become quite thin. It was still crooked, but by heating it before the fire and greasing and working it, it became more or less limber. In this crooked form, the bow was finally completed, being shaped, the nocks cut for the string, and the whole implement finished. During all this time it was constantly being worked and made more pliable, and finally, when it had become quite flexible, the bow was firmly lashed to a straight stick and left there until entirely dry and straight. Sinew was now applied to the back, and when this had been done and the glue had dried and hardened, the implement was complete and ready for use. Such bows were fine to look at, but they were more for show than for use. They did not last very long, but were likely to break when they became old. Bows were made of buffalo-horn by gluing together a number of straight pieces and wrapping the splices with sinew, as elsewhere described.

Bows made of the horn of the mountain sheep were durable and very useful, and long ago many of these were possessed by the Cheyennes. They were made by splitting the ram's horn into long pieces, which were steamed or boiled, drying them straight, and then binding and gluing them together. After this, they were backed with sinew and were very strong and springy. There was another fashion of making the sheep-horn bow: The horn was cut in a spiral about the horn and so across the grain. This worm of horn was then boiled and stretched, and again boiled and again stretched along a long stick, until the piece was made straight. The strip was thick and wide, and the bow consisted of this single piece, not of several strips. After it had been made straight, it was whittled and scraped down to proper thickness, and was then rubbed with a smooth stone until it became everywhere smooth. The sinew was now applied to the back with glue, and the sinew covering was smoothed with a buffalo-rib. The bow was now lashed to a straight pole to dry. Sometimes it was left straight and sometimes was given a double curve. In the latter case, two little blocks or bundles were placed under the bow, each about one-quarter way from either end, and the bow was firmly tied down close to the pole in the middle and near the ends. When fully dry, the bow was trimmed and smoothed down, any loose ends of sinew being cut off with a sharp knife. After this, the ends where the bowstring fitted on were wrapped with sinew, applied with glue. Finally, when the bow was finished, a coating of glue was applied to the back, and on this wet glue was scattered burnt gypsum to whiten the back of the bow. The under surface, where the horn showed, might be painted with any color. The last thing put on was the deerskin handhold, which was wrapped on the bow in a string about three-quarters of an inch wide, and held in place by glue. The whitening for the back was applied to all the best bows, no matter of what material they were made. Even hickory bows were often so treated.

The glue used in the manufacture of bows and arrows was made from the chippings from the rawhide of the neck of a buffalo-bull, or even from the shavings cut from any buffalo-hide in the process of thinning it down. These shavings were boiled with water, and made a strong glue, which was sometimes almost as thick as molasses. This jelly-like soup was often eaten, and was very good.

After a piece of wood chosen for a bow had been seasoned and shaped with a knife, and then scraped as smooth as possible with the edge of the knife, it was rubbed with a piece of buffalo-rib until smooth and polished. Then the glue was spread smoothly and evenly on the back with a stick, and the sinew from the back of the buffalo-bull, on either side of the spine, was applied fresh, and was smoothed down with the rib previously used in smoothing the wood. The layer of sinew might be a thirty-second of an inch thick, and over this was applied another coating of glue. The bow was then hung up in the lodge, and in forty-eight hours was dry and ready for use.

Not all men made bows in the same way. Different men had different methods, and each thought his way the best. Also, at different periods of time different methods prevailed—the fashions changed. In applying the sinew, some people laid it on the back of the bow in wide long pieces, while others thought it better to split it and apply it in small threads.

In ancient times they made bowstrings of the twisted bark of an unidentified tall weed (a milkweed), and later of hair, using any kind that was strong enough, and twisting it tight by means of a wooden hook. It is impossible to say when sinew bowstrings replaced those made of hair, but it was not until after women had learned that sinew could be used as thread for sewing. They had killed some large animal and had brought in the meat. A woman who was cutting up this animal noticed the great tendon which lies under the shoulder blade, and said to her husband, "I believe that from this a bowstring could be made that would be better than one of hair." They tried it and found it good, and have ever since used this for their bowstrings. So they owe their bowstrings to a woman. Bowstrings were made of the sinew of the buffalo-bull.

There was a wide variation in the power of different bows. Some men could not bend the bows commonly used by other men. I estimate the extreme range of the Cheyenne bow at about four hundred yards; in other words, it will throw an arrow to that distance. Some men declare that the best bowmen could send an arrow five hundred yards, and old men say that in days of the old smoothbore flintlock trade guns the bow at

THINNING A HIDE

long-distance shooting was a more effective weapon than the gun.

An item in one of the English papers speaks of archery records made by men in England which approached this distance. For example: in *The Shooting Times,* July 22, 1905, reference is made to "a shot" by Sir Ralph Payne Gallwey of three hundred and sixty-seven yards. This is said to have been made with a Turkish compound bow, with which some very long shots have been made. A correspondent of the same journal says, "It is recorded that the then Sultan of Turkey in 1798 shot an arrow nine hundred and seventy-two yards with one of these bows." Other shots are instanced, with English bows, of three hundred and sixty or three hundred and forty yards.[2]

At the most effective range—say from forty to seventy yards—an Indian could handle a bow and arrows more rapidly and more effectively than the average man could use a revolving pistol of that time. The effectiveness of the bow and arrow in hunting is discussed in the chapter on that subject.

Stories are told of an occasion when the Cheyennes armed with bows kept off an attacking party of Crows who had some guns. I have no doubt that the sinew backing of the Indian bow added much power to the implement.[3]

There were different modes of handling the string and arrow in drawing the bow. Some Cheyennes merely held the arrow between thumb and forefinger, and pulled straight back on the arrow and so on the string, others assisted this by having the middle finger pull on the string, while others still held the arrow between the forefinger and middle finger hooked over the string, and held the arrow in its place by the thumb. Each man's way seemed to him the best, which only means that, having practiced this method most, he could produce the best

[2] See Roberts, The English Bowman, London, 1801.

[3] For the power of the bow in skilled hands, compare Cabeza de Vaca, p. 31, Hodge ed., Scribner's, N. Y., 1907.

results with it. In other words, the methods were individual and not tribal, as has been suggested.[4]

The Arrow (Mah). Arrows were the most precious possessions of the primitive Indians. If a man wished to marry a girl, he might offer ten arrows as a gift to the girl's father. Men always gathered up their arrows, devoting much time to searching for them and trying never to lose one. They were too hard to get and cost too much effort to be wasted. In the same way, if the points were lost from the arrows, they searched for them long and carefully.

The old men who made the best arrows were proud of their skill and were greatly respected for it. There was a great difference in arrows, and it was essential for the best work that the shaft should be properly proportioned. The proportions between the shaft, head, and feather were quite definite, and if these were preserved the arrow did excellent work; otherwise it was a failure. Great skill and judgment were required to make a perfect arrow. An arrow too light in the shaft would not fly steadily; one too heavy would not carry its force long enough. A good, well-balanced arrow, when it struck the mark, tilted up at the feather-end, while the feather-end of a bad arrow dropped down. At gatherings and feasts, men often spoke of such matters, telling how their arrows acted. The subject was of general interest, and when it was under discussion, those present always listened.

The Cheyennes were thought to have the best arrows of any Indians in their country. The old-time arrow makers always made arrows by tens, and those of each ten were the same; thus each man bought his arrows in tens and all were alike. Each arrow maker manufactured his arrows after his own fashion.

Arrowshafts were usually made from the straight shoots of

[4] Handbook of American Indians, Bull. 30, Bureau American Ethnology, pt. 1, p. 93, quotes Dr. Morse as describing four methods of holding the arrow and the bowstring; but the conclusions drawn as to these methods are erroneous. The methods described are merely those practiced by individuals.

the cherry bush, but some arrow makers used the straight. shoots of the currant, and others those of "red-willow" and rose. Such shoots were employed because most easily smoothed and straightened. The shoots were cut in regular lengths, according to the rule of the arrow maker, who usually measured the shafts on his arm, from the tip of the middle finger nearly halfway up the humerus. They were then tied up in bundles and hung up in the lodge until dry.

In collecting the sticks for arrowshafts, arrow makers were always careful in peeling them to see that they were strong enough to go through the straightening process, for it was deemed very unlucky for the maker and his family if he broke an arrow-stick while straightening it. In handling his arrow-sticks, the Cheyenne always pointed them toward the fire in looking at them to see if they were straight, and never allowed them to be directed toward anyone in the lodge.

When the arrowshafts that had been hung up in the lodge were thoroughly dry, they were taken down by the arrow maker and the bundle opened and inspected. Most of the shafts were nearly straight, and those which were not so were straightened by bending with an arrow-straightener. Often this was made from the spine of the vertebra of a large animal through which had been drilled a hole a little larger in diameter than the shaft's thickness; or sometimes the straightener was the horn of a female mountain sheep, in which holes had been drilled. The arrow was passed through one of the holes and bent this way and that until perfectly straight. This work was often done also with the hands and the teeth.

In preparing the shaft of the arrow, three other important tools were used. These were: (1) grooved sandstone slabs for reducing the shaft; (2) a rib pierced with a circular hole into which extended a little projection from the margin of the hole —or a flint with a semicircular notch and a projection—for making the grooves in the shaft; and (3) a rib with a circular hole the exact size of the completed shaft, for standardizing the diameter of the arrow.

After the shaft was straightened, the two grooved blocks of sandstone, three or four inches long, with flat meeting faces, were used to reduce and to smooth and round the arrow. Placing the shaft in one groove, the other groove was fitted over it, and holding the two stones together with the left hand, the maker pulled the shaft back and forth to smooth it.

From the upper end of the feathers on one side of the shaft, toward the point of the arrow, a straight groove ran all the way to the arrow's head; on the other side a winding or zigzag groove was made, reaching from the feather to the arrowpoint. These grooves were made either with the bone or the flint instrument already mentioned. In the latter, a notch had been chipped out wide enough for the arrow to lie in, but in the middle of this notch was left a small projecting point of the flint. Holding this flint notch downward in the thumb and two fingers of the left hand, the maker placed the arrowshaft in the notch and with the right hand pulled it toward him, pulling straight for the straight groove and with a twisting motion for the zigzag one.

Much speculation has been indulged in as to the meaning of these grooves. The most popular explanation is that they were made for the purpose of permitting the blood to escape, so as to weaken the wounded animal, or that they symbolized the lightning, and so would be more fatal. What seems quite as probable is that these grooves may have been made to counteract the tendency of the wood to warp or spring and become crooked.

In a paper on the life of the Plains Indians, written by Francis La Flesche,[5] an old Omaha arrow maker is quoted as saying on this point:

Every sapling out of which the arrow is made has some defect, however faultless it may appear to be. The good arrow maker takes

[5] *The Southern Workman*, vol. xxxiv, no. 11.

a great deal of pains to smooth out and straighten the imperfections by oiling and heating. But the wood, in time, will spring back because of its inherent defects, unless these grooves are cut in the shaft soon after the seasoning and straightening.

After the shaft had been brought down to the proper size and the grooves made in it, the shaft was thrust into and pushed through the circular hole in the rib standardizer with a twisting motion. This polished the shaft and at the same time left little fine ridges running about it which could be felt as the fingers were passed over them, but were almost too small to be seen.

The arrow's flight depended largely on the feathers. If they were good and well put on, the arrow carried well. Turkey-feathers or buzzard-feathers were the best for arrows, because blood does not affect them. Feathers of hawks and eagles, if wet with blood, are injured by the wetting. However, the feathers of these birds were used for ceremonial arrows.

The Cheyennes tell of a time before the use of feathers on the arrow, when they were accustomed to shave up from the shaft of the arrow, all about the shaft, a number of fine shavings, which they left attached to it. These shavings, standing out from the shaft, acted as steadiers for the arrow's flight. After they had learned to place feathers on their arrows and had begun to use feathered arrows in fighting with other tribes, they often found on the prairie arrows shot at them by their enemies, which had no feathers, but instead bore, each one, two little bunches of fine shavings whittled up from the shaft and left attached to it by one end. These shavings were cut and bent upward toward the arrowpoint in two places on the shaft, one close to the notch and the other farther toward the point. The use of such arrows may have been general among the prairie tribes until a comparatively recent date.

The late Joseph Kipp, born 1849, told me that as a small boy (say about the year 1860) he used to see among the Mandans, near old Fort Clark, shaved-up arrows (like those described by the Cheyennes as used anciently) employed by little boys in their first hunting to kill small birds. Sometimes these boys' arrows had three small twigs tied about two inches back from the sharpened, fire-hardened point, in such a manner as to form a triangle, which gave a larger striking surface. Some such arrows were shaved up at two or three points on their length, the obvious purpose being to make them fly steadily. From what we know of Cheyenne history, it seems evident that the arrows of the Cheyennes and of the Mandans might have had much in common.

While the earliest arrows used by the Cheyennes were without feathers, feathers came into use after a time, but at first only two, instead of three. Thus, these arrows in their feathering seem to have resembled some of those used by the Eskimo, as shown in certain illustrations. The two feathers used were not split and glued to the shaft as in modern times, but notches were cut in the shaft above and below, and the entire feather was tied on each side of the shaft. One vane of each of the two feathers was thus crushed against the shaft of the arrow.

After the arrows with two feathers had been used for a long time, an old man spoke to the people, telling them that their arrows were not good and that he had a plan for a better one. He took the longest feather that he could get, split it, and wound it spirally from near the nock of the shaft as far as it would go toward the point, tying it with sinew at either end, as before. Such arrows shot well, and were better than those that they had used hitherto. Even to this day little boys sometimes make and use such arrows. It was a long time after this that the present style of arrows came into use, having three feathers cut, trimmed, and glued to the shaft.

In modern times when a man intended to make a number of arrows, the feathers were prepared in advance. The shafts were split and cut so that the feathers should all be of proper length. When applied, the tip of each end of the split feather shaft was touched with glue and put on in its proper place and then wrapped in position with a thread of sinew. This was repeated

until the three feathers were in place, when the final and complete wrapping was done above and below the feathers. The
arrowshaft was held in the right hand, the sinew in the left,
and the sinew was applied by turning the shaft with the fingers
in such manner that the sinew was laid on from right to left.
Subsequent to this came the painting of the arrow—above or
below, or both above and below the sinew—with the owner's
private mark. In putting on the paint near the feathers, the
shaft was turned in the hand from right to left.

In trimming the feathers for arrows, they were placed on a
hard surface, usually a flat piece of elk-horn. This was used so
they should be trimmed evenly, and the knife should not sink
into the surface on which the feather rested.

In the distal end of the arrowshaft a notch was cut in which
the arrowhead was set, held in place with glue, and then at once
wrapped with wet sinew, which soon dried. In applying the
sinew, the shaft was turned, so as to lay on the sinew from right
to left. The points of the arrows were of chipped or ground
stone, bone, deer antler, or of the sole of the hoof of the buffalo,
cut off, pared down, and dried; and it is possible that other
portions of the hoofs of various animals may have been used.
The Cheyennes, like the Blackfeet and the Pawnees, say that
wounds made by the old stone arrowpoints were more likely to
be fatal than those made by the arrowpoints of later times.

As soon as the white man came, metal began to take the place
of many of these piercing materials, yet for a long time metal
was hard to get, while the demand for arrows was constant.
In Elk River's young days (say from 1820 to 1840), he has
told me, arrows with stone points were not infrequently found
on the prairie, showing that they had been used only a short
time before. The thin part of the shoulder blade of animals,
ground down and shaped, was still used. It may readily be understood that if a man possessed a small portion of metal, tin
or sheet-iron, it would have been more useful to him as a knife

than if divided and used to head a few arrows, some of which might soon have been lost.

Often just above the nock in the shaft—which of course was parallel with the notch for the arrowpoint—was a little constriction caused by cutting away the wood, and on the swell below this were made little cross notches or scratches to give a good finger hold.

In making an arrowhead of stone, and later of iron, the Sioux often fashioned a barb on each shoulder, while the Cheyennes made no barb. Their arrows were either square on the shoulder, like this ⟨figure⟩ , or rounded, like this ⟨figure⟩ ⟨figure⟩

The sheet-iron arrowheads were small, and the arrows short and fine.

Quivers and Bow-cases. These, sewed together and carried by a band over the right shoulder, were often made of otter, panther, and buffalo-calf skin, the tails usually being left attached to the skin and hanging down. All these animals were believed to possess spiritual power, and the use of their skins tended to impart some of this power to the user of the quiver.

The Cheyennes in ancient times used to a considerable extent arrowheads and knives of stone. Black Moccasin, who died about 1884, remembered when such implements were still often employed. Persons recently living were told by their grandfathers that in their time, say early in the nineteenth century, such implements were in use. Some knives were made of the ribs of elk or moose.

For their cutting and piercing implements they employed the hardest stones they could secure, usually flint. When a suitable stone had been found for making a celt, it was broken off to the right length by a sharp blow of a small stone hammer; it was then held in the left hand and rested on a block of wood, and repeated blows were given it with the hammer, it being turned and chipped by these blows until the desired edge and point were produced. When a knife—or an arrowpoint—had been worked down quite thin, but had not yet received a satisfactory cutting edge, the piece was held in the left hand, between the thumb and forefinger, while a small stone punch was held between the fore and middle fingers. The punch was pressed against the edge of the blade, and was struck sharp downward blows with a hammer, each blow taking off a small flake, and this process was continued until the edge was finished. A better cutting edge was finally given by the flaking off of small chips from near the margin. The flint was held in the palm protected by a wad of hair or piece of tanned hide and a small point of antler or bone suddenly applied with force against the stone at the required point. This pressure cracked off a small chip and the operation was repeated as needed. The back of a completed knife was sometimes inserted in a split stick which served as a handle. The stick was tightly lashed with wet sinew or fine rawhide strings, and when these dried, the stone edge and its handle were firmly bound together. Such knives served efficiently for slitting killed game up the belly and legs.

The manufacture of cutting implements of stone is quite fully discussed in the Handbook of American Indians.[6]

Knives were made also of the bosse ribs—the dorsal spines —of the buffalo, with handles tied to them, the edge of the bone being rubbed down until sharp; but for a long time only a few of these—perhaps three or four—were possessed in a camp. After the Cheyennes secured hoop-iron, they sometimes inserted a metal cutting edge in such bone knives. The first metal knife told of was a flat piece of iron found on the prairie, which when rubbed down to an edge proved much more useful than the old knives of bone.

A stone axe shaped like an ordinary woodsman's axe, and

[6] Bull. 30, Bureau American Ethnology, pt. 2, p. 638, Washington, 1910.

with an oval hole drilled part way through the stone in the position and shape of the hole through an ordinary axe-head, was formerly owned by Crazy Head. The stone appears to be a hard slate, and the cutting edge is somewhat rounded. Crazy Head stated that he received the axe when a very young man (say about 1865), and that it has always been in his family, handed down from father to son. He believes that the old-time people made it for use as an axe—for cutting, but that gradually it has acquired a spiritual power. Since it came to him, this object has been used only to carry in war as a spiritual protection, being held in front of the body by the man who carried it, the cutting edge vertical and to the front. Borne in this way, it was believed that it would split and turn aside arrows or bullets shot at the holder. The shape of the implement suggests that it may have been made after white men's axes had been seen.

The woman's maul or mallet will be spoken of elsewhere. The man's so-called war-club is similar, but with a much lighter head, and a longer and more springy handle. Usually it is provided with a loop near the handhold, to slip over the wrist.

The Lance was a favorite weapon. The ordinary type was a wooden shaft, six to seven feet long, armed, in modern times, with an iron or steel point. This might be of any shape—the blade of a sabre or a knife, an old bayonet, or some other piece of iron. In ancient times the lance-head was of chipped stone, often leaf-shaped. This head was bound to the shaft with sinew or rawhide thongs. Lances were used in war and in the chase of the buffalo.

There were several types of ceremonial lances, most of them belonging to the soldier bands. These were used in the dances of the various societies; and were also carried in war, but as ceremonial rather than lethal weapons—chiefly for the purpose of touching the enemy. One of these lances was called *hōhk-*

tsĭm',[7] a word commonly translated "wheel," but perhaps having reference to the bent or curving shape. The circular wheel used in a game bears the same name. At the distal end, the shaft of this form of lance is bent somewhat in the shape of the conventional shepherd's crook. The shaft was commonly bound with otter-fur, and variously ornamented with feathers. Other types of lance, belonging to other soldier bands, were straight throughout, and the shaft was covered by a case made of deerskin—latterly of red or blue cloth—from which the feathers of eagles or turkeys or of hawks depended. All these articles are old.

The so-called "contrary lance," or lightning lance (*ho nŭhk ka wo'?*), a ceremonial weapon carried by the Contraries, is described elsewhere. It was shaped like a bow, and strung, but at one end bore a lance-head, or point of stone or metal, and was adorned with feathers of war birds. These contrary bows or lances were usually very ancient, but if one were lost or sacrificed, another might be made to replace it.

The Shield was perhaps the most important part of the equipment of the Cheyenne warrior. This was a circular piece of dried and toughened bull-hide, carried on the left arm, light, but strong enough to stop an arrow, or to turn a ball from an old-fashioned smoothbore gun. Originally carried in order to ward off missiles and spear thrusts, the shield in later times exercised a protection that was in part physical and in part spiritual; indeed, most shields were believed to possess strong spiritual power. It might exercise in behalf of him who carried it not only the general protective influence due to its sacred character, but also might endue him with those qualities attributed to the heavenly bodies, birds, mammals, and other living creatures whose images were painted on it, or portions of which were tied to it. It might afford also protection from the

[7] See Games.

elements, for some shields were sacred to the thunder and to the lightning.

A shield adorned with the feathers of the eagle was believed to give its owner the swiftness and courage of that bird. If the feathers of the owl were tied on it, the man perhaps shared the owl's power to see in the dark, and to move silently and unnoticed. The figure of a bear painted on the shield, or its claws attached, gave him the bear's toughness; and so of many of the qualities which belonged to the animals which the Cheyennes regarded as possessing superhuman powers.

Not everyone possessed a shield. For the greater part, they were owned only by men of years and discretion. Boys and very young men seldom carried them, unless some older friend or relative lent or gave his shield for this purpose. When this was done, the borrower was carefully instructed by the owner as to the spiritual power of the shield, and the ceremonies to be practiced in using it. A young man who carried a shield, and who failed to perform the ceremonies appropriate to it, would certainly be wounded in the fight in which he bore it.

There seem to have been three kinds of shields known to the Cheyennes. Of these the most important were the group shields, said to have belonged to certain groups or divisions, and perhaps never going out of them; although we may suppose that the Dog Soldiers, an organization made up of persons belonging to different bands, and which at length came to represent the old division, Masihkota, may have had members who carried shields belonging to other bands. To another class belonged the dream shields, the fashion and painting of which had been taught to some man by a dream. These shields, though made in much the same way, and with a ceremony not less elaborate, possessed less protective power than the group shields. Finally, we are told of shields without spiritual protective power; they were commonly unpainted, and were used merely to ward off the arrows or blows of the enemy—were thus literally parfleches.

The group and the dream shields were made with elaborate ceremony, and various ceremonial acts were practiced in their use. In addition, they were hedged about by various duties and tabus, which made the ownership of such a shield a matter of much responsibility. So seriously did the duties and restrictions weigh on some shield owners that occasionally a man might determine to free himself from these responsibilities by giving up his shield, and might present it to the sun or to some other power, taking it out of the camp and leaving it hung on a pole on the top of a hill. Or, he might take it down to the river, where, tying stones to it, he deposited it with some ceremony in the stream. A shield thus relinquished by its owner was never disturbed; no one would dare touch it, knowing that if he did so bad luck would surely follow.

In the more recent wars with United States troops, the Cheyennes at length came to realize that the shield afforded little physical protection against the balls from modern rifles, but they did not lose faith in its spiritual assistance, and carried shields until the fighting ceased. At present, however, old-time shields are no longer found among the Cheyennes. Many have been sacrificed or abandoned, some have been buried with their owners, or with the dead children of their owners, while a few have been lost or given to white men; so that, as far as I can learn, there does not now remain a single shield in either section of the tribe.

Constructed on the same general principle as that of other Plains tribes, the Cheyenne shield has some characteristics of its own. It was made from the shrunken rawhide of the buffalo-bull's neck, but if a deerskin cover was used over the bull's hide, the Cheyennes often stuffed the space between the shield and its covering with feathers, or with buffalo or antelope hair, thus deadening the force of arrow or bullet, and increasing the protection it gave.

When a shield was to be made, a circular hole was dug in the ground, a foot or more deep, and a little wider than the intended diameter of the shield. A fire was built near this hole, in which stones were heated red-hot. About half the fresh skin of a buffalo-bull—the front part of the hide—was spread over the hole, and pinned down all around, to hold it in place for a time. At one side near the fire there were no pins, and a place was left where the hide could be raised.

When the stones in the fire were hot, the edge of the hide was lifted and a number of these stones were placed in the hole. Water was poured on them, and the skin was clapped down on the ground and held there. The hot steam rising from the hole contracted and thickened the skin on all sides. Sometimes a single steaming was enough to bring the hide to the proper thickness, or again a second treatment was needed; in any event, the hide was kept over the steam until it had become as thick as possible. While the hide was being shrunk from beneath, hot water was poured on the hair side from above, and a man with a knife or scraper removed the hair. When the steaming had been completed, the hide was taken off the hole, and with an awl a small hole was made as near the middle of it as possible, and a strand of sinew passed through the hole. By this string it was held up, and from this as a center one-half the intended diameter of the shield was measured off on all sides, the circle was marked all around, and the hide cut off, so that it was a perfect circle of the size required. A parfleche was now spread on the ground to keep the shield from the dirt, and placing it on the parfleche it was pounded with a stone to efface all the wrinkles and to make it smooth. It was then put out to dry.

The holes through which the strings for the armhold—or for any of the attachments—were to pass, were afterward burned in the hide with a heated iron rod or wire.

A well-dressed antelope-skin was chosen to make a cover for the shield, and on this cover were to be painted the birds, animals, or symbols, which the shield-maker selected. When this painting was to be done, the shield-maker called into the lodge a number of men to sing with him. All the singers were brave men, warriors; all wore feathers on their heads, sometimes the complete stuffed skins of different hawks tied to their scalp-locks, and perhaps a lock of hair cut from the scalp of an enemy. The lodge door was shut, and a stick was put up to warn people not to enter. The paint used for the shield cover was mixed with glue made from scrapings of buffalo-hide. This made a durable paint, which did not rub or wear off.

Before the painting was begun, the shield and its cover were placed at the back of the lodge, resting on a bed of the stems of white sage, which kept the shield from touching the ground. Between the fire and this bed of sage four small sticks were thrust into the ground, forming the corners of a small square, in the middle of which a coal from the fire was put on the ground. Dried sweet grass was sprinkled on the coal, and the shield-maker held his hands over the smoke and then made the ceremonial motions. The pipe was filled, lighted, and passed around the circle. When it had been smoked out, the ashes were emptied from it, and it was filled again and placed on the ground between the four sticks and the shield. Then followed a song, and the man who was making the shield painted for a short time. Again the pipe was lighted and smoked out, another song was sung, and the shield-maker painted again. They smoked four times and sang four times, all the songs being different. Then they rested and talked for a time, again smoked and sang as before, and so it went on until the painting was finished.

After the painting was finished, the cover was rested on the shield, and to the cover were attached the feathers of the different war birds that were to go on the shield. Then the painted cover was fitted on the shield, the feathers properly arranged and over all was put a plain deerskin covering. To the outside cover, all around the border of the shield, were now attached fine feathers; sometimes only a few, sometimes many. An armhold of otter-skin, by which to carry it, was attached to the back of the shield. After all these things had been done, the singers rubbed white clay all over their bodies, and over the feathers and skins of the birds which were on their heads. Often the painting was done directly on the bull's-hide shield, to which also the protective medicines and decorations were attached.

While all this had been going on, the female relations of these men had been cooking food, and when the ceremony was over, this was brought to the front of the lodge, passed in to the singers, and they ate. After this the shield was taken close to the door, and people—men, women, and children—were called into the lodge. They passed by the shield and put their hands on it, just touching it with one hand. In front of the lodge, and not more than twenty-five feet distant, a sweat-lodge had been built. The shield was now taken out and placed on top of this sweat-lodge, and the singers and painter all entered it and sang, while taking a sweat. After they had finished, they came out, still singing, but as each one passed out the door, he stopped singing. The ceremony was now concluded.

A tripod had already been set up behind the lodge, and the owner hung the shield on it, where it remained until he was ready to go to war.

If the shield fell to the ground, it was not permitted at once to pick it up. It must be covered by a skin or a blanket, and allowed to lie on the ground for a time. When taken up, some of the "medicine"—pulverized leaves—from the bundle tied to the shield was sprinkled on a coal, and the shield passed through the smoke. After this, it was hung on the tripod as before.

A shield had very strong power. No one might handle it without the owner's permission. The shield songs were particularly sacred; they were connected with the thunder and the lightning, and could be sung only at special times, and by special men.

The old men who made shields possessed some special spirit-

RED BIRD'S SHIELD

ual power: had perhaps been helped by a bird or turtle, or a buffalo-bull, or by some spirit. They had been taught by older shield-makers how the work should be done. A man who wished to have a shield made, asked a shield-maker to help him—*i.e.*, to make a shield for him—by offering him a filled pipe; and the shield-maker, by smoking, consented to grant the request. One for whom a shield had been made, having been taught the secrets and the ceremonies, might himself become a shield-maker. If the man for whom it had been made captured a horse on his first war journey after receiving the shield, he was expected to present the horse to the shield-maker. Each maker made all his shields alike, and painted them in the same way. There is not now alive in the tribe a man of those who used to make them.

The shield was indeed a powerful helper, and every adornment it bore possessed a distinct significance. Thus, Red Bird's shield, now in my possession, had on it four claws of a grizzly bear in two pairs, a turtle's tail, a round leaden ball, and the feathers of eagles and owls. The bear has great strength and courage, and is hard to kill; therefore, the man who carried the shield would have strength, courage, and likewise be hard to kill. The turtle possesses much spiritual power, and also is hard to kill. If you cut off its head, it will still move, and perhaps even walk away. So the man who carried this shield, even if badly wounded, would be likely to recover. Moreover, the turtle knows how to hide; it can dive to the bottom of the water and stay there concealed for a long time. The leaden ball would turn aside the bullets of the enemy. The feathers of the birds gave to the man who carried the shield the powers possessed by those birds.

This shield is painted red, with a crescent moon on it. It was the last shield in the Northern Cheyenne tribe. One of the bear's claws is missing; it was shot away in a fight with the Crows, on an occasion when Big Head was carrying the shield.

This shield was made by Oak (Ōŭmsh′), who gave it to his

son Oak, who was the father of Great Eyes. The younger Oak carried it to war as a young man—before he was married. He gave it to Great Eyes, who at the age of sixty was killed at Fort Robinson, Nebraska, in January, 1879. Two Moon believed that the shield was made about 1780, and so is more than a hundred and forty years old. When the outbreak at Fort Robinson was about to take place, Great Eyes gave the shield to his nephew, Red Bird, then only a boy. In the rush from the barracks, Red Bird was shot in the knee, but managed to crawl into a hole, and there tied up his leg, cut two forked sticks for crutches, and many days later hobbled into the house of John Shettler, a mile and a half below the post. During all his difficulty and suffering, for he had almost nothing to eat all this time, he did not abandon his shield, but still had it on his back when he came to the house. He was afterward sent to Pine Ridge. Red Bird was sound and whole in 1895, but has since died. This shield is said to belong to the Mahsihkota group.

Flocco, who once borrowed a Mahsihkota shield to carry to war, was told by the owner that before it was used it must be purified in the smoke of juniper needles.

"When you put the cover on," added the owner, "the deerskin strings which hold the bear-claws must be loosened, so that they may lie down; but when you take the cover off, and go into a fight, the strings must be tightened, so that the claws will stand out stiff, and be directed toward the enemy. When purifying the shield you must pass it over the smoke in the four directions (*Niv' stăn ĭ vo'*) and last hold it over the smoke, and then raise it toward the sky and shake it. Then you must move it four times toward the right front of your body, and hang it over your body on the right side. In riding forward toward the enemy, you must keep on the right-hand side of your party, and quite away from them. Some shields may be supported on a single pole, but this must be on a tripod. In the morning it must be hung out facing the sun."

At night the women wrapped this shield up in a good blanket, moved the tripod close to the front of the lodge, and it was left there till the morning, when the women took the blanket off. Feathers of the short-eared owl (*Asio flammeus*) were tied in a bunch below the moon painted on it. The tail, made of dressed buffalo-hide (*mōhk' sĭk* or *mōhksi' ya*), was tied to the parfleche below the moon with three strings.

About 1868, Crazy Mule, then a strong medicine man and a prophet, or foreteller of events, made four shields, all alike, each with a Thunder Bird in the center, with four circular black spots—the four directions—near the border. When the first enemy was killed after the men who carried these shields obtained them, each man was obliged to eat a small piece of the enemy's heart. These shields had a special name; they were called Hole-in-the-shield (*Hoh' tăhk hō wăn*). An ordinary shield is *Hō wăn'*. The Thunder Bird on the shield was to give its owner the courage and swiftness of the eagle and the power of the Thunder Bird.

The owners of these shields seldom smoked in their lodges. Usually they smoked out on the prairie alone, and in situations where no one could approach them without being seen. If one of them wished to smoke in his lodge, the women were obliged to go out, and a stick was put across the door as a sign that no one should enter. While the shield owner was smoking, no one else might be in the lodge, unless perhaps the owner of another one of these shields. These two might smoke together. When smoking, the position of the bowl of the pipe was reversed, the opening being held toward the ground. These men might drink only from a dish made of some natural material, as a wooden bowl, or sheep-horn dish, or a turtleshell. No vessel made of tin or other metal might be used. A crockery bowl, however, might be drunk from.

The feathers and heads of the sandhill crane were often attached to shields, for this bird possesses strong protective power and his voice is alarming to enemies. The head was sometimes fastened on the center of the shield.

Mr. John J. White, Jr., of New York, owns an old-time buffalo shield, found in the neighborhood of the Custer battleground in southern Montana, which is an example of a dream shield.

This shield, about the history of which nothing was known for many years, was at length identified by the wife and son[8] of its former owner. The son, White Shield, said of it:

The man who made this shield was Whistling Elk, the father of Spotted Wolf, and my grandfather. At the time it was lost, it belonged to Spotted Wolf. He had lent it to his adopted son, Yellow Nose, a Ute captive, who is believed to have lost it from his saddle, while going from the point on the upper Rosebud where the Cheyennes had a fight with General Crook's command—June 17, 1876— to the camp on the Little Big Horn River, where afterward they fought with General Custer's men.

When a young man, Whistling Elk went to a certain lake, and out on a rocky point running into the water. He carried with him a buffalo-skull, and putting it on the ground, lay down by it, and there fasted and prayed for five days and five nights. On the morning of the fourth day, a buffalo raised its head above the water and sang a song, directing Whistling Elk to make this shield and describing how it should be made.

The painting on the shield consists of a pair of long, slender, upward-directed horns, a little above the center of the shield; below them is a large disc surrounded by dots; between the horns is a red disc also surrounded by dots, and there are four dark discs evenly distributed near the border of the shield. These discs on the outer rim represent the four directions; the disc below the horns is the moon; the red disc between the horns, the sun; and the dots are stars. The horns represent the animal that took pity on Whistling Elk and taught him how to make this shield. The moon is the spirit that during the night protected the brave who carried the shield, and the sun protected him during the day. The upper round spot to the left of the horns represents the wind which comes from the setting sun. The upper spot at the right of the horns represents the wind from the

[8] Both since dead, Wind Woman about 1915, and White Shield about May 1, 1918.

north, the lower spot on the right, the wind from the east, and the lower spot on the left, the wind from the south. The spirit which controls the south wind is supposed to have the greatest power when prayed to for help.

When carried in battle, a piece of lodge-skin was fastened to the bottom of the shield, hanging down, and across this lodge-skin were four rows of eagle-feathers.

All these statements are confirmed by Wind Woman, the widow of Spotted Wolf, who recognized the shield as soon as she saw the painting.

Four of these shields were made, two of them being given to Whistling Elk's nephews, one to his son, and one to his grandson, Little Magpie. Two of the shields were buried with their owners; one of them was left in the hills as a sacrifice, and the fourth is in Mr. White's possession, and has been lent to the Museum of the American Indian, Heye Foundation.

There have been cases where men have devised a new painting for a shield, pretending to have dreamed of the painting. Such shields, however, have often proved ineffectual, and the men carrying them have been killed by balls or arrows which pierced the shields.

Each tribal group had its own method of treating the shields before its warriors went to battle. The hill men, Hissiometaniu, before charging, used to run their horses over the prairie, stoop down to the left and sweep the shield over the grass; then raise it above the head, hold it toward the sun, and shake it. Unless this were done they were likely to be wounded.

Ivistsinihpah burned sweet grass, sage, and other medicine, which was always carried tied to the shield. They passed the shield four times through this smoke, and then held it up to the sun and shook it, and afterward moved it down toward the body four times, putting it on the arm the fourth time.

A shield belonging to the family Mowissiyu[9] was called the

---

[9] Said to be a family of Sioux which has long lived with the Cheyennes. The *Monsoni* of Mooney.

day shield. The painting on it represented the day, the sun being in the center of the shield, with blue clouds above it. The painting was done on the bull-hide; there was no cover. Eagle-feathers hung down from the lower border of the shield, and at the sides were attached the tail-feathers of eagles. On each side of the shield, tied to the strings where the otter-skin band was attached, was a small, round, polished stone, like a boy's marble. Representations of rabbit tracks were painted on the obverse of the shield.

When this shield was to be used, the man who was to carry it held it, in order, to the east, the zenith, and the west—to the rising sun, the sky, and the setting sun. The sun was believed to enter the shield, and, when the face of the shield was turned toward the enemy, to go out of it again and to blind the enemy —dazzling their eyes.

Mad Wolf carried this shield in battle several times, and on two occasions, failing to handle it exactly as he should have done, he was wounded.

A shield of the Hevataniu had a painted deerskin cover. At the top was a green crescent moon, the horns directed upward. To the right of the moon, in black, was painted a bear, and to the left of the moon a buffalo, the heads of both animals directed toward the moon, so that they faced each other. In the center was painted a red sun. From the sun, in the four directions, black zigzag marks representing lightning flashes extended to the circumference of the shield. On each of the two zigzag lines directed toward the bottom of the shield, two bear's claws were fastened with deerskin strings. About the margin of the shield a dozen tufts of yellow horsehair hung down. A long tail of dressed hide (mohksiya), with eagle-feathers tied across it at different points, was pendent from just below the moon.

In the morning the shield must face the east, and in the middle of the day must face upward toward the sun. In the middle of the day the shield was taken from its tripod, placed on the ground, and wrapped in a black bearskin, nicely dressed, painted with rings of red about wrists and ankles, and with a bunch of eagle-feathers tied between the shoulders. At night the wrapped shield was brought around to the door and left outside. At the first meal in the morning a bit of food was held toward the shield, and then placed at the edge of the fire nearest the door. This was giving food to the bear.

Each of the different divisions of the tribe is said formerly to have had its own shield; but each man knew only the shield of his own division.

Various tabus were connected with the different shields. Men who owned certain shields were not permitted to eat entrails; others were not permitted to take food from the fire with a metal implement—could not do this with knife or fork, but must use a sharp stick. Some might not eat the heart of any animal, nor anything from the kettle in which the heart had been cooked. Others might not eat of the neck, nor others of the ham of the buffalo. To some the placenta of the buffalo was forbidden. If by accident a man entered a lodge in which was a menstruating woman, he must at once purify himself by taking a sweat.

The possessor of a Hevataniu shield was not permitted to eat of the heart of any animal, nor of meat boiled in the same kettle with the heart. A tabu such as this was exceedingly inconvenient, for it was a common practice to cook the heart of the buffalo in the kettle along with other meat, and in a friend's lodge a man might unwittingly eat of it and thus invite misfortune. To free himself from the operation of this tabu it was required that the man should eat the heart of an enemy. On one occasion Wolf Chief thus escaped the danger from the violation of the tabu. He declared to me that he never tasted anything so disagreeable as the human heart which he ate. He could hardly swallow it.

They had killed a Crow in battle, and taking out his heart, cut it in thin flakes, which they dried as women dry meat. After the flesh had been dried, it was pounded up fine. A sweat-house was built, and those who were to take part in the ceremony entered it and took a sweat. After this, each inmate of the sweat-house took a pinch of the dried heart, raised it slowly to the sky, called like a crow, and swallowed it. All who had done this might thereafter eat the heart of any animal. Those who ate at this time were Wolf Chief, Bear Shield, and Big Man. On another occasion other men ate a part of a Crow's heart raw, with the same purpose—*i.e.*, purification, and to free themselves from the tabu.

In connection with the ceremonial eating of the heart of an enemy in order to remove the tabu from certain shield owners, it may be asked what evidence there is to show that the Tonkawas were cannibals in the ordinary meaning of the term. They had this reputation among their neighbors, and Mooney voices it, but did they do more than practice the ceremonial eating of the flesh of enemies? On certain ceremonial occasions, notably when they killed an enemy, the Tonkawas did eat human flesh. They took out the enemy's heart, and cutting it in small pieces boiled it in a kettle with sacred corn, and had a ceremonial feast at which each man, among other things, ate a piece of the heart. The well-known Black Beaver, the Delaware, who was present at such a feast, told what was done there, and declared that the feast was ceremonial. Such ceremonial eating of the flesh of an enemy was practiced by many tribes of Indians, and the statement of Black Beaver seems plausible.

Shield-makers always warned the men for whom they were making shields that if they did not carefully observe the ceremonies connected with the shields they would be hit in battle by bullets or arrows.

Once a shield was made which near its border had four round holes in the four cardinal directions. An arrow passed through one of these holes and killed the owner of the shield. The people believed that he must have failed to observe the law of his shield.

There is said to have been a shield for which a new covering had to be made every time the owner counted a coup.

Certain shields carried by old-time warriors have been roughly described to me. One of these had a half-moon at the upper border, a sun in the middle, and about the margin four inward directed points, representing the four cardinal directions. This was owned by the grandfather of Little Chief, Southern Cheyenne. It came from the Suhtai.

Another, called the bear's ear shield, had two bear's ears painted on it near the upper border. It belonged to the Northern Cheyennes.

A very old shield carried by Tall Bull, who was killed in 1869, had painted on it the figure of a bear.

The shield owned by Starving Elk—the father of Starving Elk killed in 1879 by Little Wolf—was a dream shield, made by Animal's Foot. It had a half-moon close to the top of the margin; four inward directed points, representing the four directions; in the center was a bat with spread wings, head upward, and about the bat, nearly opposite the four points representing the cardinal directions, were four fork-tailed (barn) swallows, their heads toward the center of the shield. This shield had a long tail with three horizontal rows of eagle-feathers. Before going into battle it was required to hold this shield four times over the smoke of burning sweet grass, and then to put it on the arm. The wearer must then turn once around till he faced as he had stood before. Before and after turning, he faced the enemy.

Somewhere near the Black Hills, east and north, is a butte or mountain—believed to be Bear Butte[10]—which is called Medicine Lodge. Some people say that the first shields came from there. It was long ago that a man went up on this butte to remain there for four days without food or drink. After he had been there two days a person came to him and said, "Come down and go into this hill with me." The young man arose and

[10] *Năvĭ vō ŏs*, Teaching Hill, *i.e.*, hill where people are taught.

followed the person, who went part way down the butte and then went into it. The man found himself in a lodge, and about it he saw hanging many different shields. An old man—the chief man of the lodge—gave the young man seven differently painted shields.

When the young man returned to his home, he brought with him these shields, and soon afterward he began to make other shields like those he had seen in the lodge, as the old man had directed and taught him. Shields, therefore, would seem to be closely related to the medicine lodge.

The man who brought these shields told his people that they must make their shields like them; so thenceforth all the tribal groups had shields which were always the same. Other shields were dreamed of by people who suffered on the hills.

At a time when Young Woman was grown, after she had married, they moved close to the hill called the Medicine Lodge, and camped there for five days. Her husband, whose name was Itching, went over the hill and dreamed that he went into the lodge in the hill and saw these shields, and noticed particularly two shields of the kind which he afterward used to make. These had painted deerskin covers.

Group shields were not many in number. At one time the Issiometaniu group had only three—owned by Black Moon, Lump Foot, and Touching Cloud (Alights On The Cloud).

MUSICAL INSTRUMENTS

The drum was an important musical instrument, and was used in doctoring, dancing, gambling, and in religious ceremonies. Its chief function was to mark time. Drums were of varying sizes, running from those so small as to be held in the hand, to large ones which rested on the ground and about which five or six drummers might sit.

Hand drums were made of a green willow stick, three or four inches in diameter, shaved thin with a knife, then heated over the fire, greased, and worked until it was gradually bent into a circle whose ends overlapped. Notches were cut in the margins of the stick over the lapped ends, which were then bound together with strong sinew. The hair was scraped from an old horse-hide (which was thought to make the best drums), and this, after having been thoroughly wetted, was bound tightly over the wooden ring, covering the upper side. From the lower edge of the ring, four or five rawhide strings crossed it, knotted together where they intersected, and serving as a handhold.

The drum was beaten with a short stick, which might be bare, or might have a little deerskin or buffalo-hide wrapped about the beating end.

The rattle, commonly used in the dance and in doctoring, was formed, in the usual way, of two hemispheres of rawhide sewed together with sinew, in the hollow of which a number of small stones were placed. The two pieces of which such rattles were made were almost circular, but running from one side of each of these discs was a strip of hide, perhaps an inch wide, and when the wet rawhide was sewed together, these pieces, from three to five inches long, were joined by two seams on either side of a straight stick which formed a handle. After the sewing was finished and the rawhide had dried, the rattle was often painted red, and perhaps, at a point of the rough sphere opposite the handle, and in the seam, were attached a few crow or magpie feathers, or sometimes the down-feathers of an eagle. Rattles were of different sizes, the sphere sometimes being from two and a half to three inches in diameter, and sometimes much smaller. Rattles were sometimes made from the scrotum of a buffalo-bull.

A rattle carried by the Crazy Dog Soldiers, and used in their dances in comparatively modern times, was formed of long strips of bull's hide, so put together that the rattle was a rough cylinder, bent around from both sides of the handle, so that it enclosed an empty space.

The handles of rattles were sometimes wrapped with red cloth, or perhaps with finely tanned antelope-skin. Rattles used by the doctors to drive away evil spirits which were afflicting people with disease were usually small. Some of these are very old, and legends or myths of various sorts are told of them.

War whistles were made from the wing-bone—humerus, or ulna—of the eagle or of the sandhill crane. Both these birds were esteemed as powerful war helpers—the eagle from the fact that he captures his prey and lives on flesh, and the whooping crane because of his resonant voice, which was felt to be alarming. Moreover, the crane is a bird of great courage, and if wounded and unable to fly away, fights hard, and will even attack a man if he comes near it. It does not seem to fear anything. Courage like this was greatly desired by every warrior.

As stated, the feathers of cranes were used in the ornamentation of shields, not because they were good to look at, but because of the bird's power in war.

These war whistles were made by cutting off both ends of the bone, making a notch in the side near the mouthpiece, and then so stopping the hollow of the bone with pine gum as to deflect the air blown through the bone and cause a shrill whistling sound. Such whistles were usually hung about the neck by a deerskin string, and were blown when men went into battle. Sometimes the down-feather of an eagle was tied to the whistle. As elsewhere shown, they were used by persons who were suffering in the Medicine Lodge.

A flute, or flageolet, much used by young men, was made by whittling out, as perfectly as possible, a cylinder of juniper wood about eighteen inches long, which was then split and each half dug out to make a shell. The two halves were then fitted and glued together, and held in place by a lashing of sinew or deerskin strings. The six fingerholes were made by burning with a hot iron. In recent times the ornamentation was usually beads of various colors, strung on a thread of sinew and wrapped close about the cylinder; but in earlier days dyed porcupine quills were wrapped about the instrument above and below the holes, and near the mouthpiece. A short distance below the mouthpiece was often carved the figure of some animal, very often a horse or a bear, standing out on a block from the surface of the cylinder. Sometimes the flute was carved at one end to imitate the head of a snake or a duck.

Flutes were of two kinds, one simply for making music, and the other—made for the owners by men who were believed to possess peculiar powers—had the property of charming the girl the man loved and making her love him. Both kinds were used in courting. They were played only at night. Not very many years ago it was common, on the Tongue River Indian Reservation, to hear the plaintive but pleasing notes of these flutes sounding from the neighboring hills.

Some men, no doubt, performed chiefly for their own satisfaction, and wandered about playing all night long. Early in the evening the faint notes of the instrument were heard a long distance from the camp, and the music might move along from point to point until the player had gone all about the camp's circle. Later in the night the sounds often drew nearer and were heard immediately outside the camp and moving around it; toward morning they might come from within the circle, and perhaps be in the middle of the camp. By daylight the music ceased.

Heard at night and from a distance, this music, strange and plaintive, was very charming, and had about it not a little romance. Sitting in the lodge at night, the occupants might listen to the distant sounds with very different feelings—the traveler merely with enjoyment of the sweet music; the older people with complete understanding of what it meant and with an amused tolerance; while the notes might quicken the pulse of some young girl busily engaged at her task and seeming to regard nothing else, until, when the sounds had closely approached, she put aside her work and, pushing open the hanging door, walked swiftly off a little way from the lodge to meet him whose playing she had recognized.

HORSE EQUIPAGE

The Cheyennes were excellent horsemen, spending much of the time in the saddle, and during the last years of their wars making their excursions against their enemies chiefly on horseback; consequently the saddle was an important part of each man's equipment.

The Saddle. The saddles of old times were high-peaked as to both pommel and cantle, which consisted of the two prongs of a forked stick, before and behind, which rested on the two flat side-pieces supported by the horse's back, to which side-pieces they were bound with strings of rawhide. Over this frame, wet rawhide was tightly stretched and sewed, making the saddle very firm. The stirrups were short, and the rider, who was obliged to lift his leg high to clear the tall cantle, mounted with some effort. In war or in the buffalo chase the man commonly rode without a saddle, or rode on pads.

Saddles of more modern time were made of two flat side-pieces of wood, lashed to a low-arched pommel and cantle, both formed from the antler of a deer, the natural bend being used. Sometimes a prong was left on the antler forming the pommel, about which the turn of a rope might be taken to render easier the leading of a horse. The whole was covered with wet buffalo rawhide, sewed with sinew. Such low saddles are comparatively modern inventions. The Cheyennes learned to make them from the Kiowas, and also from the Crows; for both these tribes used them. At an earlier date the Kiowas and Crows alike used high-peaked saddles, somewhat similar to those later used by women. But on one occasion, when the Kiowas were off on a very long war trip, their saddles from much use became worn out and broken, and they killed bulls and deer, and made saddles of the low type. In making these saddles, the horn foundation was fashioned by men, but the saddles were usually put together and covered by women.

For the making of saddles the horns of deer in the velvet

were especially desirable. Such horns were easily bent and shaped, and easily cut; yet they dried out hard and, having been wrapped with strands of wet rawhide, were very strong.

Men who had gone on the war-path on foot to take horses often made riding pads which sometimes they carried with them from the camp. These were commonly formed of a long strip of dressed buffalo-hide—a piece of a robe—or even of a strip of blanket. The hide was folded over so as to make a double strip about a foot wide and four or five feet long. The long fold and one end were sewed up with sinew, and in the other end dried grass was stuffed evenly throughout and then also sewed up. Such a pad was girthed about the horse's chest; it was long enough to come down to the rider's knee on either side, and wide enough to give him room to sit comfortably.

After the pad had been in use for a time, the stuffing became packed hard. A slit, large enough to introduce the hand, was then cut lengthwise in the top of the pad, and the stuffing was taken out and replaced with fresh grass or with buffalo-hair. Little strings, fastened to the edges of this hole, were tied together to keep the stuffing from working out. When not in use the stuffing was removed, when the pads were light and took up little room.

Women's saddles up to modern times were of Arab type— very high before and behind, and with pommel curved forward and cantle curved back. Both were usually flattened so as to be from four to six inches wide. Women's saddles were often highly ornamented with brass tacks, leather fringes, and bead- or quillwork, and often had on the front of the pommel an upright projection on which a baby-board might be hung. Highly ornamented, fringed, quilled, and beaded saddle-cloths of tanned hide were used by well-to-do young women.

Stirrups. The old-time stirrups were made by women. They were of a single piece of green wood, about two inches wide, shaved down flat and thin. On either side of the place where the foot was to rest, the wood—a willow which they call big willow—was cut almost through at right angles to the length of the stick; the green wood was then bent up at right angles, and the ends brought together to form the sides and top of the stirrup. The two long ends, which ran up from either side, were made narrow by cutting them away at the sides, and were bent toward and across each other, and on down over the opposite side of the stirrup, almost or quite to the level of the foot-rest. At different points above and on the sides, they were lashed in place with wet sinew. Over this wooden frame, green buffalo-hide was stretched and sewed together round the semicircle above the foot and in the middle beneath the foot-rest. This, when dried, made a firm, strong stirrup.

THE PIPE

The early pipes of the Cheyennes were straight (cigar-shaped), somewhat like the modern automobile pipe. Until quite recently—within my knowledge of the tribe—many men still smoked these straight pipes, made of the shank-bone of a deer or an antelope, cut off at either end, the marrow punched out, and the mouth-end pared down and made smooth. Before being much used, such a pipe was commonly wrapped with the ligament from the back of a buffalo-bull's neck, and this, when dried, made so complete a reinforcement of the bone that the pipe might last a very long time. Pipes of similar form were made of stone, but were not common, and as they grew rarer came to have a sacred character, and were smoked only at particular times. The pipe used at the Medicine Lodge is straight and of stone. The straight bone pipes were easier to carry than the more bulky and elaborate stemmed pipes, and were therefore often taken on war expeditions by preference for ordinary smoking. Such pipes were used by Kiowas and Comanches as well as by Cheyennes. The straight pipe is an old, primitive form. I have unearthed such stone pipes from prehistoric burial places in southern California.

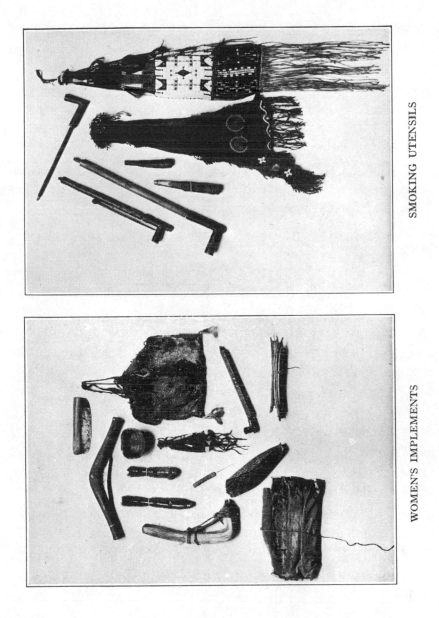

SMOKING UTENSILS

WOMEN'S IMPLEMENTS

The usual modern pipes were fashioned much like those of the Sioux and other prairie tribes, and while often of red catlinite, were sometimes of a soft black slate, which was easily carved. Frequently they were somewhat elaborate in the carving, and some of them were inlaid with lead. Such pipes were whittled with a knife, and there was a great difference in the work performed by different men. Of late years redstone pipes of this character have been turned out in quantities from white men's factories, for the soft catlinite is easily worked on a lathe.

Formerly there were war medicine (sacred) pipes. One of these is described elsewhere.

WOMAN'S WORK

Root-digger. At certain seasons of the year the Cheyenne woman spent much time unearthing from the prairie the wild roots which form a part of the people's food. This work was done with a root-digger (*his'so*), a slender, sharp-pointed implement to be thrust into the ground to pry out the roots. In modern times the root-digger has been of iron—any sort of an iron bar. In earlier days, however, these implements were of wood, usually of ash, the point sharpened and hardened in the fire. One kind of root-digger was two and one-half to three feet long, and had a knob at one end to protect the hand. The point was thrust into the ground, near the root, and as the soil was often hard, considerable force was needed to force the point in. The woman commonly folded her robe, or blanket, and putting it between her body and the blunt end of the root-digger, as she knelt or squatted on the ground, pushed the tool into the soil. A shorter form of root-digger was pressed into the ground by pushing the knee against it. A third form was a long stick, as tall as a man and forked at the upper end, which the woman used somewhat like a crowbar, as she stood erect. These long root-diggers were sometimes painted red over the lower half and black at the handhold. When the points of root-diggers became blunt, they were sharpened with a knife, and rehardened in the fire. Long ago they used prongs of elk-antler as short root-diggers—those pressed against the knee—and sometimes they used tent-pins. It is said also that still farther back the longer root-diggers were pointed with the tips of elk-antlers, lashed to sticks with wet rawhide.

The root-digger was given to them by the Creator, for their support, and it possessed something of a sacred character. The short root-digger was used in the Medicine Lodge for ceremonially digging the holes which were to receive the center pole, and other holes in which were to stand certain branches used in building the altar, and at this ceremony it was put in the Thunder's nest and sacrificed along with an arrow. The two were offered, as I conceive, as a part of the general petition that food—both the flesh of animals and the fruits of the earth—might be abundant. Besides this, the root-digger was used in connection with certain forms of sweat-house, to make, ceremonially, the holes in which the willow branches forming the frame of the sweat-house were set in the ground.

Mauls. Stone hammers were an important part of the women's domestic equipment and varied in size according to their uses. Large stone mauls were employed as axes to break up tree trunks into pieces small enough to be carried on the back for fuel, to drive tent-pins, and to break the large bones of animals. Smaller hammers were employed to break bones into small fragments before they were boiled for the grease, and hammers still smaller were used in pounding choke-cherries for cooking or to be dried for winter use, as well as for pulverizing dried roots and dried meat. These smaller hammers were used on flat, circular stones—anvils—one surface of which was often worn quite flat, or even hollowed out, by continued use. When in use, these stone anvils, which usually show that they have been taken from river beds, but which may be found on the prairie as part of the glacial drift, were often placed on a circular or an oval piece of rawhide in order that fragments of bones, choke-cherries, or dried meat, while being pounded, might not fall on the ground, but might be picked up, and if necessary pounded still further. This hammer and anvil arrangement represents, of course, the mortar and pestle so constantly used for pulverizing food by different tribes the continent over.

The mauls or hammers were formed in the usual way, by pecking out about the short diameter of an oval stone a groove in which, when deep enough, a wythe was laid, running around the stone and then off at right angles to the stone's axis, to form a handle. The wythe was held in place and protected by a covering of buffalo-hide put on wet and sewed with sinew, and this rawhide covered also the long handle. Sometimes berries were pounded with a small hammer-head which had no handle, or, where no particular force was needed, any oval stone not much larger than an egg might be held in the hand to pound berries.

Such small hammers were used for breaking up the flints for making arrowpoints.

Similar hammers, with longer handles and with longer, larger, and sometimes ornamented heads, were carried in war, and formed the weapon commonly called "skull-cracker," or "war-club," sometimes used in battle to strike the enemy.

Combs. A long time ago they used combs made of the rough skin of the end of a buffalo-tongue, scorched, so as to harden it. They still to some extent make and use combs or hair-brushes from the tail of the porcupine. The fresh skin is stretched over a stick, sewed tight, and dried, and the quills trimmed off evenly. The long seam where it is sewed together is often beaded or ornamented with quills.

Receptacles. Spoons and ladles used in cooking, filling water vessels, and in skimming off the grease from boiling bones, were made chiefly of horn of the buffalo or the mountain sheep, but sometimes of wood or of the carapace of a tortoise. What may have been used before the Cheyennes reached the plains, we do not know, but very likely birch-bark. The horn spoon was made by boiling or steaming the horn, and as it became soft, by bending it into the required shape and letting it dry. These objects were made by the women, who took great care to see that they dried slowly and did not lose their shape. Some of the sheep-horn ladles were very large, with long handles. Such spoons and ladles were practically indestructible, and were handed down in families for a long time. I have never seen spoons made from antlers.

Bowls used to hold food or for drinking, or as vessels in which to mix medicine, were made of wood or of the carapace of the turtle. The wooden bowls were carved out indifferently by men or women. Sometimes the large knots on trees were hollowed out by fire and the knife. In Oklahoma flat bowls or dishes were commonly made from the wood of the pecan or the poplar, while deeper similar bowls were carved from oak. Some bowls were flat and others quite deep. They varied much in size, and usually were not ornamented.

Vessels for carrying water were most often made from the paunch of the buffalo. The lining was stripped off smooth, and a little hoop made from a slender stick was tied about the opening of the paunch. A stick was then fastened across the hoop and to this stick a string was tied to carry the vessel. They filled this receptacle with a horn ladle, and sometimes, when it was nearly full, tied a string around it just below the hoop, to keep the water from spilling. Temporary drinking-cups, shaped somewhat like a cup or tumbler, were made from buffalo-paunch lining, with a hoop above and at the bottom, sewed to the membrane. The awl holes were stopped with tallow.

Paunch water receptacles were used as recently as 1860-1870, but without the hoop and stick. They were merely tied about the neck with a string.

Other old-time water-skins were made of buffalo bladder or

of buffalo pericardium, whence the general name for the vessel —*hĭstāĭ' wĭttsts*—literally, "heart covering," *i.e.*, the pericardium. This suggests that the original water-skin was made from the pericardium, and that the other parts of animal used were later adaptations. These membranes, when freshly taken, were blown full of air and allowed to dry. Before they became too dry they were taken down and rubbed between the hands to soften them, and this seemed also to make them thicker. Water-skins for the special use of babies or small children were usually made from the pericardium of the buffalo.

The durability of such skins in summer depended on the care taken of them. In hot weather, if they were not kept filled, they emitted a disagreeable odor after three or four days, and had to be thrown away; but if kept filled, or, when empty, exposed to the sun and dried, they lasted a long time. In the lodge they were tied to the lodge-poles at one side of the door, or they were hung outdoors on a tripod in the shade. On the march they were suspended from the platform of the travois, or, if to be used during the march, from the arched, covered roof of the travois platform.

Tanning. As the skin clothing they wore and the skin lodges they lived in were made by the women, the implements with which she tanned her skins were very important to the Cheyenne woman. These were four in number: (1) The scraper, by which the blood, fat, and flesh were removed from the inner surface of the green hide; (2) the flesher, commonly a piece of elk-horn, bent at a right angle, and armed anciently with a cutting edge of flint and in modern times with a more or less keen steel blade, so that the whole implement formed a little adze for thinning the hide; (3) the proximal end of the humerus of the buffalo, cut off just below the articulation, the rough surface of which rubbed over the smoothed flesh surface of the hide served to abrade it, so that it might readily absorb the tanning mixture; (4) the softening rope, or the shoulder blade of the buffalo, to be described later, either of which was used to break up the fiber of the hide, and to make it soft and pliable after the tanning was completed.

The scraper, in old times, was an oval, flat stone, often a slate or quartzite pebble chipped down so as to have a rather sharp and even edge all around. Sometimes it was large enough to be used in both hands. In modern times crescentic metal scrapers, shaped like an ordinary chopping knife and set in a handhold of wood, were sometimes used.

Another form of scraper was the cannon-bone of a buffalo, cut off diagonally from above downward toward the distal end, and with the sharp edge notched. Through the proximal end of such a scraper a hole was usually drilled for a thong of tanned buffalo-hide, which formed a loop through which the hand was passed.

More recent scrapers were made from a section of the barrel of an old-fashioned, smoothbore gun. A piece of the barrel ten inches long was sawed off and at one side split for two or three inches from one end, the split cylinder opened, pounded out nearly flat, and then notched or toothed. The cylindrical part of the barrel above the opening, to be held in the hand, was usually wound spirally with a thong of tanned buffalo leather.

The obvious use of all these forms of scrapers was to go over the flesh side of a green hide stretched out and pinned down to the ground, or put in a frame, and to scrape from it all blood, fat, and particles of flesh that still clung to it. To get the best results in tanning, it was important that before it dried the hide should be freed from everything that might interfere with its drying evenly.

The adze-like flesher (2) was used to chip off thin flakes from the flesh side of the hide, so as to reduce it to the proper thickness for tanning, or to remove the hair from the other side. In ancient times the cutting edge of this implement was of flint, bound to the horn with strings of rawhide, or sometimes of sinew. These elk-horn fleshers did not wear out, and were handed down from mother to daughter or niece, perhaps for several generations. It was a matter of pride for a woman to possess a flesher made by her grandmother or her grandmother's mother. I have seen many that have been so long in use that deep, smooth cavities have been worn in the hard elkhorn, where the thumbs of successive generations of women have held it while working. Women kept the metal blades of their fleshers sharp by whetting them, usually with a smooth quartzite pebble from the river gravel.

One of these fleshers was given me by the wife of White Bull, when she was sixty-five or seventy years of age. Its first known owner was Magpie Woman; when she grew old she gave it to her daughter, Sun Woman; when Sun Woman grew old she gave it to her daughter, Hole In The Nose, but Hole In The Nose fell sick and died, and Sun Woman kept it, and when she died it came to Bull Wool Woman, the wife of Frog, who was a distant relation of Spotted Wolf. From her it passed to her daughter, White Bull's wife. Bull Wool Woman had been dead nearly fifty years when the implement came into my hands, when it was perhaps 140 to 150 years old. In old times they often made a flesher for a little girl, which at first she played with and later learned to use. The girl might keep count of her age on the flesher, scratching a line across it each year until she married. After this, she recorded the years of her children on it in the same way.

An implement for removing the hair from a hide was shaped somewhat like a carpenter's spoke-shave, and might be formed of a somewhat bent willow stick an inch in diameter. In the concave part of the bend a lengthwise groove was dug out, into which was set a sharpened scale of bone, six or eight inches long and one inch wide. One edge of this blade was fitted and glued into the groove. In practical use the other sharp edge was drawn down over a hide supported on an inclined pole, to take the hair from the skin. In later times this tool was made with a blade of metal. I am not wholly clear that this is a primitive implement, though I believe it to be so.

The operation of tanning skins was similar among various Indian tribes, yet not always the same. The essential operations were the preparation of the hide, the application of the tanning mixture, and the subsequent working of the skin.

Brains, liver, soapweed, and grease were used for tanning. The root of the soapweed was gathered, peeled, and pounded up fine, and the pulverized brains, liver, and soaproot were thoroughly mixed together. Grease of any kind was then added to the compound, but when especially nice white tanning was desired, bones were pounded up and boiled, and the grease or oil extracted from them was used. This tanning material was applied to both sides of the hide, and was thoroughly rubbed in. The hide was then folded up and put aside overnight, so that the mixture should soak all through the skin. The next day it was unfolded and laid out in the sun to dry. After it was dry, the tanned skin was softened as a robe is softened, by pulling to and fro through the hole in a shoulder blade, or against a rope of buffalo sinew. The rope was tied above to a tree or a post and ran diagonally down to a peg fastened in the ground. The rope was stretched tight. The woman knelt on the ground and pulled the hide back and forth, flesh side against the rope, until it was softened. Some women preferred to use a buffalo shoulder blade in softening a robe. The inner part of the bone was cut away, leaving, however, a strong border. Then, by its joint, the shoulder blade was securely tied to a tree or to some immovable object, and the robe was passed through the hole in the bone and pulled backward and forward against the bone. Sometimes a stick, smoothed down on two sides to a blunt edge, was fastened to a tree above and to the ground below, and the robe was pulled backward and forward against the edge of the stick. I have never witnessed this process, but I have seen a woman softening a skin by pulling it backward and forward in this way against the blunt edge of an old scythe fastened as described.

The work of softening a robe was long and laborious, but the women were industrious, and, moreover, time was not important to them. A woman worked until she was tired, and then put her task aside, to be resumed at her convenience.

Dress. The early clothing of the Cheyennes was made from the dressed skins of animals. For women's dresses, and for leggings and the upper part of the moccasins, the skins of the deer, antelope, or mountain sheep were used. Such skins were smoked before being made into clothing, so that the garment might be easily softened after being wet. The leggings of old men, and the dresses of older women, were usually made from buffalo cow skin, and for this purpose old skins that had served as the upper part of lodge coverings were often employed. Such skins had been thoroughly smoked, and were always very soft and durable.

The Cheyenne women were good tanners of buffalo skins, and many of them tanned deerskin well. When tanning the skins of deer or antelope, or of mountain sheep, the most skillful were careful not to break into the epidermis when they removed the hair. In this way their deerskins had a smooth, even surface. A deerskin that was very thick might be thinned down, and so made rough, on both sides. Such a skin would be used for the uppers of a moccasin, but not for leggings, shirts, or tobacco pouches.

Sewing. There was a time when the art of sewing was not known, and when the dresses of women, like the leggings of men, were tied together at the seams with leather strings, passed through holes in the edges of the front and back pieces of the dress. The dresses of old Suhtai are said to have been so made as late as 1850-1860. In modern times all clothing was neatly sewed at the seams with sinew thread, which was very durable. Such thread was made from the sinew lying either side of the dorsal spines of the buffalo. It was taken off in long pieces, or straps, and dried, and strands of it were split off with the finger nails as needed by the women, then moistened in the mouth, rolled on the knee with the palm of the hand, and pointed for an inch or two from the end. With an awl a hole was made in the leather, the fine point of the thread was passed through the hole, and pulled tight with the fingers.

The awls used in early times were the spines taken from the side of the head of large catfish, which were strong and very sharp-pointed; or were tough thorns; or were pieces of bone, sharpened to a fine point. When metal came into use, awls and needles were among the earliest implements traded to the Indians; but we may imagine that so long as they used leather for clothing, the use of the needle as such never made any great progress among them, but that it was employed as an awl to make the hole, and that the sewing was done in the old-fashioned way. In later times, the slender piece of sharp-pointed metal used as an awl was commonly set in a wooden handle, four or five inches long, or in a handle made of the ligament from the back of the neck of some large animal, dried to the hardness of horn or bone. A worn-out knife-blade was often ground down to form an awl.

A thread used in the old days, before they discovered the possibilities of sinew for sewing, was the twisted bark of a certain plant, possibly a milkweed. This weed grows from four to six feet tall and has a stem about as thick as a man's finger. When ripe, it bears on the top two nearly spherical pods which contain something like cotton. Thread made of this bark was tough and useful.

As the women were the manufacturers of the clothing, they carried the articles for sewing. These were the awl and sinew, together with porcupine quills, dried black grass, and fine roots, which they often used in decorating the tanned skins. All were carried together in a little sack or case, usually made of dressed buffalo cow or calfskin, with the hair left on, which was tied to the belt. Such sewing cases opened at the top with a covering flap, and were often ornamented about the edges with a sort of binding of porcupine quills. The flap was tied down by a deerskin string, which met another string from the side of the case.

The porcupine quills, which (because of their extreme sharpness and their way of working through or into almost anything with which they came in contact) could not be carried loose, were always wrapped up in a little case made of the pericardium of the buffalo. Sometimes also the awl, if small enough, was put in this case, to render its point harmless.

Moccasins. The moccasins of modern times were of deerskin, the upper commonly cut in one piece, with a single seam at the back, and to the lower border of this upper was sewed the parfleche sole of buffalo-hide. In making moccasins the sole was sewed to the upper from the inside, so that when the sewing was completed the moccasin was inside out. The seam at the heel, however, was not yet sewed. The moccasin was turned right-side out with a stick, and the heel was then turned down, sewed from the inside, and turned back. The beading, porcupine quillwork, or other ornamentation, was put on the upper before it was sewed to the sole.

In ancient times the moccasin was made differently. There was one large piece, comprising what is now the upper, with a flap which passed across under the whole sole of the foot, and was sewed to the other side of the upper by a single seam. After this was completed, the parfleche sole was sewed on the outside. People now say that these moccasins were more comfortable and much more durable than those more recently in use. Almost always the moccasins of modern times have two little tails of deerskin, an inch or more long and an eighth of an inch wide, which project backward from the heel, at the point where the heel seam joins the sole. In old times it was not uncommon for a woman to sew to the heel of each of her husband's finer moccasins a buffalo-tail, or a strip from the beard of the buffalo, which trailed behind him as he walked.

Summer moccasins are without ankle flap, but those for winter have a loose piece about the foot opening, three or four inches wide, behind and at the sides of the ankle, which is drawn up and around the ankle, and tied, to keep out the snow. For very cold weather the Cheyennes sometimes used hair moccasins; that is to say, soleless moccasins, made from old buffalo-robes, the hair side in. These were a great protection against cold.

Beads, fringes, porcupine quills, and the little conical metal ornaments, so common in the old Indian trade, were used to adorn moccasins. If there was a row of tin tinklers on the moccasins, they were worn on the outside of the middle line of the foot, running from the instep nearly, or quite, to the toe.

The modern moccasin with the parfleche sole is no doubt of recent development among the Cheyennes. In ancient times, when they lived in the humid timbered country of Minnesota, and farther east, their moccasins, as described to me, were like those of the woods Indians of today, made of a single piece of deerskin and without a sole. It was only after they had come out on the high dry plains, where the cactus grows, that the need was felt of a foot-covering that would resist the thorns. The change of footgear may have come about within the last three hundred years. The old Suhtai moccasins, as described, were seemingly of a style midway between the earliest moccasins and those of modern times.

Leggings. Men's leggings were of the usual plains type; that is to say, they reached from the ankle nearly to the crotch on the inside of the leg, came up somewhat higher on the outside, and were tied to the belt, over the hip, by a long strip of deerskin. Usually they were fringed, and often were cut in what is called a "fork"; that is, there was a long, loose, triangular piece of deerskin on the outer side of the leg, running from the calf to the ground. As a man walked, this piece flapped forward and backward. Leggings were sometimes beaded, but usually the ornamentation was attached to the fringe, and might consist of shells, elk-teeth, the spurious hoofs of the buffalo, buttons, bits of chain, large beads, or anything that took the wearer's fancy. I know of no special significance to the "fork" in which the leggings were cut, and believe that it was merely for ornament. I have occasionally seen tobacco sacks made of leather in the same shape; that is to say, with a wide fringed flap toward the lower end.

Breechclout. Until recently all the older Cheyenne men wore the breechclout, which they still appear to regard as a sign of sex. Among the Northern Cheyennes, until about 1900, all still wore the breechclout under the trousers, and the string about the waist, next to the skin. They said that if they took that off they would lose their manhood. Apparently the string about the waist, on which the breechclout hangs, is as important as the breechclout itself, or perhaps the string may represent the whole article. Little boys, as soon as they can walk, have the string put upon them, and wear it constantly but wear no breechclout. Among the Southern Cheyennes I believe that this practice has passed out of use to some extent, but it prevailed much longer among the Northern people. Just before his death in 1904, it was said of Old Little Wolf that he was the only one in the camp who commonly left off the breechclout when assuming trousers.

Shirts. Deerskin shirts were a part of the ceremonial war clothing of the men. These had sleeves, were commonly fringed, and reached halfway to the knees, thus passing over the tops of the leggings. They were made of the skins of deer and also of antelope or mountain sheep. Such war shirts were trimmed along the seams with the scalps or hair of enemies, and elaborately ornamented with beads; or, in earlier times, with porcupine quills.

The buffalo robe was worn by both sexes. The head was on the left side of the body, the tail on the right side.

Ornaments. In the first half of the last century, silver plates were used as hair ornaments. Silver coins, ranging in size from a dollar to a dime, were hammered out thin, and a number of these, of varying sizes, were attached to the scalp-lock with deerskin strings, passing through holes in the center of each silver disc. The largest coin was above and the smallest below. At a later time, similar ornaments of German silver for this use were imported by traders. Men's side-braids were commonly wrapped with bands of otter-fur, and sometimes with brass wire. The braid was tied at the end with a little deerskin string. Frequently a small strand of the forehead hair, on the left side, was drawn down over the left eye, and wound with brass wire to which a few large beads were sometimes attached. Often a stone arrowpoint with a little deerskin bundle of medicine was tied to a man's scalp-lock. After the introduction of domestic cattle, some men wore cow-tails tied to the scalp-lock, and later still to their hats.

Eagle-feathers were commonly worn in the hair by older men, and down feathers of the eagle were often tied to the head at the base of the scalp-lock. There is now said to have been no significance in the use of these soft feathers, but at one time it unquestionably had a meaning. In the ceremony of the Medicine Lodge today these eagle-feathers are constantly used.

Eagles' tail-feathers were prized for making war-bonnets—either a chaplet of feathers, standing upright about the head, or with two long tails, ornamented with feathers, standing at right angles to the rawhide support, hanging down the man's back, and so long that they trailed the ground as he walked. These feathers were set in a strip of stiff parfleche, and tied so that they stood erect. In modern times these eagle-feathers often bore tips of tiny red feathers or of dyed horse-hair attached to the ends of the eagle-feathers with plaster of 'Paris (burned gypsum).

Long, long ago, we are told, the Cheyennes manufactured for themselves what might be called beads, but perhaps were small charms made of some vitrified substance—perhaps of pulverized glass—after the white people were met. Such beads are said to have been made within two or three generations. Many of them were fashioned in the shape of a lizard; that is, a four-legged object with a long tail and a small head. The ceremony connected with making such objects was secret, and he who wished to possess one was obliged to go to some person who himself had been taught the ceremony, and to ask that person to teach him how to make one. A payment was made for the service. The two went away together to conduct the ceremony in private. It is believed that in old times, long before the whites came, these beads were made from the quartz sand found on ant-hills, and that this was melted in an earthen pot. The secret of making them now seems to be lost.

In later times they melted the glass, with which to make the beads, in the ladles used in melting lead for their bullets. These ornaments or charms were made in various shapes, often in the form of a lizard, as said, or flat on one side and round on the other. Sometimes they had a perforation through which a string might be passed; at other times merely a constriction between two ends about which a string was tied. The mold was made of clay.

The first European beads possessed by the Cheyennes were white, coarse, and imperfect in finish, but were highly valued. Few of these are now in existence.

Besides the armlets of brass and copper wire, necklaces of elk-teeth, deer-teeth, and fish vertebrae, were worn in old times. The earliest known bracelets are said to have been from lengths of hoop-iron wound about the wrist or arm and kept brightened by rubbing on a stone or with a file. As soon as beads came to be easily obtained, necklaces of fish vertebrae passed out of use. Few are now to be seen.

Women's Dress. The woman's dress consisted of a smock or shirt made of the skins of deer, sheep, antelope, or elk, reaching from the neck halfway from knee to ankle. The sleeves were like a cape, open below, and hung down to the elbows. Often there was a cape from one sleeve across the back to the other sleeve. Women wore moccasins, also leggings pulled on over the moccasins and tied under the sole of the foot, and reaching up to and tied below the knee. Hanging down on the outer side of each leg, and reaching nearly to the ground, was a leather string—nowadays sometimes a narrow strap, which may be ornamented at the ends with brass-headed nails. These were the garters with which the leggings were tied below the knees. Tied about the thighs and waist they wore a sort of clout; and at night the protective string (*nĭhpĭhĭst'*) was used, as elsewhere described.

Women's dresses of the olden time were ornamented with elk-tusks, and the capes with stained porcupine quills. One hundred elk-teeth used to be worth a good horse. A dress thus ornamented would sometimes weigh ten or twelve pounds. I once counted on a single dress between 900 and 1000 elk-teeth.

It has already been intimated that the fashions in dress changed among the Cheyennes, and for the oldest modes of dressing, of which we have any knowledge, reference should be made to an earlier chapter.

THE LODGE

In primitive days, and in fact up to the time of Lewis and Clark, or the beginning of the nineteenth century, the Cheyennes to a considerable extent occupied permanent villages of earth lodges. We may take it for granted that these were not markedly different in construction from those of other earth-lodge tribes in the Plains country. The Pawnees, Mandans, Arikaras, and Hidatsas, all built houses of similar type; yet, so far as I know, no one has ever seen a Cheyenne earth lodge. We

FLESHING A HIDE

may suppose that these dwellings, the sites of some of which are known, consisted of upright posts set in the ground, that the roofs were constructed of poles, grass, and earth, and that the walls were of sod or soil, piled up to a considerable thickness.

In modern times, however, the Cheyenne lodge has been the ordinary buffalo-skin conical movable shelter so well known by its Sioux term, *tipi*.

During much of the summer and autumn little shelter from the weather was actually needed on the high dry plains of the Cheyennes' prairie home, but in winter and spring, when the weather was bitterly cold and snowy, or very rainy, the buffalo-skin lodge furnished a warm and comfortable home. Such lodges were constructed of the hides of a number of buffalo-cows, sewed together, and stretched over a conical framework of poles. The beds were ranged around the walls, and a fire burned in the middle. To the poles—all around the lodge among the well-to-do, but at all events over the bed of the man of the lodge—there was tied within the lodge-poles a buffalo cow skin lining, which reached to a height of five or six feet above the ground, and protected the person lying under it from any water which might leak through the lodge-skins or trickle down the poles, and also from any wind that might blow in under the lodge covering. The lining helped the draft in the lodge, and thus added to its comfort. Oftentimes it was highly ornamented with pictographs drawn on it by the lodge owner, or by his friends, or by some young man who painted on it scenes of battle and other adventures representing the deeds of aged men.

The skin lodge, though apparently conical in shape, is not a true cone; the windward side—that opposite the door—being shorter, that is, nearer the vertical than is the leeward side. In other words, the poles on the leeward side are more inclined, because in case of a heavy westerly wind they must offer greater resistance to its pressure. The space of ground covered by the lodge is thus not a true circle.

The size of the Cheyenne lodge was usually determined by the number of horses possessed by the lodge owner; *i.e.*, by the owner's wealth. If a man had but few horses, his lodge was small; if he had many, it was large. There was a reason for this: Two horses were needed to drag the poles of a big lodge, and one to carry the lodge itself—three horses, therefore, for the transportation of the lodge alone, to say nothing of other property and the members of the family.

For a lodge of eleven skins, eighteen poles, that is to say, sixteen poles within and two for the wings, were needed. A sixteen-skin lodge required twenty-two poles. The larger the lodge, the more poles were needed. From the great number of poles that they used, it resulted that the Cheyennes had well-stretched, nice-looking lodges. The Northern Cheyenne women declare that an odd number of hides should always be used for a lodge, and that if the number was even the lodge never came right. Lodges of different sizes might require eleven, thirteen, fifteen, seventeen, nineteen, or twenty-one skins. For the sewing of these skins much thread was needed. Each strap of buffalo sinew made a bundle of thread, which was tied up together. For a lodge of eleven skins, four sinews were required; for one of fifteen, seven sinews; for one of seventeen skins, eight sinews. These were the more common sizes; the numbers of sinews required for others have been forgotten. The Southern Cheyennes say that an even number of skins might be used for a lodge.

For the purpose of lodge making, the hides of old buffalo-cows, just shedding the winter coat—in April or May—were preferred. These hides were supposed to be the easiest to tan, possibly, they say, because the old cows were then thin in flesh, and their hides thicker, and so more easily worked.

On account of the greater ease with which they were dressed, cow-hides were used for lodge-skins and robes, though a bull-hide, up to a three-year-old, might be used for a robe. For the rest, bull-hides were used for moccasin soles, parfleches, shields, and other thick and heavy articles.

When a hide was to be tanned for a lodge-skin, the hide was made smooth, and all flesh and gristle removed from the flesh side, but on that side it was not much thinned down. The hair was then taken off, and the hide thinned down with a flesher from the hair side, thus reversing the process by which a robe was tanned. The thinning down was continued until the hide was of even thickness throughout. An experienced woman judged of the progress of her work and determined where further thinning was needed by doubling up the hide and feeling it with the fingers.

The hides were fleshed down quite thin, and were then thoroughly rubbed with the rough surface of the proximal articulation of a humerus where it had been cut off from the shaft, as before described. The smooth ball-joint being held in the hand, the flat rough cancelli of the bone roughened the surface of the hide.

When a woman who was preparing to make a new lodge had gone as far as applying the tanning mixture and drying the hides for it, she made a feast and to it invited some of her friends—usually as many as she had skins, or perhaps not quite so many. She already had provided herself with about as many softening ropes as she had hides.

When the friends had come and had eaten, she gave to each one a hide and a rope. The different women took them to their homes, wet the hides again, and on the following day softened them, so that all the hides for the lodge might be finished in one day. This was a friendly service, to be repaid in kind as the occasion arose, and was precisely similar to the old-fashioned community barn-raising, quilting, and corn-husking bees of our ancestors.

When a woman had all her skins tanned, she perhaps also had all her threads made, having been working at them at odd times for some weeks. Sometimes, if behindhand with her thread-making, she might ask one or more of her friends to come to help her. The service was a friendly one, and was not paid for. The woman had long been saving the sinews of the buffalo that the husband had killed, and now with her guest she split these dry strips of sinew, and twisted and pointed the strands. In this way she made many bundles of thread for the sewing of the lodge.

When all the materials had been made ready for the making of the lodge, the woman made preparations for a feast, for she intended to invite a number of women to eat with her, and to help her sew together the skins to make the lodge covering. Among those invited was some woman who was especially skillful as a lodge-maker. This lodge-maker possessed no patterns, but measured and fitted everything by the eye alone.

At dawn of the appointed day, the hostess sent for the lodge-maker, and when she had come, said to her, "I wish you to cut my lodge for me."

"Where are your knife and paint?" replied the lodge-maker. The woman brought out a sharp knife and a whetstone, and some paint mixed with grease, and the lodge-maker painted her own face, hands, and arms, and put on her head, in the parting of the hair, a pile of paint mixed with grease, which she would use for marking the skins.

The two women spread out the skins for the lodge on the ground, as nearly as possible in the shape which they were to assume when sewed together, and the lodge-maker stood over and considered them. Perhaps she shifted the position of several skins, so as to make a better fit and easier work. Where she wished a piece of the hide cut off, she touched her finger to the paint in the parting of her hair, and marked where the knife should go, much as a tailor marks a garment with his chalk. Perhaps she "tacked" the skins together here and there, not cutting off the threads, but leaving them long. After this was done, a messenger was sent to summon the sewers.

When they came, a meal—their breakfast—was served. After

they had eaten, the sewers went to the prepared skins, and sitting down on them, with knives, awls, and thread began to sew with the threads the lodge-maker had left hanging. As the afternoon wore on, the hostess again prepared food, and after a while the women ate. By night the lodge was completed. The last part to be finished appears to have been the bottom, where the most patching had to be done, and where the lodge covering flared out a little to receive the pins that were to hold it to the ground. The hide at the back and top of the lodge just below the wings—the one to which the pole was tied when the lodge was to be raised—was placed neck up, and two strips of hide were left at its upper edge. Not far below these two strips, the strings which tied the lodge covering to the pole were sewed on. When the lodge was to be raised, the two strips of the hide were wrapped about the pole, and the strings were tightly tied over them. The other hides were placed horizontally, neck toward the door.

When the sewing was finished, the lodge-maker went over the lodge with white clay mixed with water, which was rubbed into the covering—all the women working at it. When this was done, all turned to and put up the lodge, stretching it nicely, and pinning it down tight. The dampening which it had just received enabled them to stretch it well. After this was done, all ate again and went home.

The lodge-maker herself, if a good-natured woman, of kindly disposition, sewed on the wings, and made their pockets. If she did not possess the proper temperament, another woman was chosen for this task. If the wings and pockets were sewn by a wrangling, fault-finding woman, the lodge, it was said, would always be smoky. The lodge-maker sewed on the strips at the back of the lodge, where it was to be tied to the pole. She received a present—a pair of moccasins, a robe, a blanket, a wooden bowl, or what not. The sewers received nothing except the feast, but any one of them at any time was likely to call on the hostess for a similar service.

New lodge-poles had perhaps been made for the new lodge, or sometimes old poles were used; a new lodge did not necessarily have new poles. Some women made the lodge covering first, and then got out the new poles for the new lodge; others made the poles first. Lodge-poles were cut at the season when the sap was in the tree, and the poles were easy to peel. When this time came the camp moved up into the hills, and those who needed new lodge-poles secured them. If, by any chance, the lodge, when first put up, did not quite fit, or failed to sit well on the poles, it was altered when next taken down.

The people at large knew that a certain woman's lodge was to be made, but no one of the various lodge-makers knew that she was to be called on this particular occasion, nor did the sewers know that they were to be invited, until the time had come.

Even the largest lodges were approximately circular at the base—though actually they were oval—longer from door to back. A part of the old, worn-out lodge covering was cut up for clothing and other purposes. Sometimes the lower part of an old lodge was used as a lining for a new one. Old men used moksiya for leggings; women made sacks of it for carrying meat.

In olden times, at the making of some specially painted lodges, the lodge covering, after being painted, was spread out where everybody in the camp might walk over it. This was believed to drive sickness away from the camp. On such occasions the women took their little children by the hand and walked over the lodge covering. If the ornamented pieces of hide representing stars were to be sewed on such a lodge, they were put on as soon as the painting was finished, and in some cases, as already said, a man counted a coup as each one was sewed in position. Usually four stars were put on, and four coups counted. The day after this was done—the paint thus being allowed to dry—the lodge was spread out in a narrow place between two sand-hills, where people were likely to pass, and an old man rode about the village and shouted out that it was desired that everyone should walk over that lodge. This was done over the lodge of old Half Bear, who was the keeper of Issiwun and the father of Coal Bear, who died about 1896.

In making the lodges for the hat (Issiwun) and for the arrows (Mahuts), and perhaps the lodges of the Contraries, a special ceremony was performed. After the lodge-skins had been fitted, but before the sewing had begun, a warrior, chosen from among certain invited men who were sitting about the skins spread out upon the ground, rose to his feet, walked over the skins, and as he did so counted a coup. Until this had been done, the women might not walk over the skins and sew them.

Whenever a new lodge was made and set up, and was ready for occupancy, it must be ceremonially treated before it might be entered by persons generally. The women who were erecting it passed in and out, but no one else. The ceremony was performed by some man who had killed an enemy in the enemy's lodge. To this man, and to other brave men, a feast was given by the lodge owner.

On an occasion when I saw this ceremony performed, Little Bear was chosen to count the coup and to dedicate the lodge. After the lodge had been set up and prepared, the women all drew back, and Little Bear, with a number of the old brave men, advanced toward it. Those accompanying him stopped at a little distance from it, and stood or sat in a wide half-circle. Little Bear, holding in his hand a small stick, walked to the door, and struck the lodge on the left-hand (south) side of the door, and about halfway between the ground and the door's apex. Then facing toward the spectators, he said: "We started on the trail after Utes. All were mounted—a large party. Poor Bull and Big Bow [Kiowas] were with us. About the middle of the day in the Raton Mountains [in New Mexico] we overtook the enemy. They were in camp—five lodges of them. We charged upon them, and I rushed to the lodge on the left hand. Just before I reached the door, a Ute put his head out, and I stabbed him with my lance. We scalped him. Besides this, I took some horses." When he had said this, he turned about and entered the new lodge. The other men then rose and followed him in; first the more important ones, Little Chief, Man Above, Long Neck, Man On The Cloud—all the bravest men. The other less important men went in afterward. Man Above was said to have killed sixteen Indians in war, besides some white men.

The Arapahoes had a similar ceremony of dedicating a lodge, but with them the coup was counted by a man who, riding a white horse in battle, had counted coup on an enemy also riding a white horse. If no one could be found who rode a white horse, and counted coup on an enemy riding a white horse, the ceremony might be performed by one who had counted coup on a man riding a dark horse, but wearing a white coat.

A Cheyenne warrior might dedicate an Arapaho lodge after his tribal method. If no Arapaho or Cheyenne could be found to dedicate the lodge in the manner of his own tribe, a Cheyenne who had performed the Arapaho feat might dedicate the lodge, or an Arapaho who had performed the Cheyenne feat might dedicate it. If no one could be found to dedicate a lodge in either of these two ways, a man might do it who had touched an enemy inside of breastworks.

The fireplace in the Cheyenne lodge is usually roughly rectangular—an oblong excavation in the earth, longer from east to west, and six to eight inches deep. Sometimes it is shaped like a half-moon, and sometimes like a heart. In the southern country it is not surrounded by stones—perhaps because there stones are extremely scarce.

A fireplace is sometimes dug somewhat in the form of an equal-armed cross, the arms pointing in the four cardinal directions (nivstanivoo). This term is constantly used for the four directions, and in making a sacrifice with the five pieces of meat, held up to the east, south, west, and north, and to the sky, and then placed on the ground at the edge of the fire.

In offering to the cardinal directions, certain poles of the lodge represented them—the one immediately to the south of the door, the three which were tied together to support the frame of the lodge, and the back pole. The pole at the south of the door represented the east; the first, second, and third tied poles, the south, west, and north, in that order; while the back pole, to which the lodge covering was tied, represented the sky. These different supporting poles stood in the general direction of the cardinal points, while the back pole supported the lodge, which to those within represented for the time the overarching sky. The Cheyennes, like some other tribes, regard the earth's surface as flat, and the sky as a huge arched vault which bends down to meet the earth. It is a covering or shelter, just as the lodge is a covering. The conception is not novel.

In modern times most Cheyenne lodges were not painted. The hat and the arrow lodges were painted black below and red above—whether symbolizing the two colors of the arrow-shafts, or the night and the day, is uncertain. The lodges of the Contraries were painted red. There were some exceptions, as below, but as a rule the lodges were plain.

Old-time Painted Lodges. In old times a few of the Cheyennes had painted lodges, but the custom was abandoned long ago.

The lodge of old Yellow Wolf, killed at Sand Creek in 1864, was painted yellow, I am told. On the lodge covering, to the north and again to the south of the door, were painted two buffalo-bulls, each about two feet high, standing head to the door, and following each bull were several cows. At the back of the lodge, three feet or more from the ground, was a red disc, perhaps two and a half feet in diameter—the sun—and over this, and just below the smoke-hole, was the morning star, a green disc about ten inches in diameter. Above the door was a blue crescent moon. The wings and top of the lodge were painted black, representing the night, with equal-armed crosses, indicating stars, on the wings. Yellow Wolf was the chief of the

Hevataniu. His son was Red Moon—really Red Sun—named for his uncle, Red Sun, a younger brother of Yellow Wolf.

Old Red Sun's lodge was yellow, and above black, like his brother's. The stars on the wings were green. The morning star was green, and about ten inches in diameter. Toward the four directions (nivstanivoo) stood four men. Each had two horns on his head, and instead of hands and feet had wolf-paws, and held in his hands a pipe, bowl up. From the center of the red sun at the back two buffalo-tails hung down. The disc was about three and a half feet in diameter. The crescent moon over the door was green, and very large, perhaps two and a half feet in diameter.

A lodge marked with crosses belonged to a man called Different Tails, who was a leading man of the Himoweyuhkis. The name means a tail having feathers of various colors, from the tail of an eagle killed long ago, which was thus colored. It is an old family name. Different Tails was a cousin of Edmond Guerrier. Old Owl Man painted these lodges as described. After they were painted, four days and four nights were devoted to dancing.

Old Spotted Wolf had a painted lodge, which he was advised to make by the buffalo, in a dream. A great snake-like animal was painted all about the lodge, the head being on the left side of the door, and the tail on the right. Close above the body of the snake, as if looking over it, appeared about forty-five buffalo-cow heads. A night owl was painted on either side of the door, a crescent moon over the door, a sun on the back of the lodge, and a crescent moon also at the back, just below the smoke-hole and over the pole to which the lodge was tied. Below the half-moon at the back of the lodge the constellation "seven stars"—the Pleiades—was painted.

The painting of the lodge scarcely ever went out of the group. A man might present it to his daughter's husband, who because of his marriage had come to live with the group to which she belonged.

To the ends of the wings, and sometimes to the ends of the lodge-poles, were often tied pieces of the skin which carries the long hair from the fore leg of the buffalo. Holes were burned in the ends of the lodge-poles, and the hide attached to the ends with deerskin strings. When, as was sometimes the case, every pole in the lodge was so ornamented, it looked at a little distance as if a crow were perched on each lodge-pole. Such an ornament is called a *nǐm'hōyōh*, meaning "over the smoke" (plural, *nǐm'hōyǔn*).

POTTERY

Although the Cheyennes were without cooking baskets such as more westerly tribes used for boiling food, they cooked—in early and even in later times—in essentially the same way. Their kettle was the hide or the paunch of an animal, which either lined a hole in the ground or was suspended bag-like from sticks set in the ground. Into this tight vessel holding water, red-hot stones were put, until the water boiled. At some time, and in some fashion, they learned to make a serviceable pottery, which began to pass out of use only about 1850, when trade with the whites brought them metal vessels. Much earlier than this they had stone receptacles, similar to those told of by the Blackfeet. These were durable and useful, but were hard to make, and owing to their weight exceedingly difficult to transport.

As the earthenware vessels passed out of use so long ago, we can know little about them and the method of their manufacture, except by the stories told us by the few old people still, or recently, alive, who preserved clear recollections of the ancient art of pot-making. One of the last of these ancient Cheyenne pots was buried about 1896 with the old woman who owned it. The accounts given here come from old women, who received them from their mothers and grandmothers; but it would probably be difficult now to find among either section of the Cheyennes more than two or three old women who know how to make the old-time pottery. The accounts here given are precisely as they were repeated to me, and from them a reasonably clear idea may be had of the ancient industry.

Broken Jawed Woman—daughter of High Backed Wolf (died 1833), painted by Catlin—said to me:

In the days when we lived on the Missouri River, our dishes were made of wood, stone, and earthenware. We used a sort of clay, which was moistened and shaped, to make dishes. Pots were made for cooking, and we boiled meat in them. The small flat dishes were used to eat from, and the deeper ones to cook in.

My mother used to tell me of the time when we made earthen pots. They used a kind of stone, pounding it all up fine, and after mixing this with clay they wet the mixture with water. Taking a lump of the mixture they shaped it with their hands, first making a depression in it, and with a fine smooth stick they patted out the inside of this depression until it was large enough; then with the stick they patted it all over the outside surface, and smoothed it. They fixed pieces on the upper part of the clay for handles, to lift the pot with, and after the vessel was dry they greased it all over, inside and out, with tallow. A place was smoothed off on the ground, and on this they put the pot, and covered it over with bark, gathered from dried trees, which was then set on fire. This bark made a strong heat. They let the pots burn, until they were red-hot, and then took the fire away from them, and left the pots there to cool slowly. Then they took them out, all smooth, hard, and nice. Sometimes they burned only one pot at a time, sometimes two or three, and sometimes a great many.

Some of the earthenware pots used by the Cheyennes were shaped

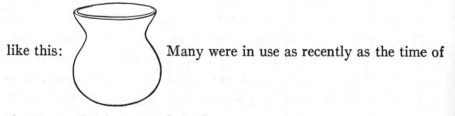

like this: Many were in use as recently as the time of

the Horse Creek treaty [1851].

Little Woman gave the following account of the way in which pots were made in primitive times, received from her mother, whose age in the year 1902 was said to be one hundred and twelve years. She was certainly very old.

When they wished to make pots (*kso ē'?*) or dishes of earthenware, a smooth round hole was dug in the ground, and was lined with a thick layer of wet clay. The clay was put on so thick that it would hold water. After this was done, the hair having been removed from the hide from a buffalo-bull's head, where the skin is thickest, the hide was cut in small pieces, put in the hole, and the hole was then filled with water. In a large fire built near at hand, they now heated stones as hot as they could get them, and with wooden tongs took the red-hot stones, one by one, and put them in the hole with the water and the hide. As the stones became cool, they took them out and put in other hot ones. Soon the water was boiling, and they kept it boiling constantly. As the scum rose to the top, it was skimmed off and put in a dish. After the hide had been boiled to rags, and all the glue got from it, they took clay—of different colors—and mixed the clay with the gluey water and the scum which had been skimmed off. This was the material for their pots.

Some pots were made of clay of only one color, and some of clays of different colors, so that some dishes were white, some red, some blue, and others of several colors, depending on the clay that had been used. The glue with which the clay was mixed made it stiff and tough. Some people shaped their pots with the hands, smoothing them with the moistened palm, while others used a flattened stick for this purpose. When the pots were properly shaped, they were put out to dry, the glue keeping them from cracking. While they were drying, a hole was dug in the side of a hill, making a kind of oven, which was filled with wood and fired. After the wood had burned to coals, these and the ashes were raked out, and the dishes were put in and left there, the hole being tightly closed with a large stone, so that all the heat was kept in.[11]

For the bails on the kettles, a strip of green rawhide was put across

[11] In such a case it would seem that the vessels were not actually fired, but were merely kiln-dried, the glue holding them together. That no great heat could have been applied is shown by the way in which the bails were put on.

the top, running from one side of the mouth to the other close to the top, and knotted there. This green hide was covered everywhere with a thick coating of clay, which kept it from cooking. Some pots, moreover, were strengthened with a strip of green hide running around the mouth, and thickly covered with clay.

Various shapes of pots and dishes are shown by the following figures, drawn by the Indian woman:

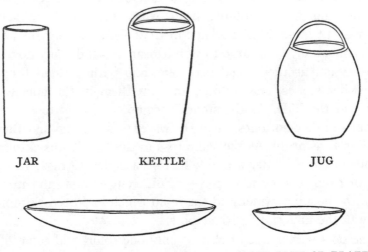

JAR   KETTLE   JUG

PLATTER OR LONG DISH   SHORT DISH OR PLATE

Another ancient woman said:

The old women used to take clay and wet it; it would then stick to their hands, and they kneaded it as bread is kneaded. Having mixed a little sand with the clay, they shaped the pots, using chiefly their hands and water, but also using a flattened stick in shaping and working the clay. While these pots were wet they were very fragile, and had to be handled carefully. They were put in the sun to dry, and after they had dried, were greased all over, inside and out. A deep hole was dug in the ground, and a fire built in it, so as to heat it thoroughly. Then the pots were put in the hole, and a fire made over them—a very hot one—so that the pots became red-hot. The purpose of greasing the pots was to make them fire properly; if they were not greased, they would not fire at all.

Of this clay they made pots, cups, platters, and dishes. The pots were not ornamented.

From all this it would seem that some of the pottery—that mixed with glue—was merely kiln-dried, but the pots for cooking were fired, as Broken Jawed Woman says. Mixed with the clay was a tempering of sand, and great heat would be required to cause this material to burn very hard. Bear Black says the pots were quite durable, and did not break easily.

Mrs. Red War-bonnet, mother of Kingfisher, a woman of sixty-five or seventy years, who has married grandchildren, gave me a small earthenware cooking-pot that had been used for mixing medicine. It is thick and heavy. Mrs. Red War-bonnet was a sister of Mrs. White Bull, Wool Woman, and Mrs. Rowland. Her mother, a noted potter, made this pot. She said that as such vessels were shaped wholly by hand, the work of making them was slow; it took from two to four days to make one, depending upon its size.

I once showed fragments of pottery, picked up on the site of a forgotten Cheyenne village on the Missouri River, to a Northern Cheyenne woman, about fifty years of age, who at once said, "My grandmother used to make dishes like that," and then described the method of making them. This woman's grandmother was born on the Missouri River and lived there till grown.

From the information obtained, it seems that the pots, made from a mixture of pounded stone and clay, were worked out of a single lump of clay, and not coiled. A flattened, bent stick was used to hollow out and shape the mass, and what was taken from the inside was added to the top, thus increasing its size. The ornamentation was once made with a string of twisted grass pressed into the surface of the plastic clay. In later times a string of twisted sinew was used for the purpose. The grass string seems to have been sometimes left on the pot, to be burned away in the firing. Previous to the firing the pot was greased. These pots were burned on the ground by piling about and over them dried bark, or dried willow wood, which by some women was thought to produce greater heat than any other wood. Half a dozen women might be making pottery at one time, and in such a case all of them would fire their pots at the same time. Such a combination saved time and trouble.

Not all the pots were fired. Some were only greased, the grease being frequently applied until the clay was permeated. The grease prevented the clay from drying and cracking. Such unfired pieces were used for platters and dishes, but not for cooking. Clay pots for carrying water, and often for cooking, had perforated ears, or lugs, on opposite sides of the rim, through which a rawhide string was passed for use as a bail in carrying.

Some years ago, the late Col. W. H. Robinson presented to the American Museum of Natural History a perfect pot found near Fort Yates, North Dakota. This was locally called a Ree pot, perhaps because the Arikaras were the people then best known as makers of pottery. It was found partially covered by soil within a few miles of the old Cheyenne village on the Porcupine, and I suspect is of Cheyenne manufacture. It is without ornamentation, has two handles, and has evidently been used for cooking.

I had thought it possible that the Cheyennes learned the art of pottery-making from the Arikaras and Mandans on the Missouri River, but the late Dr. William Jones, who made inquiry for me among the Ojibwas, told me that two or three generations ago those people made pottery of a mixture of clay and pulverized mussel-shells. This information came from Madcigado, already mentioned, who, in 1905, declared that he was seventy-five years of age and said that during his father's time pottery was made by the Ojibwas. His father died twenty-seven years before, aged ninety years.

The Ojibwas cooked by means of heated stones put into bark vessels holding water, and also cooked in birch-bark vessels

MODEL OF ORNAMENTED LODGE

filled with water and set on the fire. The bark would not burn, they say, because of the water in the vessel.

HOUSEHOLD FURNITURE

Important among the furniture of the Cheyenne lodge were the back-rests and the mattress, which together made up the formal lodge bed. Both these were made soft and comfortable by coverings of well-tanned buffalo-robes and other skins, and formed easy lounging and sleeping places.

The mattress—if it may be so called—seven or eight feet long and four feet wide, was formed of willow rods almost as thick as a man's forefinger, strung on long lines of sinew, and was thus flexible and could readily be rolled up. Its use was to keep the bed raised above the soil or to smooth out the inequalities of rough ground.

On the mattress were often spread mats woven of a certain bulrush or tule known as *mō ŭm' stăt* (?) (*Scirpus nevadensis,* S. Wats.). These mats were loosely woven and were in general use, for the plant grows abundantly in wet places. In modern times, since the introduction of the gunny-sack, which also is constantly used as a foundation for the bed, the gunny-sack is called by the name applied to this rush. The name "pretty plant" refers to its smooth and graceful shape.

The mattress and back-rests were not commonly used during the march, but when a permanent camp was made, the domicile was arranged as neatly and comfortably as might be.

At such a permanent camp, after the lodge had been pitched, the women usually cleared away all the grass, sagebrush, or roots, on the ground it covered, lowering the surface of the soil two or three inches, except for a border four or four and a half feet wide, all about the walls of the lodge, slightly higher than the general surface of the lodge floor. On this little bench the beds were spread. The earth removed by the women with knives, hands, and spoons, was piled on a blanket or a parfleche, dragged outside, and emptied on the prairie. After this soil had been removed, a slightly deeper excavation was made in the very middle of the lodge, to form the fireplace.

This left the lodge floor—in dry weather, and in certain soils—very dusty, and the dust was laid with water freely sprinkled about, either from spoons or from the mouth. This wet soil was then walked over and patted down, and when partially dried was swept and the dust thrown into the fireplace. The women and children then went off up and down the creek, and returned with great bundles of rye grass, which they spread on the little bench that was to hold the beds. On the rye grass the mattresses were unrolled and spread. Before this, however, the lodge lining had been tied to the lodge-poles and extended as far as it would go around the lodge. It covered the bed of the lodge owner at least, and very likely the couches of the women and children as well. Tied to the poles at a height of from four to five feet, the lining was brought down inside the poles and parallel to the lodge covering, and then turned in toward the fireplace, so that when the beds were put down they rested on its turned-in border. In this way, any wind which blew under the lodge covering and into the lodge never directly reached the persons sitting on the beds, but was deflected upward by the lining, passed over the heads of the occupants, and then descending, furnished draft for the fire.

If several mattresses were put down in the lodge, they were spread in their proper places, perhaps four feet distant from each other, and between the head and foot of the two mattresses was set up a tripod of slender, usually painted, poles tied together near their tops with strings passing through holes burned through the ends. Sometimes these supports of the back-rest had four legs instead of three. These were spread, and from two of the three poles, above where they were tied together, were hung two back-rests, one for each bed. These were supported by the tripods, and the vacant spaces between back-rests formed convenient cupboards for storing household articles. This was repeated between each two of the mattresses, so that each mattress had a back-rest at its head and one at its foot. In the lodge of a well-to-do person, there were likely to be not fewer than six such back-rests. From the tripods which supported each pair was usually hung by the head—either by a slit cut in the robe or by a loop sewed to it—a buffalo-robe which reached down over the whole back-rest and onto the bed, forming a comfortable seat. On the mattress were spread two or three robes.

The back-rests were formed of slender willow shoots strung on sinew. The shoots were much smaller than the rods used in the mattress, and the back-rest was usually not less than eight feet in length. At the top, where it hung from the tripod, it was often not more than eleven inches wide, but below this, toward the bed, the willow shoots became constantly longer, until finally, five or six feet from the top, they were perhaps three feet two inches in length. From this point on, the width increased very slightly. The leather loop for hanging the back-rest over the tripod was often one and a half or two inches wide, and was strongly fastened to the upper part of the back-rest. Sometimes this loop was nicely beaded or ornamented with quills. Back-rests were often painted; there might be a dozen shoots without painting, then a dozen painted red, and so on alternately. In later days the ends of the twigs on both sides were sometimes bound with red or blue cloth, with a beadwork edging, and no doubt in earlier times deerskin bearing quill-work may have been used in the same way.

When prepared for transportation, mattresses and back-rests alike were rolled up into compact bundles and lashed with strings, so that they would carry well on a horse. We may imagine that these devices for comfort are of comparatively modern invention, since it is inconceivable that in the days when the Indians were foot travelers and carried most of their possessions on their backs, they would load themselves down with luxuries such as these. The acquirement of the horse by the Indians of the plains meant a literal lightening of their burdens.

In the vacant spaces between the back-rests, and in the narrow intervals between the edges of beds and the lodge lining, were stored practically all the lodge furniture and the extra food that had been laid up against a possible season of scarcity. This food for the greater part was in the form of dried meat, though there might be sacks of pounded meat, of dried corn, dried roots, and fruit. In times of plenty, when buffalo were abundant and many were killed, the women dried great quantities of meat, and on the day following a successful hunt the camp was red with meat and white with sheets of backfat, hanging on the drying scaffolds. When the meat exposed to sun and wind had become hard and black, it was taken down and crushed flat, and put away in parfleches, in which it was carried about from place to place.

In parfleches also the women carried sacks of dried berries and dried roots, gathered during the proper seasons and kept for use during the winter and spring; and in others were ornaments, wooden bowls and dishes, small horn spoons, and any odds-and-ends. In fact, the contents of a parfleche were a perpetual surprise, for it might contain anything from an elk's tooth to a twenty-dollar gold piece.

Parflêche is a trapper French term of the Old West to denote several different things. Originally it meant a shield—Fr., *parer* and *flêche,* to ward off, or parry, an arrow. The shield being made of rawhide, the term grew broader in its significance, so that a parfleche might be any rawhide, and finally any article made of rawhide. The so-called parfleche in which the women carried their articles was, in fact, the Cheyenne trunk. Made from heavy buffalo rawhide from which the hair had been removed, it was so cut as to be from two to three and a half feet long and from a foot to eighteen inches wide, when folded. The oblong piece of rawhide was folded over for from nine inches to a foot on each side, the long way of the piece of hide, and then at both ends, at right angles to the first fold, for a foot or fifteen inches, so that these ends almost met. Leather strings laced together the two ends, and the shape of the case was convenient for packing on a horse's back. It suggested in its shape and appearance a letter envelope and was somewhat distensible, so that many things might be put in it. Originally made from the untanned hide of the buffalo, these parfleches were in later days made of the hides of domestic cattle. Often they were more or less elaborately ornamented by painting in straight lines and triangles. Women expended much effort in making and in keeping them clean and freshly painted. When a woman was looking for something that was not easy to find, she might drag out from between or under the beds half a dozen parfleches, one after another, to be unlaced and its contents picked over in the search for the missing article. A more or less cubical parfleche, shaped like a trunk, was sometimes seen. This is perhaps a survival from their earlier eastern range near the Ojibwas, who used birch-bark containers of the same form.

Other receptacles used for holding women's things were what trappers used to call "possible sacks"; that is to say, sacks which might hold almost anything—one's "possibles," or small articles. These were commonly made of tanned deerskin, eighteen inches long by fifteen inches deep, often rounded, though sometimes square at the corners below, the opening above being covered by a long flap which tied down with leather strings. Such possible sacks were often elaborately adorned with porcupine quills, dyed horse-hair, conical tin ornaments purchased from traders, and various other articles. In them were carried small ornaments; a multitude of little sacks, as those containing medicine, or sewing articles, or counters in some game of skill or chance, baskets and ornamented plum-stones used in the seed game, and many other things. Clothing for small children was packed in such sacks, and generally they were used to keep together in one package small articles that would be difficult to find if put loose in a parfleche.

At present the only basket used is the one for playing the seed game. This was made sometimes of grass, or of split willow twigs, or of split strands of yucca. Often it was made of the roots of the young red-willow (cornel), which were dug up and soaked in water for a long time. The root stems were scraped down till all were of the same size. A single slender shoot of red-willow runs up spirally around the basket, and the roots were woven over this back and forth, covering the shoot. If a single shoot was not long enough, another was added.

Although at present they manufacture only these baskets, the women were formerly expert basket weavers. As recently as the middle of the nineteenth century all women wove baskets from a certain grass (*Eleocharis*, sp.). These were of varying sizes and were used for different purposes. A very small basket was often fastened at the head of the baby-board as a shade for the baby's face. Small baskets were used for dishes, and large ones as burden baskets, to carry on the back. Mothers made tiny baskets as playthings for their children.

Only a general description can be given of the implements used by the people. Further accounts of their life will suggest other aspects of their industries.

SUBSISTENCE AND HUNTING

VARIOUS EARLY FOODS

THE most important task before the Cheyenne man was to provide food for his family—his first thought was to support life. It is commonly assumed that the Indian lived solely by hunting and fishing, and subsisted altogether on flesh, but this is not true. A considerable portion of his sustenance was derived from the soil. Like most tribes, the Cheyennes cultivated the ground, and raised corn, squashes, beans, and tobacco. At their proper season, wild fruits and roots were gathered, and these furnished an important part of their living.

We learn only by tradition about the subsistence of the Cheyennes before they reached the buffalo plains. They know nothing about when or where they first obtained the corn, but their old stories point to a long residence in a country where the sugar-maple grows, and they say that sugar formed a part of their food. They had always been hunters, and their code permitted them to eat all flesh—most birds and mammals, as well as fish and some reptiles, creatures which are an abomination to certain Plains tribes.

In that early period of their wanderings spoken of by the Cheyennes as "long, long ago, when they were in the North," they say that they had little knowledge of large food animals. There was a time when they subsisted almost wholly on small animals with long ears—rabbits—and at another period they lived chiefly on fish. At a later day, they visited in summer lakes and streams, and gathered the eggs of wild fowl and killed the young, not yet able to fly, as well as the adults when they were molting and had lost their flight feathers. In autumn, when the skunks were fat, it was their custom to move to certain hills where these animals abounded, and they secured great numbers of them. Such places were visited time after time, and much food secured. These hunts were systematized and well managed. All those in the camp were expected to take part in them and to act under the orders of designated leaders. The food secured was common property, and its legitimate share was assigned to each family.

After the Cheyennes reached the region of the Great Lakes and the country where the wild rice grows, they no doubt harvested this crop, which furnished them a winter food, as at the present day it gives partial subsistence to their relatives, the Ojibwas and the Menomini.

After they had left the Missouri River and come out on the plains, their food was essentially that of the other Plains Indians of that region, and since they ranged north and south for a great distance along the eastern flanks of the Rocky Mountains, they had a considerable variety in wild food plants, birds, and mammals.

A tea was made from the leaves of the "red leaf wood." This is a small shaggy bush, with very hard wood, very narrow leaves, and a yellow flower, growing not more than three or four feet high. The tea made from these leaves, or from the root, is red, like sassafras tea, and tastes somewhat like green tea. It does not grow in the North, but is found in South Dakota and Oklahoma. It is called "red medicine" and is used in doctoring. A tea was made also from the leaves of a certain mint.

Up to the middle of the last century the Cheyennes pounded up and boiled as a mush, with a little buffalo fat, the large acorns of one of the southern oaks. These were best prepared by roasting or parching the acorns in the shell; then, after removing the shells, the kernels were pounded fine and the meal was spread in the sun to dry. This meal furnished a fairly palatable food.

In the southern portion of their modern range they had other nuts, and gathered the pods of the knife-scabbard tree, *mŭt-ko a min' o* (*Gymnocladus*), and parched them, when they broke open, freeing the kernels, which were soft, almost like a cooked bean.

They had a sweetening after they came out on the buffalo plains, and before they received sugar from the whites. In early spring, as soon as the weather began to grow warm, they tapped the box-elder tree and used the boiled sap as sweetening. Often the sap was boiled in a kettle with the shavings from the inner side of the hides of animals, and this made a kind of sap candy, which was greatly relished. In modern days, when they had coffee, but no sugar with which to sweeten it, they sometimes used box-elder sap instead of water to boil their coffee.

They now call sugar sweet water—*vĭk' a mă' pi*, sometimes pronounced *ve' a mă' pi*. They used to call it *mĭsh kē maĭ'-măpĭ*, box-elder water; from *mĭsh kĕ maĭ'*, box-elder tree + *măpĭ*, water. They have the same name, mishkemaimapi, for the sap of the maple. The sap of the box-elder is very sweet, and a sugar may be made by boiling it, as is sometimes done today.[1] The Pawnee name for sugar, *līkĭts' u*, is said to signify wood water, but may perhaps mean rather the juice of the cornstalk.

Some Cheyennes say vikamapi is derived from mishkemai-mapi, literally, maple water; that they first applied that name to sugar, but that the traders incorrectly pronounced it *vĭk' a-mă' pi*. The word would thus be of modern coinage. It seems more probable, however, that vikamapi is from *vĭk' i ēnĕ*, sweet, and mapi, water, *i.e.*, sweet water.

The cultivation and harvesting of vegetable foods were the work chiefly of the women; and at the proper season of the

[1] Gilmore, Uses of Plants by the Indians of the Missouri River Region, 33d Report, Bureau of American Ethnology, Washington, 1919.

year—in spring for roots, and in late summer for berries—
parties of women of all ages, with their children, set out to
garner the natural crops.

Berries were dried for consumption in winter, when they
were boiled, either alone or with meat. Fresh choke-cherries
were pounded fine and mixed with pulverized buffalo meat and
tallow to make pemmican. Fresh or dried, they used sarvis-
berries, plums, choke-cherries, sand-cherries, bull-berries, and
currants. After these fruits had been pounded fine so that seeds
or pits had been thoroughly broken up, the moist mass was
pressed into flat, thin, rectangular cakes, perhaps two and a
half inches by two inches, and laid out on a skin or a piece of
cloth to dry in the sun. When thoroughly dried, the cakes were
packed away in small rawhide sacks, which again were stored
in the larger parfleches.

The *pomme blanche*[2] was gathered in June, for a little later
the root becomes good for nothing, while the tops fall off in
July. The roots vary in size from that of a pigeon's egg to a
large root four inches long and from two to two and one-half
inches in diameter. They were cooked fresh, or were dried for
winter use. Sometimes they are eaten raw, but if too freely
indulged in cause indigestion and discomfort. Raw, the taste
of the roots somewhat suggests a chestnut. The larger roots
were cut in pieces for drying, and Hinds[3] relates how he saw
the Crees cutting these roots into shreds for this purpose. The
Cheyennes more commonly cut them into thin, lengthwise
slices, which soon lose their moisture. The dried pieces are
often pounded fine on the same stones used in pounding berries,
and then are used as a thickening for soup.

The women speak of about thirty-five or forty plants which
serve them as food, of which sixteen or more are fruits, and
eight or ten roots. I do not think that the Cheyennes ever knew
the camas, which does not grow on the plains. They do, how-

[2] *Tipsin* of Gilmore.
[3] Hinds' Canadian Red River Exploration, vol. 1, p. 319, London, 1860.

ever, eat the bulbs of several lily-like plants, such as the mariposa lily.[4]

When the first shoots of the so-called red cocklebur, or wild licorice (*măt kănt no wăs*), appear in spring, these are watched, and when they have grown to the height of a foot, they are cut and eaten raw. They are sweet and tender. The tender stalks of a milkweed are used in the same way.

In wet places along the river bottoms, they say, are sometimes found plants described as like *Sagittaria* growing thick. The stalk of this is said to have been eaten.

A root, somewhat like a potato, with a red skin, many tubers growing on the root tendrils of a single plant, grows on a climbing vine. The tuber is more than an inch and a half in diameter.

Elsewhere is presented a list of the plants employed by the Cheyennes for various purposes.

AGRICULTURE

Before they had left their eastern home, the Cheyennes were an agricultural people, and they have continued to farm, with some periods of interruption, to the present time. According to statements made to me by old women and men who died between 1900 and 1915, and others living in 1918, they farmed regularly on Grand River, on the Little Missouri and the North Platte, and on the Laramie. Up to the year 1876 they kept up their Corn Dance, and retained the sacred ear of corn which is supposed to have been raised from the original seed brought out by one of the two similarly dressed young men who went into the spring and received the buffalo meat, corn, and other things, from the old woman within the hill. Watched, cared for, and reverenced, this ear would make the crops grow well. After corn-growing had been abandoned, as it was in war times, the ear was still kept as a sacred object. Incidentally they say that a long time ago the Arikaras stole their corn,

[4] DeSmet, Western Missions (p. 81), says roots of water arrow (*Sagittaria rigida*) and of wild lily (*Convallaria corealis*) are prized by Indians.

meaning, I suppose, that the Arikaras obtained their corn by taking it from the Cheyennes.

They relate that the Corn Dance came down from the time when they first planted, and was practiced up to the date of the Mackenzie fight (1876), but that since they have had agencies, and lived with the white people, the dance has been given up.

The Corn Dance was, they say, practiced by young girls and middle-aged women, who danced in a circle. Men sang for the dance, and shook a gourd rattle, which they called and which represented a squash (*ma oh?*). The woman who led the dance carried the sacred ear of corn on a stick which was fitted into a hole in the butt of the ear. In later times the dance was occasionally held as a social performance—one of rejoicing—as, for example, on the return of a successful war-party, in which no one had been wounded. They say now that in the dance no motions of hoeing corn were made. It is not known whether there was any ceremonial previous to the dance.

The corn was planted in quincunxes, four grains at the corners of the square, and one in the middle; and the grains were put in the ground with the soft end up. In plantings which have taken place since 1850, old men and old women have been seen to carry water from the stream to water the hills of corn. It is said that some of the hoes which they used in cultivating their corn were made of stones—sometimes chipped to a proper flat shape; but sometimes, also, they found natural stones, which could be lashed to a stick and used for the purpose. Hoes were made also from the shoulder blade of buffalo or of elk, lashed to a handle. Indeed, they used for this purpose any bone that they could fashion to the required shape.

Mr. Mooney's statements[5] as to the farming practices of the Cheyennes seem to indicate that he was unaware—because they are not mentioned in that locality by Lewis and Clark—that these people formerly lived on the Little Missouri (Antelope Pit) River—and that they grew crops up to the middle

[5] Handbook of American Indians, pt. 1, p. 251.

of the nineteenth century. But the early Spanish manuscript map brought back by Lewis and Clark shows a camp of "Chaquieno" Indians near the head of the Little Missouri.[6]

The testimony that they farmed up to 1865 is too general to be ignored. As already stated, the Sioux still refer to a number of old Cheyenne village sites as Cheyenne planting places, and give various details as to the crops they grew and the way in which they protected them up to the time when they moved on farther west.

Many old Cheyenne women who were born in or near the Black Hills early in the last century, and who lived on the streams flowing out from them, have repeated to me time and again that they commonly planted corn patches, as their mothers before them had done, and had taught them to do.

Accounts of the capturing of eagles, as practiced from early times down to the first half of the nineteenth century, describe as a ceremony connected with this eagle catching the preparation of a certain sort of ceremonial food, which consisted in part of balls of pulverized corn.

The growing of corn is always referred to as a common incident of old-time village life, and there is no doubt that it was usually grown. Knowing the conservatism of Indian women, we may feel certain that they would not easily have laid aside the agricultural practices that had come down to them through the generations, but that even after they had moved out onto the plains, wherever the situation was favorable, and there was a prospect that they would return during the summer, the old women planted their crops and impressed on their daughters the duty of doing likewise.

In a recent conversation with Hankering Wolf, who was a boy of thirteen at the time of the Fort Laramie Treaty (1851), he incidentally mentioned that the year before that council was to be held the Cheyennes put in their crops on a broad flat on the Platte River, just below the main canyon and above the

[6] Orig. Journ. of Lewis and Clark, Atlas, map 2.

first small canyon above Fort Laramie. It was from this point that they moved down to the treaty ground at Horse Creek.

When the Cheyennes lived along the Missouri, and no doubt later, after they had moved to the Black Hills, they had at least two kinds of beans, of which one was wild and one cultivated. One of these varieties is described as shaped like a lima bean and was whitish in color; the other was spotted yellow and white, or purple and white. According to Short Woman, the mother of Elk River, one of these kinds of beans was commonly cultivated; the other kind, believed to be *Falcata comosa*, grew wild. This plant has small beans produced from the flowers, and bears also large beans at the ends of leafless colorless branches prostrate on the ground in the dense shade of the upper branches. These are the beans spoken of as used among the Sioux.[7] In the document cited the statement was made that these beans were a favorite food of the passenger pigeon, and that they were collected by mice. Indian women often tell of finding caches in which the mice had stored considerable numbers of these beans.

FLESH FOOD

After the Cheyennes moved out to the great plains a marked change took place in their habits. Here they found buffalo in great numbers, yet more or less migratory with the seasons. The tribe, which hitherto had been chiefly sedentary, occupying permanent villages and tilling the soil, modified its ways of life when it met the new conditions. The necessity of following the buffalo from place to place led to the abandonment of permanent habitations, while the increased supply of flesh food rendered less imperative the cultivation of the soil, though it was still practiced until the active wars of 1868 to 1878 made agriculture no longer possible. In the North, cultivation of the ground began again after the surrender, and in varying degree has continued ever since.

[7] Patent Office Report for 1849-1850 (Senate Doc. 20), p. 451.

In modern times the buffalo formed the chief sustenance of the people, and, as with most other prairie Indians, practically all parts of the animal were eaten. The tongue and nose were delicacies, while the liver sprinkled with gall was a favorite dish; the small intestine, filled with chopped meat, was roasted or boiled; the marrow-bones were split and the contents eaten, and, as will be seen farther on, almost the whole of the animal, except the bones and hoofs, was used for food in some form or other.

A favorite dish was the flesh of a yellow calf boiled with *pomme-blanche* roots in a liquor made of water and the grease from the bones of fat cows. The lungs of the buffalo were cut open, dried, and roasted on the coals. They were good. The Pawnees formerly boiled them with their corn.

The Cheyennes cooked blood in the rennet of the buffalo. They built a good fire, and when it had burned down to coals, a bed of hot ashes was raked out in front of the fire; the rennet was filled with blood, and tied with sinew at the small end; it was placed on the hot ashes, and the woman who was cooking it tapped it constantly with a stick, and rolled it over and over in the ashes until the blood boiled and cooked. After it had been cooking some little time, she tested it every now and then, pulling it out of the ashes, and pricking it with a small and very sharp stick. If blood ran out of the puncture, the cooking was not complete, and it was put back again. At length, when no blood followed the pricking, the rennet was pulled out, opened, and the cooked blood eaten. It was no longer fluid, but was hard, like jelly.

The hide of the buffalo-bull was eaten. One way of cooking it was in a saucer-shaped depression dug in the ground, and lined with grass or leaves, on which were spread out large pieces of the fresh hide. Over the hide were two or three layers of green leaves, and on the leaves were placed a number of ribs or other flat bones to hold the leaves down. A layer of about four inches of clay was spread over this and was pounded down solidly and smoothed off, and on this floor of clay was built a large fire of dry wood which was kept burning for three or four hours. Then the fire was swept aside, the clay, bones, and leaves were removed, and the hide taken out. The hair slipped off easily from the hide, which was quite tender and very good.

Many women saved the scrapings from the hides which they tanned, and dried and put them in parfleches, against a time of scarcity. Then they were boiled and made a palatable food.

The flesh of the buffalo, including the back fat, was cut in thin slices and dried in the sun or on lines stretched in the lodge.

Pemmican was made by roasting dried meat, and pounding it fine with a stone maul on a hard, flat stone which rested on an oval, somewhat dish-shaped, parfleche. The operation was not unlike that of pounding cherries. The Cheyennes, however, made pemmican on a small scale—for present use only and not to store.

When young dogs were needed for a feast, they were strangled by the women of the family. A string was looped around the neck of the dog, each end of which was held by a woman, who drew the loop tight, so that the animal hung suspended between the two executioners.

Originally, it is said, the Cheyennes did not eat dogs, but were driven to it by hunger; or perhaps the custom was borrowed from some other tribe. They eat young wolves and coyotes, as they do young puppies, and also young wildcats and panthers, usually not by choice, but in case of need. Badgers and skunks are good to eat, but otters are not. They eat neither birds of prey nor crows, except under stress of hunger. The magpie they do not eat at all, because, they say, it won for them the race during the contest to see whether the buffalo should eat the people or the people should eat the buffalo. They are very fond of turtles.

Though the Cheyennes ate horseflesh, they preferred other meat. The Kiowas, on the other hand, liked horseflesh, and are

THE TRAIL FROM THE TIMBER

said to have preferred fat colt to fat cow. Young fat horse is excellent meat—tender and sweet. It is better not to cook the flesh at once, but to allow it to hang for a day to get rid of a certain taste it has when fresh killed. The flanks and breast and the back of the neck under the mane were greatly esteemed. Roast ribs and liver roasted on the coals were excellent.

Deer, elk, wild sheep, and antelope, were all taken and the flesh used.

HUNTING METHODS

The Food Quest. The hardships of the Indian war-path have often been spoken of, but little seems to have been written of the labor of his hunting. Most civilized writers seem to have assumed that hunting was all pleasure. This view is taken because to the white man hunting is a pastime, a recreation, and we assume that it is so to all people. To the Indian, hunting was work, and often work of the hardest kind.[8] This aspect of hunting has often been learned by the white man—as the market hunter—when necessity and not pleasure has been the motive for the pursuit. To the Plains Indian hunting was never a recreation, but was the chief labor by which he supported life.

Writers, quite ignorant of Indians, but who wish to give local color to fanciful descriptions of Indian hunting, sometimes

[8] This is a point apparently little understood. One writer has mentioned it—but in quite another connection—while discussing the Indian's idea of the future life. "To us Europeans hunting is more or less an amusement, but to the Indian it is a toil, and frequently a most fatiguing mode of life. In many Indian dialects the words 'hunter' and 'hunting' are synonymous with 'work' and 'working.' A good hunter is a clever and industrious workman. As, then, the idea entertained by most nations of paradise is, that it will be without toil or labor, it is to me more than doubtful whether they regard the chase as an element of their paradisiac existence. Among the Ojibbeways I never heard that they held such a view. I once asked a man of their tribe, who was describing paradise to me, and did not at all allude to hunting, 'And then you will go every day to hunt and kill a countless number of animals?' 'Oh no!' he replied dryly, 'there is no hunting or labor in paradise.' "—Kohl, Kitchigami, p. 212, London, 1860.

describe the hunters as yelling in the excitement of the chase. It would be as fitting to write of a farmer as yelling in the excitement of plowing or of milking his cows.

Although making some provision against a time of scarcity, as did most tribes of the buffalo plains, the Cheyennes yet often faced want. Winter and summer the camp must be supplied with food, and no matter how tempestuous the weather or how bitter the cold, if food was lacking, men were obliged to hunt. Often, while out in winter after buffalo, they were chilled to the bone by the bitter winds and were caught in blinding prairie snowstorms and obliged to camp for days, perhaps, without fuel, often freezing hands and feet. If the buffalo disappeared, the young men must make long journeys in search of them, and often their sufferings from fatigue, hunger, and cold were very great. At such times the women were safe at home in the camp, by the fire, having no labor to perform more arduous than gathering the daily supply of wood and transporting it to camp.

Horses and Firearms. With the advent of the horse, metal, and the gun, the primitive means of taking food began to be supplanted by the new and more effectual methods. The enclosure into which some food animals were driven was gradually abandoned; the snares with which they caught others were given up; stone-throwing was no longer practiced, and people ceased to lie in wait for animals to come to them, since now on horseback they could overtake these animals, kill them, and transport the capture to camp.

While the greater facility with which food was now secured at first seemed to make life easier for the Indians, it may also have tended to reduce their earlier industry in hunting and to make them less careful of their food supply—more wasteful. On the other hand, since Indians are conservative, slow to change their ways, and to some extent had always striven to save up food against a time of scarcity, and since, also, the acquisition of these new things—the iron-pointed arrow, the swift horse, and the far-killing gun—followed one another very rapidly, it may be doubted if at first they greatly influenced the view which the Indians took of food, and their habits of providing for future needs. Yet toward the end of the buffalo days, when traders became more numerous and more eager to secure robes, and offered almost any price for them, there was great waste of food by the Indians, who destroyed the buffalo largely for their hides, and thus brought themselves down to the level of the white skin-hunter.

Primitive Devices. Of the primitive methods of taking food, a few have been practiced by boys up to very recent times. One of these was stone-throwing; and almost up to the present time, in autumn, when blackbirds were abundant, little boys killed them by throwing stones at the thick flocks. In recent times, too, a man was occasionally found who possessed especial skill in stone-throwing. Such a man was Strong Left Hand, who died in 1905, more than eighty years of age. Stories of his skill and success by this primitive means were told and wondered at in both sections of the tribe. These are some examples of his achievements with the stone that he related to me. He said:

I was on a war-path, and we had been shooting at buffalo. They had started to run, and as the last one was going by I ran ahead of it, and as I did so, picked up a stone from the ground. As I got in the buffalo's way, it charged me, and raised its tail, showing that it was angry. Just before it reached me, I threw the stone and hit it in the forehead, and it fell over, dead.

Once, when I was out on the prairie with Sleeping Rabbit, I killed an antelope with a stone. I was lying on a hill watching, and the antelope was coming toward me, and stopped to nibble at some brush. I threw the stone just as the antelope raised its head, hitting it on the head and killing it.

One morning a man was trying to catch one of his horses that was hard to catch and would not let anyone get near it. The man who owned it had been trying for a long time to catch it, and when I passed he was angry and called out to me, "Friend, kill that horse for me!" I picked up a piece of bone that was lying on the prairie, and threw it at the horse, which was about fifty yards off, and struck it on the head and killed it.

Once there was an eagle's nest in the cliff near where we were camped. It was high up on the rocks, and could not be reached either from above or from below. Sits In The Night came to me and said: "Friend, there is an eagle's nest here that I cannot get at. I want the eagle. Will you go and kill it for me?" The nest was too high above the prairie to be reached by a stone, and it could not be seen from the top of the cliff above it. So when I went there I knew I should be obliged to wait until the eagle flew out, and by the time the bird came in sight it would be a long way from me—a long throw. When I crept up to the cliff, the bird must have heard me, for it flew out, and I let fly the stone, and hit it, and killed it, and it fell to the ground dead.

Anciently, no doubt, stone-throwing was a constantly employed and successful way of killing game. The enormous abundance of food animals and birds, and their tameness in those primitive times, make it altogether probable that men possessing anything like Strong Left Hand's accuracy of aim and his power might kill much game by this means of hunting. Many men employed this method of killing game, and of these, many no doubt became skillful and successful stone-throwers.

Until the old free life was broken up, the little boys, to secure feathers, employed an old hunting custom, now almost forgotten. It was practiced by boys of from ten to fifteen or sixteen years to kill crows and magpies for their feathers, or food birds that might happen to alight near where the hunters were hidden. This was usually on some open space near which stood small trees. More often than not it was on the bank of a river, or on some old sandbar or island in the river; at all events, where there were clumps of willow brush with open spaces among them. In these clumps of bushes the boys lay hidden. If clumps of willows were not found in a convenient situation, they cut willow branches and thrust the butts in the ground in a small circle, bringing the tops together above a shallow hole scooped out in the sand, and tying them there. A door was left for entrance, and for this door a cover was woven of coarse grass. When the hunter entered the place of concealment—the "blind"—he pulled down the door behind him. Often four or five such shelters were built in a row thirty or forty feet apart, each to be occupied by a hunter.

On the little trees and bushes they hung scraps of hide and the trimmings of buffalo-robes, and on the ground where the birds were expected to come were scattered pieces of tallow, up to within a few feet of the shelter. This bait was renewed every day. Not far from the shelter, and where the bait was scattered, little forked sticks were set in the ground in pairs, and the forks of each pair supported a crossbar on which the birds might alight. In the front of the shelter, looking toward the bait, an opening thinly covered with grass was left to shoot through.

After getting into his shelter, which he did before daylight, each boy kept very quiet, and sat watching and ready to shoot, the point of the arrow he was to discharge protruding through the grass. The arrows were either blunt-headed or perhaps had sharpened wood points, and when the birds flew down to eat the bait, they were within close range. The boys did not leave their shelters to collect the birds that they killed, nor did they make any noise which might alarm the other birds. Even if a wounded bird flew off a short distance, he who had shot it did not go out in pursuit. After the other birds had flown away, however, as they always did when the sun got high, the boys went out and gathered up what they had killed, and went home.

If a hawk made his appearance near at hand, this alarmed the other birds, which flew away. Sometimes, however, the hawks descended to the bait, and were killed. This was the boys' method of getting feathers.

BUFFALO HUNTING

The camp moved about from place to place, following the buffalo; and, as a result of the habits of these animals, a set of tribal laws had grown up to govern the hunt. Since the Cheyennes depended on the buffalo for food, it was obviously necessary that the hunting should be organized; in order first, that large quantities of food might be killed at one time; and second, and more important, that the animals which were to furnish this food should not be disturbed or frightened and so driven beyond the reach of the people. No doubt the laws governing this hunting developed slowly, but they long existed. Their utility was generally recognized, and they were supported by public opinion. Their enforcement was in the hands of the soldier bands of the camp, who rigidly carried them out.

When buffalo were plenty, small parties or single individuals were not permitted to chase the buffalo alone. There was no individual hunting. When one man hunted buffalo, all joined in the chase. Anyone found going out alone and running buffalo was severely whipped by the soldiers, with quirts, ramrods, or bows. If he were obstinate, and persisted in disobeying the law, they might cut up his lodge, chop up the poles, and perhaps even kill his horses, this of course being the equivalent of a fine, more or less heavy. Men who violated the law were sometimes beaten until they could hardly walk, and could not get about for several days.[9] When the camp moved up near the mountains, into a country where deer and elk were plentiful, and where there were only a few buffalo-bulls, each man was free to hunt as he pleased; but such a hunter, if he came upon buffalo in numbers, did not disturb them, for he knew it was wrong to do so—not just to the other people of the camp.

[9] There was a special word for the infliction of the penalty; *i.e.*, *tŭhk' a yăts*, v. t., "to punish" (for a fault committed). It refers especially to the custom of punishing for disobedience to any order or rule which had been made and previously proclaimed; as on a buffalo hunt, if a person slipped out and hunted alone, so as to disturb the buffalo before the time set for the chase, the offender was whipped and might have his horse killed or his gun broken.

The chiefs decided when the buffalo surround was to be made. They gave their orders to the soldiers, and from that time forward the soldiers had charge of the hunt. The day before the surround, it was cried through the village that on the morrow all would chase buffalo. I have frequently described the operation of killing buffalo with the bow and arrow; and the method pursued by the Cheyennes was not markedly different from that practiced by other Plains tribes. In the different stories told in this book, examples are given of the way in which buffalo hunting was practiced.

An old-time method of killing buffalo among the Cheyennes was with the lance. The rider usually ran up on the right side of the animal, and held the lance across his body, the right hand the higher. The buffalo was a little ahead of the horse, and the man, using both hands, thrust with his lance downward and forward. When the buffalo felt the prick of the lance, it usually ran still faster. Sometimes it tried to turn to charge, but as the man held the lance against it, and pressed it into its side, the buffalo always gave way, and ran on. Sometimes the lance-point might strike a rib, and the man was obliged to make a second thrust. Perhaps the first thrust hurried the buffalo along, so that the man fell behind; but he whipped up his horse, and again got near enough. Often, instead of thrusting for the heart, they thrust down for the kidneys, so striving to break down and cripple the animal. The lance was more commonly used in earlier days than it was after sheet-iron arrowheads and firearms were procured, yet it was used by war-parties in modern times, i.e., from 1865 to 1875 or 1880.

I have often adverted to the power of the bow, and the Cheyennes were good bowmen. The older men tell me that the bow was an effective weapon—that is to say, a killing weapon—up to from three to four hundred yards. This refers to the use of the weapon in war. In chasing buffalo, if the dart entered at the right point, the Cheyenne killed his buffalo with a single arrow. Big Ribs, a Northern Cheyenne at Pine Ridge, and Strong Left

Hand, at Tongue River Agency, are known each to have shot one arrow through two buffalo, killing both at a single shot. Strong Left Hand's bow was very powerful, and few men could bend it. Walks At Night, also called Wrinkled Wolf, who had once chased a buffalo-cow which stopped to fight, shot an arrow entirely through her, so that it went on and then stood free in the ground beyond her. Left-hand Wolf did the same thing with a buffalo-bull that stopped to fight, and Left-hand Bull was a powerful bowman.

In a number of instances men, in the chase, have killed buffalo with their butcher knives. This was done by a friend, who held the knife in his right hand, ran up close beside a cow, and thrust the blade several times into her flank.

Big Ribs, when chasing buffalo on one occasion, sprang from his horse to the back of a bull, and, while riding it, cut out a kidney through the flank. This was done about the year 1870, and merely as an act of bravado—to show what he could do.

In the old days, when buffalo were killed close to the camp, the women and children all went out to them, to assist in securing the meat. The men who had been killing buffalo would ask a child, often a mere baby, if it had ever before been present at a chase, and if it had not, would take a handful of blood and smear it all over its face. The children were not permitted to wash off this blood until they had returned to the camp.

In the olden time, before they had horses, the Cheyennes— as so often told of other Indians—made foot surrounds of the buffalo,[10] and also drove them into pens. Such enclosures were usually built under a cutbank or bluff, which formed one or more walls of the pen; the other sides were merely bushes or branches stuck in the ground. From the entrance of the pen diverging lines of bushes, like the wings of a chute, extended out on the plains.[11] The Indians partly enticed and partly drove the buffalo between the wings, which guided them into the en-

[10] Compare LePage duPratz, vol. III, p. 210, Paris, 1758.
[11] Compare Umfreville, Present State of Hudson's Bay, p. 160, London, 1790.

closure. Though the animals might readily break through the walls of bushes, they seldom did so, for they were afraid of them, and merely ran round and round within the enclosure until exhausted. Meantime the Indians closed in on them, and began to shoot them down with arrows. Usually most of those in the pen were killed, though often a few broke through the lines and escaped. It is perhaps better to give the account of these hunting methods received from an old Cheyenne; an account which no doubt is substantially correct, and may well enough have come to this man from people who had learned the methods through practice.

The statement that the changes in customs and the improvements in methods were revealed to men in their dreams, is merely his method of explaining the order and manner in which these changes took place. The Cheyennes are firm believers in dreams. Like the prophets of old, they often received in sleep suggestions from supernatural sources—were warned in a dream. Such visions, the Indian says, are sent to tell us what is going to happen, and the warning which they convey must be obeyed. This is White Hawk's relation:

In those days the arrowpoint was made of stone. There were birds, and so they got feathers for their arrows in order that they should fly straight. Men were always out from the camp looking for food. When any of these men found a herd of buffalo, twenty or thirty or forty, he returned to the camp and reported to the chief. Then all who had bows and arrows made ready, and went with these men to near where the buffalo were, and there formed a big circle as far as possible from the buffalo, but entirely surrounding them. The side of the circle to the leeward of the buffalo, and the two other sides across the wind were formed first. The windward side was formed last. Then the men began to close in on the buffalo, until, as the circle grew smaller, the hunters were closer together. When the buffalo began to smell the people, they ran away; but those toward whom they ran would yell and toss their robes, and the buffalo turned, looking for another place, and from being always turned back they were soon running in a circle. When the hunters got pretty close, all the most active young men—those who had strong arms to pull the bow, and who could shoot straightest—ran in close to the buffalo and began shooting their arrows at them, while the buffalo were running round in a circle, not trying to break through the line of the people. The old men say that in this way they sometimes killed a whole herd, none of them breaking out. At times a few would break out and get away, but often all were killed.

The people had dogs, and when the buffalo were skinned and cut up, they packed meat on their dogs, and then every man, woman, and child able to walk carried a pack to camp. They left nothing behind, but carried everything in. Even the bones were carried in, and the entrails, for buffalo were hard to get and were had only occasionally, and the people felt that nothing was to be wasted or left behind.

Later, after they had learned to surround the buffalo in this way, some old man was told in a dream of another and better way. That he should take the wing of some large bird, perhaps an eagle and perhaps some other big bird, and that the people should take their lodges up on the prairie and pitch them in a circle, leaving an opening at one side. When the buffalo were close, two old men, each carrying one of these large wings, should go out toward the buffalo and wave the wings in the air, beckoning to the animals, and that these would come toward them. They did this, and as the buffalo came toward them, the men moved away and the buffalo followed, and so the men led them right into the circle of the lodges, where the people killed them. The buffalo seemed to be gentle and did not run, but stood about, waiting to be killed.

In later times, another man had a dream about the way to kill buffalo. His dream said to him: "You shall take your people and have them make a large pen out of wood and brush, with a gap in one side, and a chute with diverging wings running far out on the prairie, fences which shall hide the people from the buffalo. Then you shall take certain young men of the camp and go out with them on the prairie, and you can bring the buffalo into this pen."

The man had the people build the pen and the wings as he had been told, and took his young men and told them what to do, and went out and led the buffalo into the pen without trouble. After that they could always go out and bring them.

Before they set out to bring the buffalo, the old man told his young men to strip naked down to their moccasins, and to paint their faces, arms, legs, and bodies with red earth. The medicine man and another old man, each carrying a wing, went before the painted men singing their mysterious songs. The painted young men divided into two equal parties, and followed these two old men, behind and outside of them on either side. When the old men got near the buffalo, they beckoned to them with the wings, and soon the buffalo began to come toward them. Then the old men turned about and walked toward the chute in front of the buffalo; and on either side of them, but a long way off, walked the two parties of painted young men. The young men did not sing, but if at any time the buffalo tried to turn aside in either direction from following the old men, the young men held their hands up to the sky and waved them in a certain way, and the buffalo turned back.[12] After the old men had led the buffalo in between the wings, the opening between the wings was filled by the two parties of painted men who had followed them out, and all sang. The young men who had been chosen to do the killing had been hidden behind the walls of the chute, and after the buffalo had passed them, they climbed over this fence and followed them, hurrying them into the pen. While they did the killing, the painted men stood there at the gap of the chute, and kept on singing until all were killed.

When the buffalo that were following the two men who called them with the wings had come to the entrance to the pen, these medicine men walked a little to one side of the entrance, still singing and waving the wings toward the entrance, and the buffalo walked into the pen. Then, while the painted young men walked up and formed a line in the entrance, the medicine men walked along outside of the fence, and close to it, around the pen to the back, opposite the entrance. They stood at the back of the pen and sang their mysterious songs all the time while the men were killing the buffalo, and when they were through killing, sat down on the ground and re-

---

[12] Compare this method of directing the buffalo with that practiced in more recent times by the Red River half-breeds. Hunting at High Altitudes, p. 258, Harper & Brothers, 1913 (*Forest and Stream*, vol. LXXIV, p. 969).

mained there till the skinning and cutting up was finished, and the meat was taken to camp.

The best pieces of the meat were selected for the two men who had called the buffalo, and the painted men were then allowed to go into the pen and to select for themselves the next best portions.

Such were some of the primitive methods of taking buffalo, when they first hunted them on the prairie; but long ago, in the North, before they reached the plains, and when they lived in a country of heavy snowfall, they followed them in winter on snowshoes and chased them into snowdrifts in ravines. When they had driven buffalo into such drifts, they set the dogs free to worry them, and ran up and killed them with the lance, in the manner figured by Catlin, and described for killing moose in the *Jesuit Relations* and in Perrot.[13] They led the dogs on the hunt and had trained them how to act. After the buffalo had been killed, the dogs stood about, and the owners, while cutting up the buffalo, fed them freely. Then they put packs of meat on the dogs and started back to the village. After the packs had been taken off, in the village, all the dogs would start back to eat more. Bitches that had pups would come back to camp and disgorge what they had eaten for their young to feed on, and then the mothers would run back again to eat more.

This, the old men tell us today, was the easiest and most successful of the old methods.

Near some of the places where the Cheyennes brought the buffalo into a pound or enclosure and killed them, there were formerly to be seen piles of buffalo-horns heaped up, which, as described to me, were similar to the piles of horns made under like conditions by the Blackfeet that I have seen near their killing places. Remains of such piles of buffalo-horns used to be seen at a point west of the Black Hills in the latter part of the last century, but must long since have disappeared.

The dangers of the modern buffalo hunt to the men who

[13] Blair, Indian Tribes of Upper Mississippi Valley, etc., vol. I, p. 107.

practiced it have been described in another volume.[14] They were many, and almost every year a few men were killed in hunting. One danger, not commonly recognized because unusual except at one season of the year, was the pugnacity of the bulls, and their occasional pertinacity in pursuing men.

The rutting season was in June and July, and then the buffalo-bulls, when chased, were often ready to fight. Many years ago a bull followed Four Bulls five miles before the man managed to get out of sight behind a hill, when the bull stopped. Four Bulls was riding a fast gray horse, and had gone to help Crooked Neck, who was being chased, when the bull left Crooked Neck and followed Four Bulls. This was a four-year-old bull.

Wolf Chief described a similar experience:

In the spring of 1868 I set out with a boy to hunt buffalo. We had four horses, two to ride and two led horses to pack. We had gone ten or twelve miles from camp when on looking over a hill I saw buffalo, and we changed to our running horses. A herd of cows was near us, and beyond them a herd of bulls. This was in May, when the buffalo were shedding their coats. I was riding a sorrel horse, captured in Texas, which was very fast. The country, on the head of the Washita where we were, is level. Our camp was on the Beaver, above where Fort Supply is now. I had two pistols, each with six loads, and the boy had a bow and arrows.

I said to the boy, "Do you kill some calves, and I will kill some of the larger buffalo." I rode fast down to the herd of cows, and they started to run, and soon I shot three. When the cows began to run, the bulls started too, and ran after the cows, and I thought that I would kill one or two bulls, for in May they are fat—much fatter than the cows.

I raced up to the herd, and shot a fine four-year-old bull that had large smooth horns. Then I rode on to another bull, and shot it. When I rode up to the second bull I turned in ahead of the first one, and after the second one had fallen with a broken back, I looked

[14] American Big Game Hunting, p. 195, Forest and Stream Publishing Co., N. Y., 1893.

behind me and saw the first bull coming. A little blood was dropping from its mouth, and I thought it was badly hit.

I turned my horse to finish it, and rode alongside and shot it again. When I fired, the bull turned away, and I supposed that I had not hit it in the right place, and rode on after it to shoot again, when suddenly the bull made a short turn and rushed toward me. I shot at it, but it still came on. I turned my horse in one direction and another, trying to avoid it and get out of sight, but the bull followed every turn I made, and I saw that it was going to chase me.

The boy, Little Bear, was a long way off, and I did not ride toward him because his horse was not very fast. I turned and tried to run away from the bull, but he came on, running fast, and kept following. He came after me, sometimes going slowly, and then suddenly would begin to run fast and try to catch up to me. He seemed to measure his gait by that of the horse.

Several times I turned about and shot at the animal, but I do not think I hit him. I did not fire the last two loads in my pistol; I saved them in case my horse should be run down. It was a busy ride. With one eye I was obliged to keep watching the bull, and at the same time it was necessary to look out for holes in the prairie. If my horse had stepped in a hole, and had fallen, that would have been the end of me.

Above the river, where the village was, there is a hill, and when I reached the top of this hill, looking over toward the camp, I kept right on, but the bull, surprised at what he saw, stopped, and stood looking down toward the big camp.

Soon he began to bellow and paw the ground, thrust his horns into it, and throw the dirt on his back. After he had done this for a little while, he turned about and went straight back as he had come. My horse was wet with sweat, and staggering from fatigue.

I went down to the camp and got a fresh horse, and started back to where I had left the boy. When I reached the place, I found Little Bear up on a hill looking for me. He said to me, "I saw the bull close to you, and I made up my mind that he had killed you."

By many of the buffalo-eating tribes the white buffalo, on account of its rarity, was deemed mysterious, and in this matter the Cheyennes were like other Indians. White buffalo, and the way in which they were regarded by the Cheyennes, seem worthy of special mention.

George Bent was the last surviving son of Colonel William Bent, an historic character of the early West, whose name suggests a host of recollections to anyone familiar with western history. His mother was a Cheyenne woman. He was born in 1843 near Bent's Old Fort, one of the early trading posts of the Arkansas River.

George Bent traded with the Cheyennes and Arapahoes for many years, and during these years met other tribes of Plains Indians. He stated that in his time he had had five white robes. In the first one, the tips of the hair were white and the bases black, giving the effect of a silver gray. This was a five-year-old cow, killed by Crazy Mule, whose wife dressed and painted it, after he had performed the required ceremonies. Crazy Mule was a medicine man, and possessed the power to remove the tabu against dressing a white robe, which existed among the Cheyenne women.

The second robe was that of a three-year-old bull, obtained from Big Wolf. It was white.

He procured the third from Heap o' Birds, whose proper name was Many Magpies. This was a three-year-old cow, described as "claybank" in color—a dark cream.

The fourth robe was from a two-year-old heifer, a dappled gray obtained from Wolf Man.

The fifth was that of a two-year-old bull, described as yellowish fawn color, obtained from Starving Elk.

The Cheyennes regard a white buffalo as mysterious—sacred —and in ancient times, if a Cheyenne killed a white buffalo, he left it where it fell, taking nothing from it, and not even putting a knife into it.

Some of them say that the white buffalo belongs far to the north; that it comes from the place where, according to tradition, the buffalo originally came out of the ground. They regard it as the chief of the buffalo. This feeling was confirmed by an observation made many years ago. A war-party went up north against the Crows. One day they came to a hill, and when they looked over it they saw great numbers of buffalo, lying down, and among them a perfectly white cow. When the buffalo got up and went to water, the white cow went too, and it was noticed that none of the other buffalo went very close to her. They did not seem to fear her, but they did not crowd upon her, but gave her plenty of room, as if they respected her.

In old times the hide of a white buffalo was not used, but was sacrificed to the Sun or to the Great Power (Heammawihio). Such an offering has been made within sixty years; and a story of the sacrifice was told me by Bent, as he witnessed it. He said:

In 1867 I happened to come into Eagle Chief's camp just after a white buffalo had been killed. The man who had killed it came in with the hide tied on his horse; he rode into the center of the camp-circle, stopped there, and dismounted. He did not take the hide off his horse, but stood there in the center of the circle holding his horse. The Indians began to look through the camp for some one who might take the hide from the horse with the prescribed ceremony. This could be done only by a man who had counted a coup by pulling an enemy off his horse in battle. Presently Left Hand, an Arapaho, came up carrying a stick in his right hand. He stopped by the horse, pointed with the stick in the direction of the place where the event had taken place, and then told how he had seen a Ute coming, had stepped behind a tree and waited until the Ute rode by him, and then had sprung upon him, pulled him from his horse and killed him with a knife. Then he struck the white buffalo-hide with his stick, and took it from the horse and placed it on the ground, where it remained. The man who had killed it had brought in no meat, for the carcass of a white buffalo may not be eaten; it must be left on the ground. If the meat were eaten, the buffalo might never again return to that place.

The next day a pole was set in the ground to which the white hide was to be tied. Before this was done a very large sweat-house was built, and many of the old men went in to take a sweat and pray.

DIGGING POMMES BLANCHES

Before they went in, women came in crowds, bringing their children, and various offerings—calico, beads, moccasins, and other gifts— which were to be tied to the pole and given to the sun. Before it was folded up to be tied to the pole, the hide was painted on the hair side with blue paint. The folded hide was tied to the pole by an old man who was naked, and was painted. While he was tying the hide to the pole he was constantly praying, and as each child was brought to him with an offering he prayed, passing his hands over its head, arms, and sides, and asking for good luck for it, for long life, health, and abundance of everything. Other old men stood about the man who was tying the hide, praying fervently.

Unless specially painted by some medicine man who has the power to do this, and prayed over, and so absolved from the consequences of violating the tabu, no Cheyenne woman may dress a white buffalo hide. The painting is done with red paint applied about both wrists, both ankles, and on the face—a ring over the forehead, down the cheeks, and across the chin below the mouth. Some of the hides obtained by Bent were dressed by captive women of other tribes—one, for example, by a Kiowa woman, and one by a Pawnee woman—who were not bound by Cheyenne customs and subject to Cheyenne fears. The ceremony of tanning the white buffalo hide procured by Bent from Many Magpies is described elsewhere.

HUNTING OF OTHER BIG GAME

Elk, Deer, and Wild Sheep. According to tradition, the Cheyennes, when they lived in the timber in the East, used to surround the elk and the deer, and sometimes drive them into enclosures. This has been known as a practice of some forest tribes since the seventeenth century.[15] They say, too, that in ancient times when they found, in the timber, a place where an elk trail passed under a tree, they tied a rope of rawhide or sinew to a branch, arranging the rope so that the noose would hang down over the trail at about the height of an elk's

[15] Lahontan, Voyages to North America, vol. 1, p. 65, London, 1703.

head. If an elk in passing ran its head into the noose and became frightened, it gave a quick jump, drew the rope tight, and so was strangled. Obviously, if elk were trapped in this way, deer, moose, and caribou were also thus taken in the ancient days when they lived in the timber to the eastward.

This tradition is well founded. The Cheyennes of modern times on the plains, when they tell of snaring elk, speak, of course, of the only large deer which they know. They have no tradition of the moose, nor of the caribou. These animals have been forgotten. Yet we are told by Perrot[16] that the Saulteurs, or Ojibwas, made a practice of snaring moose, and so successfully that in one winter (1670-1671) they snared no fewer than 2400 moose on the Island of Manitoulin. Caribou were captured in the same way, the animals being driven among "trees and poles planted at intervals, in which they stretched snares of rawhide, which enclose a narrow passage purposely left. When all these snares have been prepared, they go far away, marching abreast and uttering loud yells; this unusual noise frightens the animals and drives them to flight on every side; no longer knowing which way to go, they encounter this obstruction which has been made ready in their course. Not being able to clear it, they are compelled to follow it until they reach the passage in which the snares are laid with running knots, which seize them by the neck. It is in vain that they strive to escape; rather, they tear up the stakes and drag these with them as far as the larger trees; in short, their utmost efforts to extricate themselves only serve to strangle them more quickly."

Wistar[17] tells us that certain tribes of California Indians that he met practiced snaring the elk after the year 1850. He speaks of it as commonplace, and saw the snares and how effective they were. He says:

[16] Blair, Indian Tribes of the Upper Mississippi, vol. I, p. 221, 1910.
[17] Autobiography of Isaac Jones Wistar, vol. I, p. 196, Philadelphia, 1914.

Before taking leave with reluctance of the Bald Hills I must not forget to mention the extraordinary skill of those Indians in snaring elk and other large animals in nooses of stout rope made by themselves from bark, which sometimes got them into trouble with the whites as in the following case: At Durkee's some of his friendlies once confided to me with much secrecy a mysterious accident they had met with which they feared would peril their friendly relations with Durkee, who while protecting them from others was sometimes disposed to be rather violent with them himself. Accompanying them therefore at their urgent request some miles to the top of the ridge they pointed out an unlucky ox belonging to Durkee which must have been dead for a fortnight and still lay just as he perished in a running noose set for elk on a well-marked runway. The noose had been skillfully arranged by placing a log for the game to step over and a branch necessary to stoop under, the two together well calculated to divert attention from the snare itself. Two long brush fences extended from the spot on either hand obtuse angled toward each other so that any animal traversing the runway would surely be led directly to the noose and get entangled while avoiding the obstacles placed to distract his attention. Unfortunately Durkee's ox, unaccustomed to such fiendish contrivances in the far-off Missouri prairies of his youth, had in this case fallen an easy victim and perished by a lingering and solitary death.

This method was practiced also by the Beaver Indians of the Liard River. Keith, describing the way in which these Indians kill large game animals, says that "they sometimes entangle them in snares made of green cords," and gives details similar to Perrot's account:

The method by which they entice the moose deer into the snare is performed thus: they clear a narrow road by felling the underwood and placing it on each side of the road so as to make an impediment for the animal to get in; in this road they leave small openings here and there upon each side, into which they set their snares with a piece of wood five or six feet long tied to the end of the snare, in order to entangle the animal in the thick woods, when taken.[18]

[18] Les Bourgeois de la Compagnie du Nord-Ouest, vol. II, p. 66, Quebec, 1890.

The Cheyennes appear to have no definite traditions of a time when they were accustomed to drive elk over a bank or a cliff into an enclosure or pit below, yet no doubt this was done, for the affiliated Arapahoes tell of the capture of elk in numbers by this method in old times, and Blackfoot stories refer to the practice. The ungulates, which collect in great herds, readily lend themselves to this method of capture. West of the Black Hills is a place where in early times the Arapahoes drove elk over the cliff, and after they had finished killing and caring for the meat, it was their practice to carry the horns of the animals to a great pile of elk-horns already heaped up and add them to it, so that at length there was an immense pile of these antlers. This heap of elk-horns was not far from where the Cheyennes had a place for killing buffalo and where they piled up the horn-sheaths of buffalo in the same way.

In his report of the trip up the Missouri River in 1850, published in the Smithsonian Report for that year, Culbertson speaks of a great pile of elk-horns heaped up, no one knows how long before, which gave its name to Elk Horn Prairie lying sixty or seventy miles above Fort Union. Culbertson visited the place and declares that at the time neither whites nor Indians knew anything about the origin of this pile of horns, and that the Indians had no traditions about it.

It is altogether probable that all the Plains Indians—certainly Arapahoes, Blackfeet, and Cheyennes—captured elk by this method.[19]

Deer were usually shot with arrows, something that was not difficult, since in old times they were very numerous, seldom frightened, easily approached, and the arrow made no noise. We may presume that the animal shot at, if wounded, did not connect its hurt with the hunter, even if it saw him.

In the country which the Cheyennes occupied in ancient times there were no wild sheep, and it was only after they had reached the plains that they met with these animals.

[19] Compare Napi story, Blackfoot Lodge Tales, p. 158.

In early days wild sheep were very numerous, and very unsuspicious and gentle. Of all the larger food animals they are said to have been the easiest to kill—less shy, even, than the buffalo. Moreover, they were exceedingly abundant in many places, as, for example, on the prairie, near the bad lands of all the streams running through the northern plains country, and about the high buttes that rise from the prairie. In the bluffs along the Yellowstone, White River, the branches of the Cheyenne River, and along the Little Missouri, as well as in the Black Hills as recently as 1860-1870, sheep were very plentiful and were usually killed with arrows.

It is well understood that most hoofed game—buffalo, antelope, deer, elk, and sheep—usually travel by certain established trails. In the days of their abundance, they always followed such trails and were not turned from them except by some alarming object. The Indians, who were constantly studying the habits of the animals on which they subsisted, were well informed as to their ways, and commonly built their pens, pitfalls, and other traps, lay in wait for, and laid their snares on or near these trails. The Indians expected the game would come to them, instead of their being obliged to search for the animals and bring them to the traps. This was not only a labor-saving practice, but also added greatly to the probability of success in securing food.

Antelope. Few people today realize that in old times the antelope in their range were probably more abundant than the buffalo. They were found in vast numbers over all the plains, but because of their small size and inconspicuous coloring, they did not impress those who saw them as did the black herds of the larger animals. The Cheyenne captured antelope in great numbers, leading them into enclosures as they did the buffalo. The methods by which this was done varied, for each man who possessed the mysterious power to accomplish the work exercised that power in his own way.

The older people have always said that when the Cheyennes first came west of the Missouri River and had worked out toward the Black Hills, they found many antelope pits already existing along the different streams. What tribe had dug and used these pits is not known. The pits or ditches were usually found near where two branches of a stream came together. The wings—often bushes piled up close together—which guided the antelope toward the pit were built along the borders of these small streams. Behind the fences and the brush wings the men, women, children, and dogs lay hidden. Resting on the piles of brush at frequent intervals were poles with one end on the ground whose weight should hold down the brush. The Cheyennes repaired many of these old pits, and used them. In those days it was very easy to pit antelope, since they were enormously abundant and overran the whole country. It may be that it was from their neighbors the Kiowas that the Cheyennes learned how to catch antelope in pits.

I shall let White Bull tell how Red Lodge did this. He said:

When I was a young man, more than fifty years ago [say 1855], my people had only a few guns. Not many white men had come into the country, and we still took the food animals in the ways that our people had always used.

When they were going to catch antelope there was always some one medicine man who told the people what they must do, and who watched to see that they did it. The man whom I saw do this was named Red Lodge. His lodge was always painted red, and from this fact he had that name. When the people needed antelope to eat, or their skins for war shirts, and when the spirits were favorable, then Red Lodge determined that antelope might be taken, and told the people what they should do.

In a broad flat they began to build two straight, tight, brush fences, eight or ten feet high, as if for the opposite sides of a square pen. From the ends of these fences on one side two lines of brush heaps about five steps apart stretched away onto the flat for 400 or 500 yards, the ends of the two lines constantly becoming farther and farther apart. This made two wings, which ran out from the ends of the tight fences, to direct the antelope to the pit. Between the ends of the tight fences opposite the side from which the wings extended, the people dug a big hole in the ground, reaching from the end of one fence to the end of the other. The side of this hole toward the opening between the wings was straight across, stretching from the end of one fence to the end of the other; the other side of the pit was rounding—a part of a circle. They dug this pit about five feet deep and

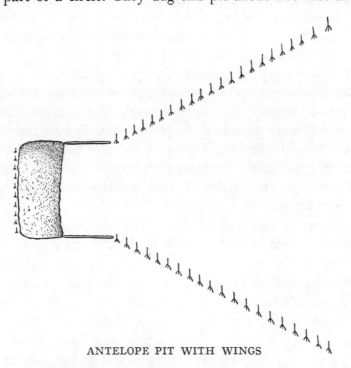

ANTELOPE PIT WITH WINGS

with sides straight up and down. On the rounding side of the pit they drove stakes in the ground and tied low bushes to them, but on the straight side they stuck in the ground bunches of grass, some of it standing up straight and some hanging over the edge of the pit so as to hide it. Outside of both the straight, high, tight fences and outside the wings they dug trenches, deep enough for people to get into and to be hidden when they were lying down. After all this had been done, they made many clubs, which were put on the ground at each end of the pit close to the ends of the high fences.

When all this was nearly finished, Red Lodge had his lodge cleaned up and prepared for the ceremony. The beds were taken out; all the family moved out and slept elsewhere. Only Red Lodge remained in his lodge. If the camp was new, and the ground not yet worn bare, and roots of grass and of weeds were still left on the floor of the lodge, the women cleared these away, so as to leave the ground bare and smooth. Then they gathered white sage, and covered the floor of the lodge next to the walls with these stems, the tops of the stems pointing toward the fire. From one of his sacred bundles Red Lodge took many antelope feet, which had been cut off at the pastern joint, and had been bent and dried so that they would stand upright on the ground. One of these feet was the right fore foot of a buck, the foot with which he paws the ground. This pawing foot Red Lodge put down on the floor of the lodge, about three feet from the wall and to the left of the door, and so to the right of the lodge man's bed. The other feet were placed on the ground, standing on their soles in circles all about the fire; but in front of the door these circles did not meet. Here, opposite the door, was left an opening about three feet wide. There were four circles of these antelope feet about the fire, one inside the other.

After the lodge had been prepared, Red Lodge went into it alone and made his medicine [*i.e.*, exercised his spiritual power]. No one knows what he did while he was there. For one day and one night he ate nothing, and all night long he sat in the lodge and sang. After he had made his medicine and was ready to call the antelope, he painted himself like an antelope—his mouth black, his back red, his belly, arms, legs, rump, and face white, and painted red streaks across his upper chest. On each temple, and running down on his cheeks, he painted an antelope horn, black. Then he was ready, and he came out of his lodge, naked except for his breechclout and moccasins. In his hand he held his own medicine pipe, which was painted red over bowl and stem. Now he walked to the opening in the pen where the wings met the fences; there he stopped and filled and lighted his pipe, then walked between the wings out onto the prairie, sang his sacred songs and held his pipe up to the Great Power [He-ammawihio], and then out toward the prairie where the antelope live. Then he walked back, still singing, between the wings and the fences until he reached the edge of the pit, where he rested the bowl of the pipe upon the ground, and prayed. Four times he went backward and forward, and sang his antelope songs. The fourth time, after he had touched the ground with the pipe bowl, he went around to the back of the pit, and placed his pipe on the ground there. The bowl was toward the pit, and the stem was leaning against a support, so that it pointed diagonally upward.

When he had placed the pipe on the ground, two young men, who had already been told what to do, started out toward the prairie, one on the right and one on the left, following out the wings so as to come in behind the antelope, and all the people hid themselves in the trenches that were dug outside the high fences and the wings.

Now, after this, Red Lodge walked about within and without the fences, holding in his hand a feather which he waved in the air, and as he walked and waved the feather, he was singing his sacred songs.

After a little time, the young men who had been sent out and were running on the prairie far beyond the ends of the wings, discovered antelope coming, and when they saw them they gave a loud, high-pitched call, which could be heard a long way. This was a signal to the people that the antelope were coming, and when they heard it everyone was glad. When the antelope had passed these young men, they turned in and ran along behind the animals, keeping up this calling until the antelope had come between the wings and were close to the pen. After the young men themselves got within the wings they began to call differently, and to imitate the hooting of an owl.

As soon as the antelope had come to the opening between the fences, all the people who had been hidden in the trenches rose and rushed toward the opening and closed it by crowding into it. They ran toward the antelope, which now were frightened and were going so fast that they could not stop, and rushed on and fell into the pit. Then men and women seized each a club, and jumping into the pit, knocked the antelope on their heads. After all were dead, the people climbed out of the pit.

Now Red Lodge went around behind the pit, took his pipe and filled it, and then sprinkled on top of the tobacco a little powdered buffalo-dung. Then he went back thirty or forty steps from the rounding side of the pit, struck fire, and lighted his pipe. He looked about on the ground until he found a small flat stone, which he picked up. He went around the fence, and entering the opening, went close to the edge of the pit, placed this little flat stone on the ground, sat down, and, resting the bowl of his pipe on the stone, he smoked there alone.

As Red Lodge smoked, he pointed the stem of his pipe at the antelope, trying to point at each one, and to offer a smoke to each. Next he smoked to the little flat stone and then gave four smokes to the direction from which the antelope came. After he had done all this, he smoked his pipe out. When he was about to begin to clean his pipe, he first pointed it in the direction whence the antelope came; then he knocked out some of the ashes on the flat stone, and pointed the pipe in the same direction. He knocked out more ashes and pointed again, and so until he had pointed four times and knocked out all the ashes on the stone. Now he took the stone, holding the ashes on it, went down through and across the pit to the other side, where he climbed out, holding the stone carefully, and going slowly, so that he should not spill the ashes, and walking away a few steps, poured the ashes off the stone to the ground in four places, finally putting down the stone and leaving it there.

After this had been done, the people went into the pit and began to cut up the antelope. First they picked out a young fat antelope— one about two years old—fat and tender. That was taken out to some high hill where everything could see it, and without being skinned it was cut up into small pieces, and left there to be eaten by the birds and by the wolves. It was a sacrifice.

After these ceremonies had been performed, the meat was divided. The medicine man let his lodge remain as it was over the next night. That night he cooked, and called in his friends, and they sat around the lodge behind the circles of antelope feet and ate. When the medicine man put away these antelope feet, he did it alone. No one knew what he did.

If after the antelope had come between the fences and before they reached the pit, they should by any chance turn back and get away without falling into the pit, it was certain that some one of the medicine man's family or relations would die.

This is the way, my friend, in which we made our living in old times. Then the animals which we ate were plenty, and our maiyun (mysterious power) was strong. Now there is nothing to eat on the prairie. Those were happy days.

In 1858, on a creek running into the Arkansas which the Cheyenne called Short Timber River,[20] antelope were captured in a similar way. William Bent's train was traveling with the Cheyennes.

At this time White Faced Bull, the father of Porcupine Bull —who witnessed the occurrence and was still living in 1914, when he gave me his recollections of what took place—made the medicine for calling the antelope, and the next day brought them in. This White Faced Bull was the uncle of old White Faced Bull and of Ē hyōph′ stă, Northern Cheyennes, who have died within a few years.

During the preliminary ceremonies White Faced Bull with a number of older men began to sing in the lodge, but before the singing began certain young men, Porcupine Bull among them, stood outside the lodge and with sticks beat on the poles in the time of the song which was to be sung. They struck the four important poles, the three which are tied together and the one at the back, to which the lodge covering is tied. They tried to strike first the pole to the east, then the one to the southwest, then the one to the northeast, and last the pole to which the lodge covering is tied. After those outside had struck these poles the singing began. During this singing, if all was to go well, antelope hair would begin to fall in the lodge. The amount of antelope hair that fell showed how successful the drive was to be. If only a little fell, few antelope would be taken; if much, many antelope would be killed.

This was the song that all sang, addressing the medicine man:

White Faced Bull, come crying, and bring with you your antelope arrow = *Hotūa′ wō′ hē ĭs wo′ kai hi′ ma hŏts′ nīh′ no a ka nĭhsts* [*nĭh no a ka nĭhsts*, addressed to a single person].

[20] Now Wild Horse Creek.

They sang this three times, and as they sang it the fourth time the air in the lodge suddenly became filled with antelope hair, flying about the lodge. When the hair commenced to fly, White Faced Bull said to his fellows: "There, I told you that if plenty of antelope hair fell from the lodge-skins we should have good luck: You can see how it is for yourselves!"

The next morning two implements called antelope arrows (*wō' kaī hī mā hŏts'*) were made. They looked like this:

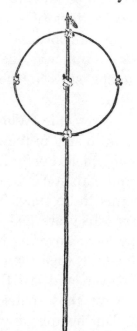

The pole is three feet long and the hoop about ten inches in diameter. At four places about the hoop and to the pole at the center of the hoop, were tied strips of rabbit-skin, and with each strip a single raven-feather. To the upper end of the upright, by a string, was tied a gray-eagle feather. The pole and hoop were of slender willow twigs, a half or three-quarters of an inch in diameter. Hoops and uprights were painted black. They were made in public, out of doors, and without ceremony. All might watch the operation.

After these antelope arrows had been made, White Faced

Bull took them in his hands, mounted his horse, and rode off in the direction in which the antelope were thought to be, and the whole camp—men, women, and children—followed him. After a time White Faced Bull stopped and dismounted. All the different bands of soldiers formed in one broad-fronted line, abreast. White Faced Bull on foot stood about thirty feet in front of the line. He spoke and said, "Have two young unmarried women come up here." Cow Woman (Ō ōhk′ stǎ) came and sat on one side of White Faced Bull, and then Single White Buffalo Woman (Wōhk′ pǐ mǐ hǐh′) came and sat on the other side. Both young women were strong and plump and of good, kindly disposition. If the women selected were ill-natured, the antelope would act badly and could not be caught. If one or both women were lean or thin, the antelope caught would be thin and poor. White Faced Bull sat down on the ground between the two young women, wearing his robe hair-side out. The young men—the soldiers—who had been told what to do, began changing their horses.

White Faced Bull held the antelope arrows, one in each hand, and raised and crossed his arms four times, at each crossing drawing his arms toward his body, for the purpose of drawing antelope toward him, to call them. While doing this, he told the girls what to do: they must go straight ahead and look straight ahead; if they looked back or to either side, the antelope would do the same. He crossed his arms a fifth time, and the girl on either side grasped from the hand of White Faced Bull the arrow which was nearest her, each seizing the shaft above White Faced Bull's hand. As soon as they had taken the arrows, the girls started on a run diagonally forward. After they had gone a little way, they were followed by two young men riding fast and long-winded horses, who were supposed to be their sweethearts and to be trying to take the arrows from them. After the young men had started, the soldiers moved forward in two long lines on either side, following these two young men, and all the young men followed the soldiers. White

Faced Bull sat there. No one knew where the antelope were or even if there were any antelope.

Soon the young men riding each on the outside of one of the girls overtook them and reached down and took from each her arrow, and the girls dropped back.

After the young men had gone, the old men, the women, and the children stepped up into the places where the young men had been, and stood on either side of White Faced Bull, making a long line, reaching forward at the ends—a crescent—so as to make the beginning of a circle. At the ends of the line were many young women who were riding good horses. They held in their hands the forked poles that women use to support their drying scaffolds.

The leading young men, who carried the antelope arrows, rode fast out on the prairie, getting farther and farther apart, until at length the distance between them must have been two miles; and now it was seen that between them there were many antelope, which, instead of running away, began to run toward White Faced Bull. When the young men in either line—those who were following the men who carried the antelope arrows—saw that there were many antelope between them, and that they were running thick together, then the two men with the antelope arrows turned and rode toward each other, and those who followed them began to close in. The leaders continued to ride toward each other, and then passed each other, and each rode back on the outside of the lines to where White Faced Bull was standing. The other mounted men did not follow them, but met and closed in on the antelope, riding not behind the antelope but rather at the sides of the herds. The young men were whooping and calling, to drive the antelope toward White Faced Bull.

The leading young man who reached White Faced Bull first handed him his antelope arrow. Then the other came up and gave him the other arrow. Now White Faced Bull stood holding one antelope arrow in each hand.

Porcupine Bull was back near his father, and he had seen, a long way off, the soldiers tossing their robes as a signal that something was coming. The women and children now dismounted and formed a circle about White Faced Bull, and the old men began to call out to him to get into the center of the circle. The people in the circle all held their blankets or robes spread out behind them, and got close together so as to make a barrier that the antelope could not get through.

White Faced Bull called his son to come with him into the middle of the circle. Now the antelope were coming fast, and soon they entered the circle, which by this time was almost complete. It was still large, but was growing smaller all the time. White Faced Bull held the antelope arrows in his hands and made motions with them, and whenever he did so the antelope turned in the direction toward which he motioned. There were many antelope, and when one band suddenly turned and ran into another, the antelope piled up in a struggling heap, so that many were knocked down and broke their legs, or were hurt in other ways.

When the antelope began to run around inside the circle, they made the old man dizzy, and he said to his son, "Let us get out of here!" As he started to move, the antelope stopped and looked at him, and the old men on the outside cried, "Do not move!" He stopped and made a motion with his arrows, and the antelope moved in the direction in which he motioned. He caused them to run first one way and then another. He did this to confuse them, so that they would run first in one direction and then in another, and against and over one another. They soon became entirely exhausted.

When this took place all the people broke out of the circle and ran toward the antelope. It had been ordered that morning that neither guns nor bows and arrows should be used. The women were armed with forked sticks, poles, and axes with short, straight handles, even root-diggers, which they used to knock down the antelope. Men used ropes and boys did the same, catching the antelope and dragging them away. Women who knocked down antelope claimed those that they had killed. Some stranger Indians were present in the village, but they were not allowed to enter the circle for fear they might shoot and hurt someone.

The very few antelope which got out of the circle were followed by the mounted men and all killed. With the antelope were wolves, coyotes, kit foxes, and rabbits.

The antelope killed in the circle were all dragged to its center where White Faced Bull had stood, and were placed in rows— all the oldest bucks in a row together, then a row of younger ones, and then others still younger in rows, till they reached the kids. The females were all placed in similar rows by age. White Faced Bull selected his antelope, choosing only two for himself, but all the tongues came to him. The two girls and the two young men who carried the antelope arrows were called up and told to choose each an antelope. Then the men cut out the tongues, and two women carried them in a big blanket to White Faced Bull, telling him that there was his food. They made heavy loads for the two women.

There were six hundred lodges of Cheyennes, and every woman had an antelope. The antelope were so many that the leanest ones were not saved—only their hides were taken off. Bent's wagon train had all the antelope it could use.

A buck antelope had helped White Faced Bull and once coming up to him had sung this:

Hĭs tŭm ĭ ŭm' Hī tă īn ī' ŏm.

The words of the antelope song sung by White Faced Bull are mostly forgotten, but one of the songs was recalled and sung by Porcupine Bull:

Hī tā īn ī' ō mŏn ĭ, Nā nĭss' ōn ĭ.
(All will   be gone   My children)

This is repeated in several songs.

WHITE BULL,
ONE OF GENERAL MILES' SCOUTS

On three occasions afterward White Faced Bull did this same thing, but none of the other surrounds was as successful as this one.

Old Indians say that in leading the antelope into pits, antelope arrows were often used and moved in the same way, and that the medicine man who was drawing the antelope to the pit motioned toward it with the antelope arrows.

Antelope were last called into the pits on Antelope Pit River —the Little Missouri—in 1865, by Curly Hair. His daughter was still alive a few years ago, at Cantonment, Oklahoma.

This account of the antelope drive may be compared with the very similar description of the same operation among the Kiowas,[21] who appear to have carried antelope arrows not unlike those used by White Faced Bull. There are minor differences in the two accounts, but on the whole the resemblance is close. Mr. Mooney, however, intimates that the antelope drive was made only in seasons of scarcity, and only in winter, at which season the antelope were accustomed to gather in large herds, while in spring and summer they scattered. The Cheyennes, on the other hand, made antelope drives at any season of the year, whenever antelope skins were required for women's dresses. It is true that in winter the antelope went in large herds; but it is also true that in early days they were enormously abundant, and in favorable localities large numbers were seen at any season of the year.

A woman born in the winter of 1851-1852 described an antelope pit she had seen as a girl, which was made additionally safe by having erected just beyond it a sort of fence made of poles set in the ground at an angle and crossing each other near their upper ends, and there tied together. Behind these poles branches and weeds were piled up so that it was impossible to see through the obstruction. Across the top of the pit were laid several large logs, on which, after the antelope were in the

21 Mooney, Kiowa Calendar, p. 288.

pit, women walked out and lying down on the logs reached down and killed the antelope by blows on the head.

The antelope arrows described by Porcupine Bull were used only on the flat prairie and for the purpose of drawing the antelope into a circle of people. Other antelope arrows, described by Little Hawk, consisted of a long upright, with a short cross-piece tied to it near the upper end. The upright and the cross-piece were wound with a strip of wolf fur, and to the top of the upright was tied a magpie feather.

In ancient times, long before they had horses, certain men are said to have possessed especial skill in calling the antelope and to have devoted much of their time to this work. It is said that these men often remained in certain favorable situations to perform this function while the tribe moved off and left them. These men gave all their time to leading the antelope into pits, killing them, and drying the meat and skins, which the tribe found on its return.

The number of men and women still alive who have witnessed this method of securing antelope justifies the belief that it was in use up to the year 1870 or even later.

Bears. The Cheyennes killed no grizzly bears on the plains for they feared them. That black bears were often killed, however, is shown by the frequent statements that the skin of the black bear was commonly used as a covering or wrapper for a shield.

She Bear told of the killing of a black bear that must have happened not long after 1860. While riding over the prairie with a friend of his own age, a bear came out of a ravine not far off. The two boys raced after it on horseback, overtook and shot it with arrows, and finally killed it.

Stories are told of man-eating grizzly bears, animals that habitually preyed on the people, lying in wait for and capturing them, and even driving large camps away from favorite camping places. Such stories go back to a time before the coming of the whites, for the acquisition of horses and of iron-pointed arrowheads tended to put the Indian more nearly on an equality with his brute enemy than he was when he traveled afoot and his piercing weapons were of stone. In primitive times every advantage was with the bear. It was swift of foot, enduring, and hard to kill. Its tough muscles, heavy fur, strong hide, and thick coating of fat were hardly to be pierced by the primitive arrow.

Horses. While in later years the Cheyennes secured their horses chiefly by capture from their enemies, in earlier days— say in the latter part of the eighteenth and the first half of the nineteenth centuries—they captured many wild horses. There were professional horse-chasers, who devoted much time to this work, and who possessed swift and enduring horses, which were kept always in good training, so that they should be strong, tough, and long-winded.

The first horses on the recent plains were brought by Coronado, who, on his march from Mexico to Quivira in Kansas, penetrated almost to the Missouri River, and not very long before this the mounted troops of De Soto had crossed the Mississippi and come almost to the edge of the plains. No doubt horses were lost by both expeditions, and those that thus escaped found themselves in a favorable environment, in which there were no natural enemies. Since there was nothing to check their increase, they multiplied astonishingly. As early as 1680 there were horses among the Pawnees and other tribes of the Missouri, and from that time on horses spread with great rapidity from south to north.

The Spaniards in Mexico possessed great herds, and while many of them were branded, many escaped the iron and became truly wild. These wild horses were captured by the Spaniards in various ways, usually in corrals toward which the horses were driven between diverging wings until they entered the pen. They were seldom run down and captured with the rope. The Kiowas followed the practice of penning wild horses employed by the Spaniards, but among the Cheyennes I find no tradition of any such method of taking horses.

However, in the year 1836, members of Cheyenne war-parties who had gone from the Black Hills southward almost to the Washita River, in what is now Oklahoma, found a great corral which had been used for.catching horses. This pen was situated in a park or opening in the black-jack timber which formerly covered much of the country of central Oklahoma, but was later largely destroyed by prairie fires. This pen was not circular in shape, but was oval, the opening being at one end. The fence was not made after the fashion of a white man's fence, but was a stockade formed of black-jack posts set on end in the ground and close together. On the outside of the fence brush and the limbs of trees were piled against the stockade. The wings of underbrush were heaped up high and wide, so that a horse could neither see through nor jump over them. The corral showed that it had been used for catching horses, yet not for a long time, for in many places the posts which formed the fence were partly rotted and were falling down.

Though at first greatly puzzled by this enclosure, the Cheyennes who discovered it at length reasoned out what it had been used for, and years afterward, when peace had been made between the Cheyennes and Arapahoes on the one side and Kiowas and Comanches on the other, the Kiowas explained to the Cheyennes the purpose and the manner of use of the structure. Of the horses driven into this corral the best young ones were roped and dragged out to be used, while the older and otherwise less useful animals were butchered for their flesh and hides. The Kiowas used horse-hide for all purposes for which the skins of large animals are employed—for moccasins, lodge linings, lodge coverings, and even for robes and sheets.

It is impossible to say whether the Kiowas may have borrowed from the Spaniards this custom of impounding horses, or whether it was an adaptation of the old-time Indian method of catching buffalo and antelope. The latter conclusion seems more probable, and it is certain that the methods pursued in getting the horses between the brush wings leading to the corral were the same as were practiced in bringing in antelope and buffalo.

The Cheyennes did not become expert in the use of the lasso, or reata, employed by Mexicans and cowboys before the second half of the nineteenth century. They used the slip-noose, to be sure, but did not throw the rope. Their method was to hold the loop open by tying it with light strings to a hoop formed of a long willow twig, which was passed over the head of the wild horse, if the rider could come close enough to do this.

A further development of the use of the slip-noose was a change by which the rider carried a light pole, to which the loop of the rope was attached by strings, so that this loop might be passed over the head of the horse. It was probably not until after the year 1850 that the horse-chasers learned to throw the rope with much success. Still later, as certain horse-catchers became more skillful with the rope, they began to carry extra ropes coiled and tucked under their belts. Another man on a good horse followed the one who used the rope, and when the wild horse was noosed, the second man took the rope and choked down the wild animal, leaving the roper free to follow another wild horse.

It will readily be understood that, provided things were otherwise nearly equal, a horse running free could not be overtaken by one that was carrying a hundred and fifty or two hundred pounds of weight, and from this it follows that the horses captured were chiefly old and slow ones, and that the best horses always escaped. For this reason a favorite season for chasing wild horses was toward the end of the winter or in early spring, when, through insufficient food and cold weather, a proportion of the wild herds had become thin and weak. The horse-chasers, on the other hand, watched their running horses with care and endeavored to keep them in good condition, and at this season it was not difficult for them to overtake mares that were thin from suckling their colts, or those that were heavy with foal.

When the wild horse had been caught, the work was only half done. It was necessary that the animal should be kept from running away, and yet the men of the party could not be constantly occupied in watching the horses. This difficulty was overcome by the device of taking with them on their expeditions for horses a number of gentle mares to be used in handling the wild horses when first taken. Some of these gentle mares were commonly driven out on the chase. The captured wild horse was choked down, thrown to the ground, and its feet tied. A head-stall, or hackamore, was put on its head, a rope tied about the neck with a knot that would not run up, and the rope passed down through the head-stall. A gentle mare was then brought up, and after a knot had been tied in her tail, the rope leading from the wild horse's head was tied about the mare's tail with a slack of three or four feet between the head and the tail. To keep the struggling wild horse from injuring the mare during its first efforts to escape, her tail was bent around to one side and the loose end of the rope was passed along her side to the base of the neck, where it was tied about the neck just in front of the shoulders by a knot that could not draw up. To prevent this large loop from slipping forward, it was tied to the mare's mane, just above the withers, by a deerskin string.

The feet of the wild horse were now untied. When it sprang up it plunged and struggled for a time, but soon became quiet and thereafter followed the mare without trouble. Three or four days later, when it had come to know the mare well and perhaps to be attached to her, it was set free, and thereafter followed her about wherever she went. The mare was then used to tame another horse, and if the party was out for a long time some mares might have eight or ten captured horses following them about. These wild horses were readily broken to the saddle. While they were "tailed" to the mare, the owner would occasionally go up to the mare, pat her for a little while, and then pass on to the young horse, handling it and gentling it. In this way it became accustomed to the sight and smell of man, and no longer feared him. Sometimes after the horse had become somewhat gentle, a young man would spring on its back and at once jump off again. The wild horse soon learned that it was not to be hurt. The man who mounted would presently sit on the horse for a little while, and then the old mare might be led about by someone while the young man was sitting on the wild horse's back. Thus the work of breaking it to ride was not long.

It rarely happened that a horse tailed to a gentle mare would attempt to drive her away from the camp and out on the prairie —in some direction that he wished to take. This was provided against, however, by hobbling the mare so that she could go only slowly.

The wild horses ran on the prairie in bands of from thirty to fifty mares and young animals, all of them under the leadership of some old stallion who kept them together and drove intruders away. Such an old stallion drove out of the herd all of the young colts, two, three, and four years old, and these were often found on the prairie by themselves in considerable herds. Indian horse-catchers, if such a herd of young horses was seen—and they were readily recognized by their shorter manes and tails, and light frames—often drove out toward such a company a few gentle mares, when the wild horses usually ran toward and mingled with them, and after a time the herd could be approached, driven together, and perhaps many of the young horses caught. If it were practicable to give them time to become acquainted with the old, gentle mares, they often did not attempt to run away, and many of them were captured.

Beaver. Until intercourse with white men had taught them that the skins of beaver had a value for trading purposes, the

Cheyennes made no systematic effort to trap these animals. They killed them for food and used the skins for clothing, and they trained dogs to hunt them.

When a beaver-dam and houses were found, it was the practice to break away the dam so as to lower the water about the houses, and then to find the hole by which the beaver entered the house or the bank. The dogs used were small enough to enter this hole and yet were of fair size. A dog, sent into the hole, found the beaver and barked at and worried it until it became angry, so that it fought back and finally followed the dog out. As the dog gradually backed away, barking at the beaver, it made short rushes at him, and finally the dog backed clear out of the hole, and when the beaver jumped out after the dog, the man standing there knocked the beaver on the head with a club. They also shot beaver with arrows, watching for them by their ponds; and in the same way they occasionally shot otter. The fur of the otter was highly valued for covering for bow-cases and quivers, and for hair wrapping.

In connection with the first method of catching the beaver, a mysterious story is told:

A long time ago a beaver-dam had been found and broken down. Close by was a large camp of Cheyennes, and people came out to see what was being done. When the water had receded, an unusually large hole was seen, leading into a beaver house. One young man said to the others, "I will creep in there myself and see if I can find the beaver." He went into the house, feeling with his hands as he went; presently he felt something alive, and supposed it was a beaver's hind leg. He called out, "I have got him by the hind leg!" By this time many people—men, women, and children—stood about on the bank watching.

A woman in the crowd called, "Hold him! I will run and get a rope, and you can tie it to the leg and we will pull him out!" The woman ran to the camp and got a buffalo-hair rope, and it was passed into the hole to the young man, who tied it to the leg and himself came out. Men and boys took hold of the rope and began to pull on the beaver, but it seemed heavy. They could hardly move it. They kept pulling and pulling, and presently there appeared at the hole a man's foot, and then the whole of a person appeared, sitting up and holding back, but hitching himself along as he was pulled. It was an old man with long white hair—an Indian.

Just as he came in sight the rope slipped off his foot, and the people, who were frightened at what they saw, all ran away. Only the young man remained; he stood there coiling the rope, and when he had finished he hung it on the limb of a tree, when he too ran away. No one ever went back there again, for they were afraid of the place. They often talked of this, and the people thought that this must have been a mysterious beaver that had changed itself into a man, to keep the Cheyennes from killing it.

Toward the end of the eighteenth century the Cheyennes no doubt had learned the value of beaver-fur from the French traders who had penetrated the Black Hills. According to Perrin du Lac,[22] they were great beaver hunters and killed many, which they sold to the Sioux. Before this they had perhaps learned the uses of the steel trap, yet it may be doubted if they were ever a tribe of trappers. I have heard in modern times of only one Cheyenne who made a business of trapping with steel traps. Trudeau[23] says that in 1795 the tribes living on the Cheyenne River, above the Cheyennes, did not gather fur at all, and that a good trade with them might be set on foot if horses were furnished him with which to take trade goods to these people.

Gray Wolves. Big wolves were caught in pitfalls, made so deep that the animals could not jump out, the sides being dug away toward the bottom, so that the hole at top was somewhat smaller than the width at the bottom, which was about six feet. On opposite sides of the opening of this hole, two pairs of stakes were driven in the ground, two inches or more apart, and between these stakes on either side, and reaching across the

[22] Travels in Louisiana, p. 63, London, 1807.
[23] Missouri Hist. Soc. Colls., vol. IV, p. 9, St. Louis, 1912.

hole, was laid a pole to which a bait of small pieces of meat was tied. The horizontal pole at either end was lashed to the two stakes between which it lay, and thus could not be moved.

Large weed stalks were split and laid close together from the pole to the ground on either side, and over these grass and earth were scattered, so that the covering of the pit looked as nearly as possible like the ground about it. The wolf, attracted by the bait, ventured out on the split weeds, which broke with his weight and let him fall into the pit, either as he was reaching for the bait or leaving it.

Trapping Foxes. Except for purposes of ornamentation, the old-time Cheyennes made little use of small furs. For clothing, shelter, and bedding they used the skins of large animals. Nevertheless, they trapped foxes in deadfalls.

In constructing the trap a little trench was dug in the ground, and over it was built a small house of willow twigs, thrust in the ground on either side of the trench and bent in a half-circle. Over these twigs was put grass, and then earth, and on the earth were placed the thorny leaves of the prickly-pear (*Opuntia*), so that the fox should not dig nor scratch at the roof of the house, which was open only at one end. Leading up to the little door of the house a fence was built on either side of the trench, and at the door a dead-fall of ordinary type was arranged, the fall log and the bottom log being lodge-poles. The bait was a bit of tallow slightly roasted, and placed on a spindle inside the house. A pull at the bait dislodged the spindle and the supporting stick (called *mō wǐsh kǔn'*, finger), and the log fell on the fox's neck or back, killing it.

After a trap had been set, the person who had made it often went off to one side a little distance and sang, calling the foxes. Sometimes when one of these traps was first made, the women and children would gather around the singer and dance to the time of the song, the words of which ran as follows:

Come, fox, I have meat for you—
Ni nāī' ĭs mā hō' ĭs tām' ĭ na' hĭt hō ē' wō
Come, fox, I have food for you—*Ni nāī' ĭs mā hō' ĭs tām' ĭ na' hĭt*
Come, fox, I have food for you—*Ni nāī' ĭs mā hō' ĭs tām' ĭ na' hĭt*

Small Wolves. Sometimes larger traps of this type were made, in which coyotes were caught, and sometimes, but not often, big wolves got into them and were secured. However, such deadfalls were not set for these large animals, which were usually too strong for them.

Eagle catching. The feathers from the tail of the eagle were highly valued for use in adornment and for trade with other tribes, and at the proper season of the year some men devoted much effort to catching the birds. This, however, might not be done by everyone, for the eagle catchers were regarded as possessing much spiritual power. They alone might make the eagle medicine.

Eagle catching was practiced in the spring, when the birds first appeared, and again in the fall, when they were going south. Only certain people engaged in this work—chiefly old men—those who had ceased going on the war-path. The young men who wore war-bonnets rarely caught eagles themselves, but procured the feathers from the old men. While engaged in the work of eagle catching, these old men used only one certain vessel to drink from in the evening, and this vessel no one else might use. At this time these men were obliged to keep to some extent apart, and were not allowed to touch even their own children; each one slept by himself.

Each man had his own method, and each thought his own way the best. The Cheyennes always declared that they were the most successful eagle catchers, and that after them came the Arapahoes.

Two or three of the different methods practiced by men who were well known as eagle catchers are given here.

A man who wished to catch eagles for the first time offered

299

the pipe to one who understood this, and by him was taught the secrets of the work.

One who intended to go out to catch eagles made his preparations in his lodge, alone. The lodge was cleared out and the floor about the fire was covered—not very thickly—with white sage, the stems pointing away from the fire. While the eagle catcher was making his medicine, the fire was burning brightly, and he sang alone in the lodge all through the night.

After he had made the medicine, he left the camp without telling where he was going. In a suitable place on a hill he dug a pit large enough for a man to sit in with outstretched legs, but not long enough for lying down. Often the pit was small at the top, but hollowed out under the sides. He carried the earth from this pit far away, and scattered it. He covered the narrow hole by laying across it lengthwise a pole, to which was tied long grass, which hung over on each side and concealed the hole. Spaces through which he could look were left in this grass, or sticks covered with grass were put over the opening of the pit.

The digging of the pit was a work of time, for eagles are keen-sighted and wise, and the earth and rubbish must be carried a long distance. Before going into the pit, the eagle catcher took a sweat-bath, so as to dispel the human odor. He went to the pit for four successive days, and on the evening of the fourth day, when he returned to his lodge, he took four sweat-baths.

The bait, tied down so that it should not be carried off, was often a fresh wolf skin to which a piece of the meat was attached, laid flesh side up across the sticks; or it might be a rabbit. The sticks laid across the mouth of the pit were far enough apart so that the hands might be passed between them. The floor of the pit was covered with white sage, which men carried up in their blankets from the lower ground. Very early in the morning, before he started to go to the pit, the man combed his hair and painted himself all over with red greasepaint, the grease being the fat of eagles. He set out long before daylight so as to be there before the eagles were moving about.

After all had been made ready, the man went to the place and entered the hole while it was still dark. When in the pit he did not eat or drink. He must go for four successive days. If he tried for four days without success, he thought that some mistake had been made—that the laws had not been properly followed. He had with him a small rope of buffalo hair to be used to kill the eagle by strangling it. Some people used a bowstring for this purpose, while others merely broke the eagle's neck. The man sat in the hole and waited for the eagles to come. Perhaps a bird flying over saw the bait and kept circling about it, getting lower and lower.

Until it began to eat, the eagle was very cautious, hovering around the bait, stretching out first one foot and then the other, before alighting. The man heard its feet strike when it alighted, and while the eagle was tearing at the bait the man very slowly reached up through the grass and grasped the bird by the feet. He pulled it into the pit, slipped over the head the noose of the rope, or a bowstring tied to his foot so that he could pull strongly, and killed it by strangling. Men have been known to catch as many as twenty eagles in one of these pits, and to have caught several in one day. Once a man named Wolf Fire got hold of an eagle so large that it nearly pulled him out of the pit.

Each night the man took his eagles home, for it was the law that the eagles must be brought to camp just as they were caught. Not a feather must be pulled out in the pit. At the camp, close by his lodge, two forked stakes had been set up in the ground, in the forks of which lay two slender poles, like lodge-poles. These were tied together at one end, but were loose at the other. When the man brought home an eagle he slipped its foot between the two poles at their loose ends, brought the ends together, and slid the foot along until it was firmly held. There he left it hanging. Some men were free to leave the pit at any time, but might not enter it except at night, when it was dark; others might not leave the pit until sundown, no matter how many eagles had been caught.

When a man had caught as many birds as he needed, he stopped. After this he began to pluck the feathers from the birds, taking only those from the tails and the wings. He put the feathers away, carried the bodies off a long way from camp, placed them on the ground side by side in a row, and left them there. The feathers he gave to the people, who gave him something in return, perhaps a horse for twenty or thirty feathers. Four kinds of eagles are known—the eagle that has a white head, and the gray one that is its young, and the war-eagle and its young.

The method of eagle catching was closely similar to that practiced by the Arikaras and the Blackfeet. It was not without its dangers. It is related that an eagle once killed a Sioux Indian by piercing an artery in his arm with its talons, so that the man bled to death.

Another method practiced in the early part of the nineteenth century was described by Ridge Bear, who had it from his mother, who was born before 1820.

When a man purposed to catch eagles, he, with his family, moved away from the main camp, put up his lodge wherever he had decided to stop, and near it put up another lodge. The floor of the second lodge was smoothed and leveled, and all around its border next to the lodge covering was spread a nice bed of white sage. This lodge was for the eagles that he expected to catch: they were to be placed on the bed of sage, with the heads pointing toward the fireplace. The man prepared a number of balls of pounded corn and a number of balls of pounded meat, and these were placed about the edge of the bed in pairs—a ball of meat and a ball of meal together—as many pairs of balls as he hoped to catch eagles.

The man greased his whole body with eagle fat so as to conceal the human scent. He entered the pit in the morning before daylight and remained there until after sundown.

In the evening when he returned from the pit with the eagles he had caught, he called to his family as he approached the camp and told them to enter the eagles' lodge. He went in and placed his eagles on the bed of sage, the head of each one being near a pair of the balls of food. Then to each one of his family the man gave a mouthful of food from two of the balls. The family then left the lodge and the man remained there for the night.

Four days were spent thus in eagle catching, and at the end of this time the man moved to the main camp with his eagles.

Some people were fortunate in eagle catching, while others never caught any eagles. It was thought that those who were continually unlucky were not likely to live long.

Often there was great rivalry among eagle catchers, each one trying to outdo the other, and some would not stop at anything to attain their desires. A story is told of Ridge Bear's grandfather, who is supposed to have sacrificed his daughter to the maiyun in order that he might have success in eagle catching.

Some eagle catchers, especially those beginning the work, did not offer the eagles food when they brought them in. They were laid in a place by themselves. He who had killed them took a pipe and held it to each bird, asking it to take pity on him. This was in his own lodge, which had been cleaned out and the floor covered with white sage. Every time he caught birds, he called in the old eagle catchers who had taught him, and filled his pipe and offered it to each bird, saying: "I did not kill you without thought [i.e., without a reason]. We want to wear you." Food and water were then passed into the lodge, and one of the old eagle catchers put medicine on the food. After that the novice drank the water, then ate, and did not drink again before he started out before daylight the next day. Before sleeping, he removed the feathers and piled them up in his lodge, but took out the bodies and left them a long way off. The feathers were not touched again till he had finished his four days' hunt. Then he divided the wing-feathers among those whom he wished to have them. The old men used wings for fans. There were always many buyers for the tail-feathers. Eagles were the only birds in connection with the killing of which there was a ceremony.

On the highest of the three bald hills in the Muddy Divide a little east of south of Lamedeer, to the northeast of the house of the late William Rowland, Sr. (now occupied by Ed. Powell), are two unroofed shelters—eagle pits—of stones and logs, the walls being about four feet high. These hills are about as high as the Tongue River Divide. On two of them are monuments, a few great stones heaped up to a height of four or five feet, and of about the same diameter at the bottom. One of the hills that bears a monument has at the other end of its highest part the eagle pits referred to. These constitute a single structure, or perhaps two adjoining structures, roughly built of the irregular, large, burned rocks which crop out in a ledge on the summit of the hill. Advantage has been taken of this outcrop in building the shelters, and one great rock projecting from the ground to a height of six or seven feet forms the wall of a part of each pit. Other rocks, estimated to weigh several hundred pounds each, appear to be in place. Other stones, large and small, have been used to make a wall for the two structures, the ground-plan of which is something like the rough sketch which is shown on the following page.

The long chamber lies about north and south; the oval chamber is east of the long chamber and at its north end. The walls within and without are irregular, for some of the stones project more or less into the chamber. The lesser width of the long chamber is 1 foot 11½ inches, and its length 7 feet 2 inches, or long enough for a man to lie down in. The average height of the wall of this chamber is nearly four feet, but the great stone at the north end, already spoken of as apparently

POUNDING CHERRIES

in place, is higher than a man's head—seven or eight feet. The wall of the oval chamber is not quite so high as that of the long chamber. The width of the oval enclosure from east to west is 5 feet 3 inches, and its length about 6 feet. This would be too short for a man to lie in, because of the irregularity of the walls.

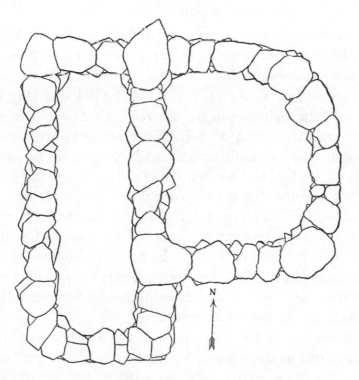

Compared with the country immediately surrounding it, the elevation of this construction is considerable, and a bait exposed here would be more likely to attract a bird's eye than one at a less altitude. It is thus very favorably situated.

Such pits were used not for catching eagles only, but also the larger hawks, whose feathers were much used for purposes of ornamentation.

When I first saw these pits, many years ago, no vegetation grew in them, though they showed no signs of recent use. In

1916, however, seeds of the black currant, presumably dropped by birds, had sprouted, and several hardy plants were growing in the enclosures.

The structures are old, but how old no one can tell. It is possible that they may have been built by the predecessors of the Cheyennes in this country, Crows or others, but they have undoubtedly been used by the Cheyennes. There are said to be other such shelters in these hills.

The monuments spoken of are watchers' stations for young men looking out for enemies or for game. They appear to be not so old as the eagle pits.

Such enclosures were roofed with slender poles or long weed-stalks, and the bait spread on the roof. Certain old men say that the eagle catcher, after going into the enclosure, remained there night and day until he was ready to give up his attempt to catch eagles for the time being. He did not leave the shelter; he neither ate nor drank, nor wore any robe or blanket while he remained in it. This was partly an act of sacrifice, but besides that, if the eagle catcher was hungry, the eagles that he was trying to catch were likely to be hungry also, and so would descend to his bait. When he was successful in catching eagles —getting perhaps ten on one expedition—he was permitted to paint his hands in token of his success.

The main use of the feathers was for war-bonnets, and in those days two or three horses might be paid for a war-bonnet. The small feathers were sometimes used to feather arrows.

In later times eagles were secured also by finding a place where the birds roosted. Under the tree a bark house was built, which the man entered, carrying his rifle, and patiently waited there until the eagle alighted in the tree, when he shot it.

The old method of eagle catching began to pass out of use when the Cheyennes obtained guns. It has not been extensively practiced for about three generations, but was in common use by the grandfathers of the old men of the present day in the early part of the last century. The last man who ever used one of the pits was Red Wolf, who died in 1893. Since about 1860-1861 such pits have not been used much, if at all. The people say they came to fear the practice, and abandoned it.

Turtles. In the country of the Northern Cheyennes there are few water turtles, but they are abundant in the southern country, and are commonly captured and eaten. In the pools and streams where turtles are plentiful, those searching for them often watched on the bank for the turtles to come to the surface of the water to breathe. When the men or boys saw them, they dived into the stream, swam under the turtles, and usually caught them in their hands.

Sometimes men waded along in the water in a long line, feeling for the turtles with their feet. If one was felt, they tried to determine the direction it took in trying to escape, and one man after another plunged under the water and endeavored to grasp it with the hands. Often they succeeded.

Sometimes a circle was formed of men, women, and children, surrounding a place in the water where turtles were known to be abundant. The people closed in slowly, and sometimes the turtles all moved to the center of the circle, or some of them tried to pass through the ring of people to go to the bank. If a man chanced to step on one of the turtles, he kept his foot on it, pressing it against the bottom, and called one of his fellows, who dived down and, following the man's leg, caught the turtle. When a man put his foot on a snapping turtle, he knew what it was by the notched ridge on the back, and could tell where it should be caught; that is to say, either by the tail or the hind leg. These turtles were not to be caught near the head, because they bite; indeed, people were sometimes severely bitten by snapping turtles. Soft-shell turtles were hard to catch, for they swim fast, are smooth and slippery, and so are hard to hold.

Where there is moss on the bottom of a stream or a pond, the turtles are easily caught, for they become entangled, but where there is no moss on the bottom, they are hard to catch, for they can swim and walk fast. In such a case horses were sometimes driven into the water, and the turtles kept moving until they became tired and remained in one place.

Sometimes when turtles were abundant, and only one or two men or boys were together, they tied grass and willows about their heads, and very slowly approaching a turtle at the surface, put the hands under it and caught it.

Turtles were killed by putting their heads in a fire, after which the side, near the hind legs, was opened and the entrails drawn out and thrown away. Then a large fire was built, and the turtles were placed about it, standing up on the edges of their shells, and thus roasted. Some people boiled the turtles in their shells.

Fish catching. The Cheyennes formerly caught fish, and in this respect were quite unlike some of their neighbors on the plains. It may be conjectured that they brought from their earlier eastern home their fondness for fish, as well as the methods which they employed in taking them. A story describing the earliest fish catching practice treats of a period long, long ago, but after the people had obtained bows and arrows:

A long time ago a man and his wife who were traveling alone far from the main camp had almost nothing to eat. The woman dug roots and gathered berries when she could find any, and the man hunted hard and tried to kill either game or birds, but they were near starvation, for they found little to eat. They were camped by a small stream, and, as the man was walking along the bank one day, he saw something dart through the water. He looked again, and saw fish, many little ones, and some big—half as long as his arm. When he returned to camp he spoke to his wife about this, telling her that he had seen fish in the stream. He said, "If we could catch some of these fish, then we should have something to eat."

He thought much about this, and at last decided what to do. He went to where willow bushes grew near the camp, and cut many small, slender shoots, which he took to camp. Then he and his wife tied these sticks close together, and made something like a back-rest, long enough to reach across the stream, which was only two or three steps wide and about half a leg deep. Then he said to his wife, "Come now, take one end of this and we will go to the stream." When they had got there he said to her: "Now, let us put the edge of this into the water so that it reaches the bottom, and then drag it slowly up the creek. The water is shallow, and if any fish come against it, we will try to catch them."

As they went along they watched for fish, and if one got against the willows near the woman, she reached over very slowly and grasped it and threw it out on the bank. If one got against the willows on the man's side, he did the same. In this way they caught many fish—all they wanted. They pulled the willow net out of the water, and the man said: "Ah! in this way we can live. We can catch fish. We will save this and keep it." They went to camp with their fish.[24]

Standing All Night, the aged man already mentioned as having died in 1869, used to tell how the Cheyennes subsisted before they reached the buffalo country. At certain seasons they were accustomed to make journeys to some great lakes, which constantly appear in their traditions. These lakes were so large that one could not see across them to the other side, and in their waters were many fish, some of them quite large. It was their practice to make nets of willow twigs tied together with strings of bark and sinew, and to stretch them out diagonally from the shore into the shallow water. These nets were often very long. Men stationed along the net held it in place, and other men, with women and children, went farther along the shore of the lake and entered the water in a line, some of them going out as deep as they could go, and walked toward the net, driving the fish before them. When they reached the outer end of the net, it was slowly moved in toward the shore, enclosing a large space; then it was gradually dragged up into the very shallow water, and men, women, and children got within it and

[24] Compare, as to the Pima, Lloyd, Aw aw Tam Indian Nights, p. 60, Westville, N. J., 1911.

threw the fish out on shore. In this way they commonly caught many fish, some of them very large, possibly sturgeon. After being secured, these fish were carried to the camp on the backs of people, or packed on the dog travois. The larger fish were cut in pieces before they could be put on the travois. In the camp they were dried in the sun, the larger ones being cut in strips. The bones of the larger fish were pounded and boiled for grease, just as in later days buffalo bones were pounded and boiled. From the largest of these fish they got a white sinew.

In modern times they caught fish in a pound or pen made of willow saplings. Such a pen was built by the direction and under the charge of a medicine man, who during the night, when the fish were expected to enter it, remained in his lodge, not going out. His face was painted red, and his robe was drawn up over his head so that he was wholly covered and could see nothing. All night he sat alone and silent in his lodge.

The people who built the fish-weir drove into the ground in the stream-bed willow saplings as thick as a man's wrist, and fastened them together with strings of rawhide. The saplings were in a circle as close together as possible, an opening or gate being left on the up-stream side. The weir was ready for the reception of the fish in the evening. Pieces of meat to serve as bait were laid in the water at the back of the weir.

A man was appointed especially to watch this trap. While it was building he took willow twigs, and from them wove a sort of oval basket about twenty inches long, and eight inches in diameter, with a hole about six inches in diameter in one end; to the other end were fastened two short willow sticks which served as handles for the basket. In the morning, after daylight, the man went to the trap and looked about its walls to find a place where he could work his hand and arm in between the willow saplings, so as to feel whether there were any fish inside. If he felt fish, he called the people to come. Then taking the basket, he went to the lower part of the weir and squeezed the saplings apart, so as to leave an open space, against which he put the opening of the basket. The fish began to come out through the opening in the walls, and to pass into the basket. From that the man took them in his hand and threw them out to the people on the bank. As long as he could get fish, he kept throwing them out on the bank. Sometimes he might be at it all day long.

Sometimes, but not often, the fish in the trap became frightened and swam out at the up-stream opening. Such traps have been used, certainly later than the year 1860, to capture suckers and whitefish in the Laramie River.[25]

[25] See also The Boy and the Girl, page 113.

GAMES AND AMUSEMENTS

LIKE people the world over, the Cheyennes had their sports. From their earliest years the children played about the camp, grubbing in the dirt, dabbling in the water at the edge of the stream, heaping up along the trails piles or ridges of dust, which represented breastworks or the walls of lodges; or, as they grew older, swimming in the streams, and making mud images in summer, while in winter they slid down hill, or played upon the ice. So it went through life, at least to middle age; and if the games of older people were more serious than those of the children, they still furnished the amusement which is as necessary to primitive as to civilized man.

The amusements of these people, like their very lives, were simple. Without books and without any of the varied forms of public entertainment known to civilized life, their diversions were almost altogether social. Visiting, feasting, the dance, and competitions of skill in various games, constituted their forms of recreation. It resulted that they were great gossips, visiting from lodge to lodge, carrying to each other items of news, on which they commented at great length. The frequent feasts furnished opportunity for the discussion of news, and for bringing forward suggestions bearing on the welfare of the tribe. Much as in many of the simpler communities of our own country in earlier days, the religious ceremonies at which from time to time they assembled were regarded by many of the people less as occasions for worship than as exciting and interesting entertainments.

Some of us have known of country districts where formerly a funeral was regarded as an event which no one would miss on any account—a gathering which for weeks afterward furnished subjects for conversation to the country-side. So it was with the Cheyennes. The great ceremonies of the Medicine Lodge, or the renewing of the medicine arrows, while to many of the older people occasions of much solemnity—seasons of prayer and humiliation, and devout worship—furnished to the younger people also an opportunity for meeting friends and relatives from whom they had been long separated, and for indulging in a more or less protracted course of social excitement, from which for months or years they might have been or might be debarred. On such occasions young men had the opportunity to see young women who had grown up since they had last met; girls attended the social dances so frequently held, and young people generally renewed earlier acquaintance—and met other young folks hitherto known but slightly, or not at all.

If this was true among the Cheyennes as a tribe, it was equally true when the whole great camp of the Cheyennes met that of some other tribe, perhaps as large, and mingled more or less freely with its members. Then, sometimes, a boy courted a girl of the other tribe who took his fancy; or a Cheyenne girl was sought in marriage by a young man of the strangers.

Among boys and young men there were many games and sports—contests of skill, usually in some athletic struggle. Each one was eager to outdo the others, whether in shooting at a mark, or throwing sticks, or wrestling, or at the kicking game. At this last sport the Cheyennes were skillful; and while most often it took place within the camp, it was sometimes practiced on a larger scale when the Cheyennes were camped near some other tribe, and the contest was between the boys of the two tribes.

These competitive games continued from childhood to middle life, and when men became too old to take part in them, they still enjoyed watching the games and seeing practiced by those coming after them the sports in which as young men they had participated. Besides the different diversions of the children, such as holding mimic camps of their own, and pretending to hunt buffalo, or to fight other groups of boys, who represented enemies, as already described, there were many games for children, or young folks, closely similar to those played by civilized children.

In winter the Cheyennes used to slide down hills on sleds made of buffalo-ribs placed side by side, with a stick tied across each end. This was done not merely by children, but by young men and boys and even by older active men, but not by women. For sliding down hill they chose a long slope, preferably ending on a frozen river. Girls and young women made toboggans from a slab split from a tree and used these, but not the rib sleds, for their coasting. The rib sleds went faster than a horse could run.

In winter, little boys and very small girls slid down snow-covered hills on pieces of rawhide (*ăn ha sī yăn'*?, sliding down hill); and even in summer very little boys might be seen sliding down steep banks in similar fashion. Their mothers encouraged them to do this, for it was a convenient and labor-saving method of wearing the hair off the buffalo-hide that they wished to use for the soles of moccasins. The removal of this hair is said to have been a slow process in ancient times, but later, after they devised bone scrapers for removing the hair, or had obtained metal ones, it was more easily accomplished.

Very small children were and are fond of playing in the dirt, in which respect they do not differ from children of other races. They often built up ridges of dust, making them like breastworks. They were straight, or circular, or took the form of squares, perhaps, with a gateway in one of the sides. Often today they build houses, stables, and corrals in imitation of those of their parents, laying out the ground-plans with rows of stones, and sometimes having in the corrals mud images of horses, buffalo, and cattle. In the cutbanks along the streams I have found niches dug out in which children had stored figures whittled from clay—some like little cubes or rhombs, some shaped like bricks, while others had a bottle-like form. Some of the niches were packed full of such geometrical forms, and were evidently children's storehouses for their blocks. Little boys were much given to modeling figures of animals and men from clay, and some of these were remarkably good.

In summer children spent much time in the water, and boys and girls alike were expert swimmers.

The little boys spun tops (*nĭ tō' hō yĭn* = "whirling," *i.e.*, whipping tops) on the ice or on the hard, frozen ground, whipping them with a whip-lash of several strands, and trying to see who could keep his top spinning the longest, or could drive it farthest over the rough ground, before it fell over. On the contests they bet their tops. One of two boys whipped his top along the ground until it fell; the place was marked, and then another started, and if his top went beyond this place he won the other top.

The little boys had tops also which they spun with a string, much as white boys spin theirs. The tops were made of cottonwood or ash, and were provided with a bone point or peg, or, in later times, when it could be had, a brass tack was used. These tops were spun on ice, or on hard ground, or even on a circle tramped hard in the snow. The strings used were twisted from the milkweed (?) that grows along the streams. The boys wagered their tops as to which one should spin the longest.

These were winter games played chiefly on the ice, as stated. Mr. Petter has pointed out the well-known fact that when the ice broke up in spring, tops, whips, and other implements of winter games were thrown into the water. It was believed that to play winter games in summer would make hairs grow on the body, and these it would be necessary to pull out.

Some of the games[1] played by the children were these:

Nē ē' wăt sē' ŭm (Carrying head downward). Two parties of

---

[1] Many of these games had a wide currency among North American tribes, and most of those played with the implements have been described by Mr. Culin in the 24th Annual Report of the Bureau of American Ethnology.

girls and boys sat opposite one another, about thirty feet apart. A boy was chosen, who went out midway between the two parties, closed his eyes, and turned around two or three times. The children of both parties called to him, "Come this way! Come this way!" He went to one line or the other, and caught a child, put it on his back, holding it by the feet, head downward, and carried it to a certain place, where he left it. Those whom he left there were obliged to remain. When all had been carried there, he lay down in front of them, as if to watch them and keep them from running away, and all began to pat him with their hands, and to sing in chorus, "Poor wolf! Poor wolf!"

Ŏk ō mē' hĭn ĭm (Coyote game). One boy, whose part is to attack, acts as the coyote. Another boy stands in front of his fellows, to protect them. All the others stand in line, one behind another, and each holding to the boy before him. It is the part of the leading boy to keep the coyote away from the line of boys behind him. In front of the protector stands the coyote, making dashes at the boys and trying to get behind the one who is holding him off. The protector runs toward the coyote, and then, when the coyote dashes toward him, jumps back and keeps jumping back and forth in front of the coyote, throwing up his arms. The coyote tries to touch a boy in the line, and one so touched is out of the game and retires. The boys are ranged in order of size, the tallest in front and the littlest one at the tail of the line. As they move from side to side, the end of the line of boys is likely to move rapidly, so that in this respect the game is somewhat like the white children's game "snap the whip."

Mă mau' ĭs kăn ĭt' (Jumping from side to side). This may be called a game or dance. The tallest child was in front of a line, and the others followed in order of size, each one holding to the one in front of him. They danced along, jumping from the ground, with both feet, a little forward at each jump, and calling out in time, *"Hagh! Hagh! Hagh!"* If one of them laughed aloud, all the others fell on that child and beat it with their hands.

Sūhk' pa khĭt (Running through the line). In this game the children stood in a circle, holding hands by locking the bent fingers of each hand in the bent fingers of the children on either side. A boy was chosen to be in the middle of the ring. He constantly tried to break out of the circle, by separating the handhold of some two of the children. If he succeeded in doing so and escaped from the ring, all pursued him, and those who overtook him slapped him with the open hand.

Nāh' kăn ĭsts (Playing bear). A boy was chosen to go into the underbrush where there were cherries or plums, and sit down there. He was the bear. Boys and girls went to the place to gather fruit, and while at work picking it, the bear charged upon them. As soon as he appeared, all would cry out, "Look out for the bear!" Often he caught a child and threw it down, and pretended to be eating it. The boys gathered about him, and pretended that they were shooting at him, picking up handfuls of dust and throwing them at him, at the same time making with their mouths a noise like the explosion of a gun. At last the bear appeared to be killed, and fell down, and the boys pretended to cut him up, using their hands for knives, as in the sign for skinning.

There are several variants of this game.

Sham fights. The small boys used to have sham battles, in which the weapons were a lump of stiff, moist clay, held under the left arm, and a slender switch, four or five feet long, carried in the right hand. A boy pressed a small lump of clay about the end of the switch and threw it, just as a white boy throws a green apple from a switch. Groups of boys, so armed, often had mimic combats with one another, two parties on foot carrying on a battle in which they retreated and attacked like real warriors, or sometimes several boys on foot would attack one mounted on a pony, following him up as he retreated, or, with shrieks of excitement, seeking cover if he charged.

Nĭt aī ĭs tai′ wa (*hŭs*) *tūm*. This game is sometimes called throwing fire. It is played like the preceding, but at night. Each party has a big fire, and after they have put the clay ball on the end of the switch, the ball is thrust in the fire. Coals are likely to stick to the clay, and the ball of clay is then thrown with the switch. If fire clings to the clay, the missile can be seen and so avoided.

A favorite game with small boys and young men was that of throwing a straight, slender stick. They held the stick by one end and pressed the other end against the ground, bending it once or twice, and then, by an underhand throw, darted it along close to, and parallel with, the ground—less than a foot above it.

Ē′ hyo ăn ĭs′ ko (Arrow mark). Boys and young men threw arrows at a mark, the first arrow thrown being the mark at which all subsequent throws were made. If an arrow thrown at the mark lay across it, this was a good throw; but if another one stuck in the ground, so as to touch the feathers of the mark, this throw was better. The boy whose arrow struck closest to the mark won.

Young and even middle-aged men sometimes engaged in the sport of throwing arrows, which often were really darts. The sticks were about twice as long and thick as an arrow, had a slight swell or enlargement toward the point, a spike three or four inches long for a head, and feathers reaching a considerable distance—*i.e.*, much farther than on an arrow—up the shaft. Just above the feathers, little tufts of down of various colors indicated the ownership of the darts. The distance thrown was forty or fifty yards. The one first thrown stood in the ground, and formed the mark for the succeeding darts. At the end of the throwing, the arrows stood in a fairly close sheaf, within a space of three or four feet. Sometimes the arrows of two throwers stood so close to the one first thrown that it was difficult to decide which one was nearest, and the distances had to be measured carefully with a little stick or with two matches held side by side.

Crowds of young and middle-aged men often stood about the mark at which contestants threw, and by exclamations or grunts, approved or derided the throws.

Ōn ĭmo' tăn' hăs iyo wūhk' ĭvst (Swinging around horn). A man's winter game was played with a limber twig, fifteen to eighteen inches long, one end of which was fastened in a hole drilled in the center of the butt of a point of buffalo-horn, while to the other end a bunch of feathers was attached, to make it fly well. The player twirled this twig a few times in his hand, and threw it down on the ground by an underhand cast, so that the horn-tipped end struck the ground, perhaps eight feet in front of him, at a very slight angle. The stick then glanced up, and flew a long way before the tip again struck the smooth ground, or the ice, and so scaled along, constantly ricochetting, often for a long distance. Four or five men might play at this game, preferably on ice or crusted snow, each trying to throw his stick farther than the other.

Hēk ō nĭm (ŭhk) stŭm' (Throwing (*i.e.*, sliding) bone) (*hēk*, bone; *ŭhk*, throwing). In another game, which the Cheyennes were especially fond of playing on the ice in winter, they used a slightly curved piece of buffalo-rib or elk-rib, eight or ten inches long which was cut away on each side to make it sharp in front, and at the other end pierced diagonally with a hole on each edge, in which holes were fixed the quills of feathers, so as to make the instrument fly evenly. This bone the men threw underhand. When it struck the ice on the convex side, it glanced up from it, and flew along, sometimes ricochetting several times. The object was to see who could throw the farthest. Two different parts of the rib were used to make this implement. If made of the distal portion, the bone had a curve slightly different from that made of a part of the rib near the spinal column.

Ē wō' ĭs tsĭm' tsĭs. The kicking matches which frequently took place were in the nature of sham battles. While these contests perhaps never had any serious results, nevertheless they were violent. The boys and young men kicked each other with one or both moccasin-shod feet, kicking either from the ground, or jumping up in the air and lashing out sideways with both feet. The blows dealt were often severe, yet the contests were always good-natured.

Sometimes, when the Cheyennes were camped near the Sioux or the Arapahoes, the boys of the camp assembled and went out on the prairie near the other camp, and called out, *"Co'ho! Co'ho! Co'ho!"* This was a challenge, and soon the boys of the other camp were seen gathering, and came out to meet the Cheyennes. When the camps were large, the contestants might number several hundred, ranging in age from twelve to twenty-five years.

It was the rule that under no circumstances should the hands be used; also, if a boy sat down, no one kicked him until he rose to his feet. Thus, a small boy might sit down if he saw a big boy or a man about to kick him. There was nothing disgraceful about this. Of course, if a boy continually sat down to avoid being kicked, he was laughed at, and soon was considered a coward.

A young friend of mine was once kicked in the back of the head, with both feet, by a larger boy, and knocked about twenty feet.

Grown men occasionally played the kicking game, and sometimes, just before the Medicine Lodge, the different soldier bands challenged one another to kick.

Nĭ' hĭ wăn ŭh'' (Wrestling). The Cheyennes were great wrestlers, and practiced it from the age of seven or eight years to middle life. They never used the feet or legs in tripping; but

DRYING MEAT

endeavored to swing the opponent off his feet, or bend him back by main strength. They were tremendously wiry and strong, and very difficult to handle.

The wheel game, so widely distributed over the continent, was played in several forms. In one of these, called *ē' ū tsŭhk-nia,* the wheel (hohktsim?) was used. It was practiced chiefly by boys and young men, and was played in two ways.

Hohktsim appears to mean "binding something together," and refers to the lashing together of the two ends of the stick which forms the hoop or rim of the wheel. The wheel, the shinny-ball, and the football are all so called. Old people used to call wagons *hŏhktsĭm'e,* because of the shape of the wheels. Wagons are now called *ă mō' ĭn ī" u,* which carries the same idea.

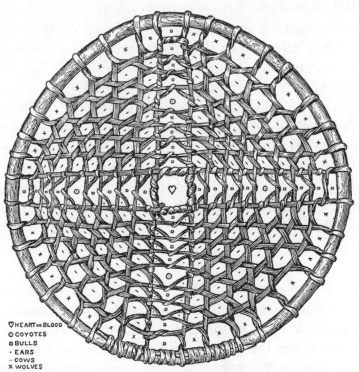

♡ HEART or BLOOD
⊙ COYOTES
▢ BULLS
· EARS
– COWS
✕ WOLVES

Some wheels of the Southern Cheyennes were divided into rough quadrants by double lines of rawhide, cross-laced, as above.

The center hole was called the heart (*hĭstsĭs*), or sometimes the blood (ma?); the rectangular spaces which crossed the pairs of dividing lines, close to the heart, represented bulls (*hotu'ao*); the small spaces in each quadrant were cows (*mĭh'*, singular; *ĭs'sĭwŭn*, plural); while the triangular meshes just within the wooden rim of the wheel were wolves (*hōhnē'*, singular; *hohne'hĭū*, plural). The four small circles between the parallel lines separating the quadrants, and dividing the groups of bulls, are called *o kōm'*, coyote. The small triangles within those parallel separating lines are *he tsista' ha ya*, ears.

They generally played with hohktsim in spring, after the cold had gone, and when the buffalo were shedding their coats. This was called the "clear day game," for when the players threw their wheels up into the air, each made a prayer that as his fell it might bring with it good weather.

The wheel varied in diameter from eight to fifteen inches or more. It was rolled along the ground, and the sticks thrown at it were straight, peeled, and from three to six feet long. Usually they had two or three prongs, three or four inches long, projecting from the end which was to strike the wheel, where small branches had been cut off from the sapling. The players commonly wagered their throwing sticks on the game. These sticks were often ornamented by wrapping them, sometimes spirally and sometimes horizontally, with strips of bark, and then by holding the stick over the fire the unprotected part was smoked or charred black, while the protected part remained white. This white part they painted yellow with the dung of the buffalo fetus.

The game was played between two opposing parties, perhaps a dozen or fifteen on a side. Each lad had a stick, and some might have two or three. From six to ten wheels might be employed. When the game began, all the wheels were in the hands of one party, whose members rolled them swiftly, by overhand throws, to the opposing party, which stood forty or fifty yards distant. These threw their sticks at the wheels as they approached or passed. To merely strike and throw down the wheel counted nothing; but if the point or one of the prongs of the shaft passed through the meshes of the rawhide netting, and held it, the wheel was "killed," and was not rolled back, but was retained by the side that killed it. The party that had received the wheels now rolled back all those which it failed to kill, and the opponents killed such of them as they could. The others were again rolled back. After all the wheels had been killed, each party started in pursuit of some of the opposing party, throwing at the boys the wheels that they had killed and so retained. They threw them hard and tried to hit. Those thrown at strove to protect themselves with their robes, or to catch the wheels on their sticks.

A wheel might be thrown only once, unless the boy thrown at was able to catch on the fly, and hold on the point of his stick the wheel thrown at him. If he could do this, he might throw it back at one of the opposite party. A hard blow could be dealt with one of these wheels—quite hard enough to knock a boy down.

There were different methods of throwing the wheels toward the opposing party. If a boy threw a wheel high in the air, it was understood that he was trying to bring good weather. If he threw it in a curve, he was very likely to call out, "I am beckoning it [*i.e.*, good weather] to come!" When one wheel was thrown, closely following another, the boys would shout out, "Ha! He is following his wife!"

Hohktsim was also used in a game for men alone, in which from two to six players might compete. The wheel was rolled by a disinterested man, and the players were armed with throwing-sticks. A place was marked in the ground where the feet of the thrower should stand. The first player took his position there, and threw at the wheel as it rolled by him and then retired to give place to another, and so on until all had thrown, each thrower standing in the same place.

The man who threw the wheel stood at a little distance, and

to one side, and rolled it in front of the thrower, perhaps two yards from him, perhaps six or eight yards. Five points made the game. If the point of the thrower's stick pierced the larger center mesh of the wheel—the blood (ma?)—it counted five, or game. If his point, however, pierced one of the four large circles, in the divisions of the four quadrants called *okōm'* (coyote), it counted nothing, but the man was entitled to another throw. If it entered one of the small meshes called *hē'-tsĭsta' hā ya*, it counted one, and the man kept on throwing until he missed. The place where the string passes over the rim is called *wĭhĭokōts;* to catch the stick on this was to win the game. On this game players bet anything they might choose, as horses, blankets, robes, or arrows.

Another game, *āh'koinĭs,* was played with a wheel (*ahk'-ōi yū*) nearly two feet in diameter, not cross-meshed with rawhide, but open. The sapling that formed its circumference was an inch or more in diameter. This game was perhaps borrowed from the Sioux. It is described in Mr. Meeker's paper[2] on Sioux games, under the name *pain yan kapi.*

The rim of the hoop was adorned with beaver-fur, beads, and other ornaments. The hoop was marked at the four quarters successively with one notch, two, three, and four notches. Two sticks about four feet long, tied together with two four-inch strings, were used to throw at the hoop, which was rolled slowly by the players, who threw the two sticks held together in one hand in such a manner as to make the hoop fall on them. If the single notch rests on either stick it counts 10 for the player; if the second notch rests on one of the sticks it counts 20, the third notch counts 30, and the fourth 40. The game is 800, for which there are counters of 10's and 100's. Often it takes a long time to play the game. As always, there was much outside betting on it.

This game of the old life seems essentially like the Blackfoot

2 Bull. Free Mus. Sci. and Art, Univ. of Pa., vol. III, no. 1, p. 23, Jan., 1901.

game *ĭtsē'wah*. It was not a boy's pastime, but was played by men of all ages up to middle life. Different wheel games were apparently played in some form among all North American tribes. In ancient cliff-dwellings of Colorado, one or more of these rawhide netted hoops have been found, indicating that this game—like many others, civilized and savage—was played in ancient times.

Nĭ tāi' āh tsĭm' a kūh' ŭm (Going to play). The wheel was placed on the ground, and the first boy, holding his stick in his hand and standing by the wheel, jumped from it as far as he could. His back was now toward the wheel, and without turning around he looked back over either shoulder, and threw his stick over his shoulder at the wheel behind him.

None of the other throwers jumped from the wheel before throwing their sticks. All took their places in the tracks made by the boy who had jumped from where the wheel lay. Often no one of them all hit the wheel, but the player whose stick was nearest to it took the sticks of all the others. The sticks were left lying on the ground where they had fallen, and the winner picked them all up.

Ŏhŏ knĭt' (Knocking the ball). The shinny game was not originally a Cheyenne game, but was borrowed from the Sioux. It was played by two parties, armed with curved sticks, somewhat like hockey sticks, and a flattened ball, from 2½ to 4 inches in diameter, made of deerskin, often beaded or quilled, and stuffed with hair. At each end of a level space of ground, 200 to 250 yards or more in length, two low mounds were heaped up—or sometimes poles were erected—20 or 30 yards apart. Sometimes, indeed, the field was as much as a quarter of a mile long. The object of each party was to drive the ball between the mounds its opponents defended. The number of players on each side must be equal. The ball must be driven between the mounds. If it passed outside of either mound, this counted nothing. Usually the players were afoot, but occasionally they were on horseback, which, of course, suggests the game of polo. Most of the players on either side stood near the goals, but the fastest runners stood off at either side. In the middle of the field stood the two leaders, and at the same time each tried to strike the ball with his stick, and to knock it off toward the fastest runner at his own side. If one of these got it, he usually kept it for a long time, for it was often difficult to overtake him. The ball might thus travel a long way over the prairie before it came near the goal posts, where the crowd of players was thick. There might be interference, one player getting in the way of another, or running against him, so as to delay him or to prevent his getting the ball. The ball might not be touched with the hand, nor might the hand be used in grasping a player. It is evident that the swiftest runners were the most successful players, and they were in great demand.

No' o its in is' ta (They are hiding). The well-known game usually called "hands" was played constantly. The man who manipulated the bones was called *i nō ō its ăn iv, i.e.,* one who is hiding (something). Each of the two parties who gambled against each other had two bones or small sticks, one marked— as by a string tied about it—and one plain. The two parties sat in a line or half-circle opposite each other, and between the two lines lay the eight, sometimes ten, counters, which must be gained by one side or the other before the game was won. Each side chose a man to guess for it; that is, one whose duty it was to announce in which hand the man held it who was hiding the bone. Certain men were considered especially expert in detecting the position of the marked bone, while others were almost equally skillful in hiding it. This skill was so well recognized that an effort was always made not to have two good guessers on the same side, the players protesting that this would not be fair.

All the players commonly sang one of the many gambling songs, and several beat time to the song, either on the ground with a stick, on a parfleche, or on small hand-drums.

When all was ready for the play, each guesser sat a little in front of the line of his own party, holding in his hand the bones that belonged to his side. Each player had already made his bet, usually with the man opposite him; but if a bettor could not wager enough property to cover the whole bet offered by any man, the wager might be shared by someone else; so that one man might be betting with two or three others.

The guesser of one side now gave his bones to someone who was skillful in passing and hiding them. This man, moving his hands in time to the singing, and making many gestures to confuse his opponent, raising his hands high, bringing them down close to the ground, and putting them behind his back, at length thrust out his closed hands, holding, of course, the marked bone in one hand or the other, and the opposing guesser, after a time, chose the hand which he supposed held it. If he was successful, his party then hid their bones, and if the opposing guesser also chose the hand which held the marked one, the game began again. If, however, he failed to guess right, his party gave up their bones and one counter. If both guessers were unsuccessful, the game began again.

After one side had secured both marked bones, the two might be manipulated according to the directions of the guesser on that side, one man or two men handling the two bones.

The guesser used various signs to indicate which hand of the opponent he chose. The simplest sign was to point with the forefinger at the hand chosen, but there were many others, some of them devised to puzzle the opponent. The forefinger and thumb of right hand extended, all the other fingers closed, palm held toward opposing player, meant (where two men were manipulating the bones) the two outside hands, that is to say, the right hand of the man on the right, and the left hand of the man on the left. But the same gesture, with the middle finger also extended, meant in the middle; that is, the hands of the two men which were toward each other, or the inner hands of the two men. The first two fingers of the right hand extended and pointing to the left, the back of the hand being toward the opposing player, meant the hand in the direction opposite to which the guesser was pointing; one finger meaning the direction in which the finger pointed, while the two fingers reversed the sign apparently made. If the guesser held in the hand a little stick, or some small object, like a small pebble or a bit of charcoal, this when shown—as it must be by the guesser, who must at once open his hands just as the holder of the bone did—reversed the apparent guess.

The game was won when one side had taken all the counters.[3] Sometimes the game lasted all night; sometimes it was finished almost at once. For high stakes, like a horse, it might be arranged that six games, or 48 points, must be won.

To drop the bone to the ground was to lose the game, all the counters being given up to the opposing party when this happened.

A variant of the hand hiding game, known as beaver game, is played by two persons. The object to be hidden may be held in the hand or may be placed on the ground on either side of the hider.

Another variant is the moccasin game, played with a pair of moccasins on the ground before the hider. He may put the object to be hidden in the moccasin, or may hold it in the hand. There were two sticks to be hidden, each bearing a different mark.

Certain signs for the four places where the sticks may be hidden are as follows: The forefinger, pointed toward the hider's right arm, would signify that the objects were in the right hand and the left moccasin; pointed to the left arm it would signify left hand and right moccasin; the thumb and forefinger extended means that the objects are held in both hands, while all the fingers extended and pointed a little downward means that the objects are in both moccasins. The name

[3] Compare this with Mooney's account of the same game among the Kiowas, in his Calendar History of the Kiowa Indians, p. 348.

of this game is *hōma' ĭ yŭts mōts ăn ĭv'* (*hōma'*, beaver; *ĭ yŭts*, I play; *mōtsănĭv'*, moccasin).

Women and girls, as well as men and boys, had their sports and games, which tested their strength, skill, and agility. They were often swift runners, good swimmers, and excellent horse-women, and skillful at ball and at throwing sticks. They were industrious and faithful in performing their daily tasks, at which they chattered and gossiped, yet they found abundant time for active recreation, whether in throwing the long and slender willow sticks, in kicking the football, in playing the finger game, or in gambling at the seed game. Usually girls and women played by themselves, yet occasionally a lad of thirteen or fourteen might be seen with a group of girls older than himself, kicking the football.

Nĭt' ăn ĭ tai' sĭn ŭn. In winter young girls played on thick ice a game which suggests bowling. The two parties sat on the ice, perhaps ten feet apart, and in front of each, lying on its side, was a small cylinder of wood, four inches long and as thick as the finger, one of twenty or forty equally divided between the two parties. Each girl was provided with several—sometimes ten—small spherical stones, about an inch in diameter, which they rolled at the sticks in turn. When a stone from one girl hit the stick lying in front of the others, a mark was made on the ice. If the stick was not hit, the opposing side rolled the stone back, trying to hit the stick in front of the other group. Each hit counted a point, and when a certain number of hits had been made, the game was won, and the girls who had lost the game tossed over to the others the beads that had been wagered.

Ĭn' nĭ tŭn ĭs' to (The finger game). This was played with the "fingers," *nē tŭ yē sūn'* (the bone). This implement consisted of four of the phalanges of a deer or an antelope, in which holes were drilled lengthwise, and also from side to side.

329

These four bones were strung lengthwise on a thread of sinew
or a string of deerskin, and this in turn was attached to a long
pin made of wire, or in old times a pin made from a slender
bone. To the holes in each end of each bone were tied small
loops of beads, and at the free end of the most distant bone,
a larger loop. The pin was held in the right hand; the string
attached to its hand-end swinging forward; the bones were
thrown forward and upward, and an effort was made either to
transfix a bone by driving the pin through the holes drilled, or
to catch one of the beaded loops. The four bones were marked
—beginning with the one nearest the pin—I, II, III, IIII. To
pass the pin lengthwise through any bone counted 10, 20, 30,
or 40, according to the number of the bone pierced. To catch
one of the beaded loops at the juncture of two bones, or the
large loop at the end of the last one, counted but one; but to
catch two of the beaded loops at the juncture of two bones,
each loop being attached to a different bone, won the game. To
catch the end of one of the bones, and the first side hole,
counted game, provided the opposing side had not yet made a
count; but if the other side had counted, the game began again,
all the counts being canceled.

To catch one of the bones through one of the transversely
drilled holes gave the player the game. To catch any two of the
bones lengthwise counted but two. The game might be played
by any even number of persons, but there were two sides, the
players sitting alternately as to sides. It is still played, chiefly
by young people—girls and men—but it is really a girls' game.[4]

Ō ăssi' ŏph (Football). This game was played by young
women. The ball used was eight inches in diameter, stuffed with
antelope hair, and covered with deerskin. Three hundred slender sticks, twelve or fifteen inches long, were prepared for
counters, and were placed in the center of the circle where two
women stood to care for them. The players were even in number
—eighteen or twenty—divided into two parties. They stood

[4] Compare Hind, Labrador Peninsula, vol. I, p. 277, London, 1863.

alternately around the circle in a close ring. The one who began the game took the ball, and, balancing it on her instep, kicked it up a little way, caught it on the instep, kicked it again, and continued this as long as she could. The object of the game was to keep the ball on the foot or in the air—off the ground—as long as possible. Usually they began to kick with the right foot, but if that foot became tired, an expert player might kick the ball over and catch it on her left foot, and continue kicking with that foot. Some people among the Northern Cheyennes say that only one foot could be used (they could not change feet), and sometimes the players grew very tired from standing for a long time on one foot. Sometimes the side which kicked first chose its best player, and she might perhaps keep the ball going until the three hundred counters were exhausted, and the game was won. While she was kicking the ball a girl might support herself by a stick four or five feet long, held in the left hand, or under the left armpit. If the girl dropped the ball, the one standing next to her, and so of the opposing party, took it up and began. If she missed, the one next on the left took it and tried. The girl who was kicking counted aloud, and the opposite side watched her kicks, and listened to her count. Among the Southern Cheyennes it was not usual to have two women in the center of the circle to care for the counters.

When the girl who had been kicking finished her turn, she stepped up to the counters and took away as many sticks as she had made kicks, and put them to one side. The next one took her share of the sticks. Each one who kicked afterward put the counters that she gained with those of her side. When the counters in the center had been exhausted, they began to take from each others' piles, until one side or the other had won all the counters.

On this game the women wagered beads, earrings, bracelets, everything they possessed. Sometimes they had a regular feast before the game began. This was a winter game, played chiefly by unmarried girls, though young married women often took part in it.

I' whū stĭsts (Throwing ball at one another). This was a modification of the football game. The players agreed on the number of times the ball was to be kicked, perhaps 150 or 200 times. The one who kicked the most out of that number seized the ball and threw it at another girl; if she was hit she picked up the ball and threw it at someone else. Of course, the slowest girl was likely to get hit. A girl who thought she was about to be hit by the ball usually got hold of a piece of brush or a forked stick, and protected herself with the branch, knocking the ball away, so that it should not touch her person.

I kō' kōē hăs ĭn ē' ya, also *Boe hă sĭn' ĭsts* (Throwing up in the air). The Cheyenne seed or basket game was played with a shallow bowl or basket and five plum-stones, or flat pieces of bone or antler, *mōn shī mō ŭt'*. The bowl was from two to three inches deep, eight inches across at the top, flattened or not on the bottom, and woven of grass or fiber of yucca or strips of red-willow twigs. It was nearly half an inch thick, and was strong. The five dice, which were usually plum-stones, were unmarked on one side, but on the other, three were marked alike and two bore a different mark. A common device was

this: representing the paint pattern often used by girls

on their faces, the cross being on the bridge of the nose,[5] the side marks on the cheeks, and the upper and lower ones on the forehead and chin respectively. The other two stones were

sometimes marked thus: representing the foot of a

---

[5] The paint cross on the girl's nose represents the morning star, and so indirectly Cushing is right as quoted by Culin, 24th Annual Report of the Bureau of American Ethnology, p. 59.

bear. Sometimes a small spherical "lucky" stone (*nō ă nī′ o′*, mixer) was thrown up with the seeds.

The plum-stones were placed in the basket, tossed up, and as the basket was brought to the ground were caught in it. The combination of the marked sides which lay uppermost after the dice had fallen determined the count of the throw.

The players sat opposite one another, and, if several were playing, in two rows facing each other. Each individual bet with the woman opposite. Each player was provided with eight sticks, which represented the points that she must gain or lose to win or lose the game. When a player had won all the sticks belonging to her opponent, she had won the game and the stake.

There were several combinations of marks and blanks which counted nothing for or against the player making the throw, except that she lost her chance to make another throw. Others entitled the thrower to receive one, three, or even all eight sticks, and each throw that counted anything entitled the player to another throw. Each player on the side of the thrower, *i.e.*, in the same row, won from or lost to the one opposite to her as the thrower won or lost. If the woman making the first throw cast a blank, she might make another throw and on failure she passed the basket to the one sitting next her. If this one made a throw that counted, she had another, and another, until she threw a blank, when the basket passed on. When the basket reached the end of the line, it was handed across to the woman at the end of the opposite row, and in the same way traveled along the opposite line.

In making the throw, the basket was raised only a little, and the stones tossed only a few inches high. Before they fell, the basket was brought smartly down to the ground, against which it struck with some little noise. Some of the throws are given below, the sides of the seeds being designated by their marks:

2 pairs counted 1 point, or 1 stick.
5 blanks counted 1 point, or 1 stick.

The marked sides of all the seeds uppermost gave the highest possible count, and the game was won.

3 blanks and 2 of a kind counted 3 sticks, or 3 points.
3 similarly marked seeds and 2 blanks counted 3 points.

The lucky stone had no value in the count, but it was said that it made the counters turn over. Any of the players might put in the lucky stone, and if beaten was privileged to keep it in the basket. If she won the round, however, one of her opponents might ask her to withdraw it and might put in her own lucky stone.

After each eight points were won, the loser "washed" the bones or seeds—rubbed them between her hands—and threw; and then the winner washed them and threw.

In the South the counters were usually of black walnut or of mulberry wood. In the South, too, the count is sometimes 10.

The seeds might be marked according to the fancy of the maker; perhaps with a lizard, a bird, a horned toad, a skunk, buffalo tracks, or a bug.

The women did not sing at this game, but they chattered and joked continually as the play was in progress.

Ē' hyo ĕs tsĭm' as. An athletic game in great favor among the women was the contest with throwing-sticks. These were straight, slender sticks, usually of willow, about twice as long as the men's throwing-sticks—not far from six feet—but like those, carrying on one end a tip, usually of elk-antler or of buffalo-horn, although I have seen some made from the horn of the domestic cow. Sometimes these tips were six inches long, and quite heavy, but usually they were not more than three or four inches in length. The horn tips were drilled out to a depth of an inch or two, to receive the end of the throwing-stick, which was simply twisted into the hole. Women threw these long sticks by an underhand throw, the object being to make the stick slide a long distance over smooth ground, ice, or crusted snow. Many women were extremely expert, and over favorable ground would send the stick to an astonishing distance. The motion of throwing the stick was exceedingly graceful, and the contests were very well worth watching.

On this, as on most other games, the women bet quite heavily.

The Twenty-fourth Annual Report of the Bureau of American Ethnology contains, in Mr. Culin's splendid monograph, a vast mass of information on Indian games. In the Cheyenne Dictionary prepared by Rev. Rodolphe Petter there is much detail regarding Cheyenne games.

TRIBAL GOVERNMENT

THE government of the prairie Indians, while varying in some particulars among the different tribes, was democratic in form and in fact. The will of the people was the force that controlled, and the chiefs, however great their power and influence, seldom attempted to run counter to public opinion.

CHIEFS

Among the Cheyennes there was a governing body of chiefs, not all of equal authority, which decided a variety of questions coming before it, its decisions, if necessary, being enforced by power of the soldier bands. Yet this council of the chiefs, always endeavoring to act for the best interests of the tribe and striving to lead public opinion, seldom attempted to force it.

In the Cheyenne view, the first duty of a chief—though not always the one first spoken of—was that he should care for the widows and the orphans; and the second that he should be a peacemaker—should act as mediator between any in the camp who quarreled. The dignity of a chief did not permit him to take part in any quarrel; he might not take personal vengeance for an offense committed against himself; to do so would result in loss of influence.

Since so much depended on his example and precept, a chief must be brave in war, generous in disposition, liberal in temper, deliberate in making up his mind, and of good judgment. A good chief gave his whole heart and his whole mind to the work of helping his people, and strove for their welfare with an earnestness and a devotion rarely equaled by other rulers of men. Such thought for his fellows was not without its influence

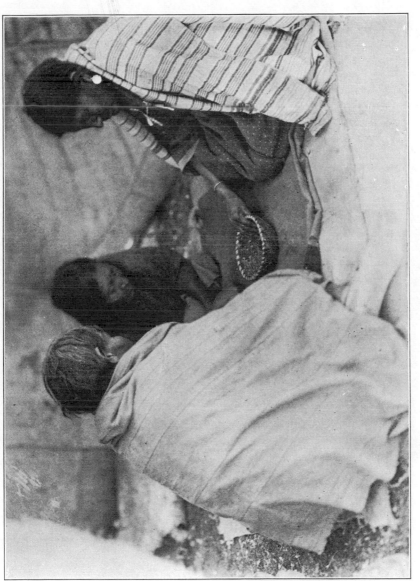

PLAYING THE SEED GAME

on the man himself; after a time the spirit of good will which animated him became reflected in his countenance, so that as he grew old such a chief often came to have a most benevolent and kindly expression. Yet, though simple, honest, generous, tender-hearted, and often merry and jolly, when occasion demanded he could be stern, severe, and inflexible of purpose. Such men, once known, commanded general respect and admiration. They were like the conventional notion of Indians in nothing save in the color of the skin. True friends, delightful companions, wise counselors, they were men whose attitude toward their fellows we all might emulate. We do not commonly attribute to Indians a spirit of altruism, but it was seen in some of these old-time chiefs.

Among the Cheyennes there were forty-four chiefs—four principal chiefs, and four from each of the ten bands of the people. The four chiefs of each band, who were in constant touch with their own constituents, knew and accurately reflected their opinions. Each group was thus equally represented in the council of the chiefs, and presumably by men of sufficient intelligence and influence effectively to present its views to the council. The four head chiefs—though usually men of special influence and importance—possessed, in weighty matters, little more actual authority than other members of the council, yet from their position, and the qualities which had raised them to that position, their advice and opinions usually received greater consideration than those of other speakers.

Of strong influence in the government of the tribe was the sentiment of the soldier bands. These were the police and chief fighting force of the tribe, and at different times one or another band might possess special influence on account of its bravery, its success, and the self-confidence which followed this success. If for a series of years one of the soldier bands had been generally fortunate in war, had performed feats of daring which reflected special credit on it, and for this or any other reason had come to have an exalted opinion of its own importance, it might at times exercise pressure on the chiefs, and induce the council to act in some particular way that it desired. Or, the chiefs, recognizing the popularity and influence of the band, might defer to it, ask advice of its chiefs, or might even submit to it the decision of weighty questions. It was thus sometimes possible for the council of the chiefs and one of the soldier bands to overrule the wishes of the majority of the tribe. Yet this was not likely to occur, or, if it did happen, some change of sentiment soon took place, and the pendulum of public opinion swung back again.

At the meetings of the council of chiefs, questions of interest to the tribe were considered. Concerning minor matters, one of the principal chiefs was likely to express his opinion, and, if supported by another principal chief, the council assented without debate. Questions of greater importance, such as moving the camp when buffalo could not be found, of undertaking a tribal war, or of seeking an alliance with other tribes for the purpose of proceeding to war against a common enemy, were discussed at great length, the deliberations perhaps extending over several meetings. In such debates the talking was done chiefly by the older men—those of greatest experience—yet after the elders had stated their views, middle-aged men expressed theirs, and even younger men might speak a few words, suggesting a different point of view, or giving new reasons for or against a certain course.

Such councils were conducted with much form and with a degree of courtesy that could hardly be exceeded. Usually the subject of the council was known in advance and to some extent had been discussed. When all the chiefs were present, a few minutes of silence ensued, then one of the older men arose and introduced the subject at issue. His remarks were followed by a brief silence for consideration, when another old man followed him and the discussion continued. Sometimes there were wide differences of opinion among the men, yet each was listened to gravely and with respect, and no matter how earnest the debate might become, no man ever interrupted a speaker, nor did anything like wrangling occur.

This has always been a characteristic of public meetings among Indians, and in old times such courtesy and deliberation were invariably practiced. So long ago as the end of the eighteenth century Le Page du Pratz said of the Natchez:[1]

When the natives converse together, however numerous the assembly be, never more than one person speaks at once. If one of the company has anything to say to another, he speaks so low that none of the rest hear him. Nobody is interrupted, even with the chiding of a child; and if the child be stubborn, it is removed elsewhere. In the council, when a point is deliberated upon and debated, they keep silence for a short time, and then they speak in their turns, no one offering to interrupt another.

While these discussions were commonly confined to the council of the chiefs, and only a few other old men were present in the lodge, the meetings were in no sense secret; for in summer, when the weather was warm and the lodge-skins were raised, a considerable audience might gather and listen to what was said.

When a decision had been reached, it was announced to the camp by the crier, who, mounting his horse, heralded the news as he rode about the circle, from the opening on the east, toward the south, then to the west, then to the north, and so back to the east again. After the council was concluded, the different chiefs talked of its proceedings with the people generally, so that full publicity was given without delay to all acts of the governing body; whatever they did was thoroughly canvassed through the camp, and the public feeling about it at once known. If by any chance this public feeling was adverse, and personal argument by the individual chiefs and the soldiers who favored it failed to convert the people to their views, the action taken was likely to be modified to meet the public opinion.

[1] Du Pratz, History of Louisiana, Book III, p. 238, London, 1763.

In practice, however, this did not happen. The popular pulse had been felt and the public sentiment well ascertained before the council met. The older men were always conservative and slow to take any action that was radical; it was seldom that a decision had to be reconsidered.

The war chiefs of the Cheyennes were the chiefs of the different soldier bands, and led these bands when any duties were to be performed. They were not especially leaders of war-parties, for any man who could enlist followers might lead a party to war.

The four principal chiefs of the tribe were equal in authority, and the others of the forty-four chiefs were really counselors, whose authority as chiefs extended no further than over their own immediate following. However, their positions as counselors commanded respect, and led the people to listen to the advice which they gave.

Chiefs were chosen to hold office for ten years, for it was thought that this period was long enough for anyone to serve. Yet, if, at the end of ten years, a chief had proved himself a good one, he might be chosen to serve a second term. The soldier chiefs—that is, the chiefs of the different soldier bands— were elected and changed at the same time.

Of the forty-four chiefs who had held office for ten years, four, or sometimes more, were usually elected for a second term, and of these, four were likely to become the head chiefs. While the soldier chiefs held office for ten years, as did the others, still, if one did anything wrong he might be removed from his office, and a new chief chosen for the remainder of the term. A soldier chief elected for a second term became the head man of all the soldier chiefs.

Any one of the four principal chiefs of the tribe might, at the end of the ten-year period, choose his own successor, and so might name his own son to follow him at the end of his ten years of office. If a son was chosen, he was likely to be a good man and the choice to be acceptable to the whole tribe. Thus in a sense the office of principal chief was hereditary. The son might decline to serve, as in the case of Bull Hump, son of Dull Knife, of the Northern Cheyennes. Bull Hump, though named by his father and the choice of the tribe, refused to take his father's place, on the ground that chiefs were then (1883) no longer needed. If a chief had no son whom he wished to succeed him, he might choose another man, who in turn might select his son. If the son of a dead chief was a boy too young for the position, someone was elected to fill the father's place, but when he became a man the boy might be made a chief, if he had proved himself fit.

If, as often happened, a principal chief died or resigned and failed to nominate anyone to take his place, his successor might be chosen from among the forty-four head men, but was quite as likely to be selected from among the braves of the tribe who did not belong to this council.

The choice of a chief was an important matter, and there was much discussion as to the best man for the place. A large lodge was pitched, a feast was made, and all the chiefs were called together to consider the man for this position—one who was brave, whose heart was strong as well as big—a man generous and wise.

They endeavored to choose a man of even temper, liberal and brave; they never selected one who was quick-tempered or stingy. They used to say that a man of mild temper and generous disposition was wise. Regard was had for a man's judgment and discretion, and for the quality of his mind as respects justice.

Among those qualified for the position of chief, there was no strife as to who should secure it, no "wire-pulling" or intrigue. If a man who had been chosen as chief declined to accept the office, he might have to be persuaded to accept, or he might definitively decline. In not a few cases men have refused the office, often on the ground that the responsibility was too great.

Roman Nose,[2] who was several times selected as chief, was an example.

Each chief of those who exercised the right to nominate his successor was careful to choose a good man—one who would be acceptable to the chiefs and to the people. When the time came for the assembling of the new chiefs, it was the duty of each outgoing chief to fetch his successor to the first meeting. For this service his successor presented the outgoing chief with a horse.

In old times, when the chiefs wished to take some action, a council was called to consider the matter, often without notifying the head chief. When the council had decided on a certain course, the head chief was sent for, and the decision announced to him. If two of the principal chiefs were in the camp, both were sent for to attend the council. After these head chiefs had been told of the decision, and had considered it, they very likely approved the action of the council and directed that it be carried out; but if they thought the decision unwise, they said so, and gave their reasons for it, telling the council that they must not act as proposed. The council usually accepted this decision. In such a case the head chiefs thus possessed the veto power.

Sometimes, on the other hand, the head chief gave a feast, called the council together, and told them that he thought it would be well to do some particular thing—for example, to move away to a certain place—and asked the guests what they thought of this. If, after talking the matter over, they did not agree with him, he usually said no more about it. Having asked their advice, he felt that he must abide by their decision.

It is said that when the forty-four head men were first chosen, forty-four official sticks were made, to represent them. Each stick was about a foot long, as thick as the finger, and sharpened at one end. They were always carried about with the camp—by one of the chiefs, or, as is believed by others, in the bundle with the medicine arrows. When the chiefs were to

[2] Killed in 1868 at Beecher's Island. See The Fighting Cheyennes, p. 277.

be called together, one of the forty-four sticks was set in the ground before the seat of each chief, and messengers were sent to summon them. As each man came to the place of assembly and sat down, the stick before his seat was taken up and put back in the bundle, until, when all were present, the forty-four sticks had been returned.

When one or more chiefs were to be elected to take the place of men who had died or resigned, as many of the forty-four sticks as there were vacancies were taken into the lodge where the council was held, and for each vacancy to be filled a stick was thrust into the ground in front of the place where each new man was to sit, to be removed when he had been called and had taken the seat to which he had been elected.

Middle-aged warriors and old men attended such meetings, and in public speeches talked over the various men available, saying what they thought of each. The discussion and the expressions of opinion usually showed very clearly who was the most popular man for the place. There was no formal balloting, but when the sentiment had crystallized on the one man, two messengers were sent to bring him to take his place among the chiefs, and when he came he was asked to sit in the seat of the man who had died or resigned. Sometimes, and especially often in later times, the man chosen might decline the office, and another man must be selected. Old men resigned from this council when they had passed the period of active usefulness. The intention of a man to abandon the office was usually known in advance and his successor chosen before he formally resigned.

It is said that long ago if the man chosen for the position refused to accept it, misfortune was likely to happen to him; he would not live long. It was held to be a man's duty to accept.

At the decennial election of chiefs, ten small sticks were prepared to mark the years that had elapsed since the last election, and after the choice had been made, these sticks were put aside—some say in the bundle with the arrows, some say with the sacred hat.

The two youngest of the forty-four chiefs acted as door-keepers, and also as messengers for the chiefs, and sometimes they held over for a second term. When the chiefs had decided on any course of action, the doorkeepers were sent to summon the two principal men of one of the soldier societies—perhaps of the *Hĭm' ŏwē yŭhk' ĭs,* or of the Fox Soldiers. When these soldier chiefs came, the chiefs told them what had been decided on, and directed them to inform their soldiers, which they did at once. The orders of the chiefs were conveyed to the men of the camp in this way. A little later the old crier on his horse rode about the camp, calling out the orders, so that all the women and children might become informed.

There were certain old rules governing chiefs which have long passed out of use. One of these was that if a woman went to a chief's lodge to borrow fire, he was expected to give her a horse. If a chief, riding a fresh horse, met on the prairie a woman whose horse had become exhausted, the chief should dismount and give to the woman his horse to ride into camp.

Long ago it was unusual for anyone to go to the lodge of one of the principal chiefs to borrow anything. If an individual asked the chief to lend him something, the chief at once presented the article to the borrower, so it came about that people seldom tried to borrow anything from a chief.

A chief, after a man had shaken hands with him, was supposed not to become angry with that person under any circumstances. The man might quarrel with, or abuse, or even whip, the chief, and he would not resist. But this might happen only four times; the fifth time the chief was ill-treated he was free to resent the injury.

Nothing definite is known about the origin of the system of selecting chiefs, but some short tales are told about it. One of these attributes the system to the culture hero Motsiiuiv, and comes from Tangle Hair, an old man whose mind was well stored with legendary lore. In substance it is as follows:

The man who had brought the buffalo said, "Now you must make chiefs." He took four sticks and stuck them in the ground, one at the door, one at the back, and one on each side, so that there was a stick toward each of the four cardinal points. Between each pair of these first sticks, ten others were set in the ground, making in all forty-four. The people were called in, and from the four bands of soldiers forty-four chiefs were chosen. Then he said to the people, "Now, the smartest men among you must look about over the earth and examine the plants and herbs that grow, and you will find medicine with which to doctor the sick, and you can cure them. Now you have buffalo, and you must kill them to eat, and to make robes for your beds, and clothing. From their hides you can make everything that you need to wear. When you go out to hunt, you will find many other animals, deer, elk, and smaller creatures, and you can use their skins also to make clothing."

Two other stories are more modern, dating back only to the time of the Cheyennes' active wars with the Hohe, or Assiniboines. The first is this:

Before the Cheyennes saw any white people, or had any guns, the Assiniboines came to war against their camp, and, as they already had guns, they used to kill many Cheyennes, who had only bows and arrows, and to take many prisoners—women and children.

In one fight the Assiniboines captured a handsome young Cheyenne girl. The man who captured her was a principal chief of the Assiniboines. He already had a wife, but he took this girl home, and had her also for his wife. His first wife used to abuse the girl, and was always quarreling with her, and at last the chief who had captured her said to the girl:

"I am tired of this. I will have something made up for you to eat, and some moccasins made for you, and you will take your moccasins and what I give you to eat, and you will start off from here in the night, and go home to your people."

While she was in the Assiniboine village, this chief used to make

345

feasts, and call to them forty-four men, all chiefs and head men of the tribe. He had a fine large pipe, and they used to smoke this pipe.

The girl went away to her home as the Assiniboine chief had ordered. When at last she got to her own village, she had been gone a year or more. After she had been at home a little while she said to her father, "I want you to kill forty-four buffalo, and bring the hides to me. I want also forty-four pipes."

Her father did as she had asked, killing for her the forty-four buffalo, and bringing in the hides, and also getting her the pipes for which she asked.

She had all the hides dressed, and ornamented the robes and the pipestems with porcupine quills, just as the Assiniboine robes and pipes had been ornamented. After they were finished, she asked her father to call to his lodge all the principal men of the Cheyenne camp. After they had gathered, she herself selected forty-four men, to each of whom she gave a pipe, and about each one she put a robe, and told them that this was the number of head men in the tribe with which she had been living, and this was the way they were marked, and that these forty-four men, who were now the heads of the tribe, must assemble whenever anything was to be done, and must hold councils and make laws for the tribe. So this became a custom in the Cheyenne tribe, and has been followed ever since. Whenever one of these men was killed, or died, some one was chosen to replace him; so that until recently the number was always forty-four. All the men chosen must be good men, brave, wise, and generous.

This happened a long time ago, before the Cheyennes crossed the Missouri River. The last time they did it was in 1874. Before this woman made that law the Cheyennes always had only one chief.

Another version is more detailed, and is made more credible by its supposed connection with a well-known man who was killed about the middle of the last century, and whom people living recently still remembered. It is as follows:

The Assiniboines captured a Cheyenne married woman. Her husband's name was Red Painted Robe. Her name was White Buffalo Woman. She was the last woman that the Assiniboines ever captured.

While the Assiniboines were taking her back with them, she gave birth to a child. White Buffalo Woman was very handsome. When she reached the Assiniboine camp she was taken into the lodge of the man who had captured her, and put on the north side of the lodge. This man had a handsome young wife.

After some days the wife cut some parfleche soles and moccasin pieces, and gave them with some sinew to the Cheyenne woman, saying to her, "Make yourself some moccasins, and make them strong." While White Buffalo Woman was doing this, the wife made a large parfleche sack, and put in it dried meat and back fat. When the moccasins were finished, she put them in it also, and in one of the moccasins she put some parfleche, some sinew, and an awl.

When she had done this, she said to the Cheyenne woman, "When your moccasins wear out, make others for yourself with these things." "Take this rope too," she added, and she put in the sack a line of buffalo-hide.

After all was ready, the Assiniboine woman put the sack behind her own bed, so that no one should suppose that it belonged to the captive and ask questions about it. After a few days she said to the Cheyenne woman: "Tonight we are going to have a big dance, and my husband is going to it. I wish you to go to your home. I will go a little way with you and help you. You know the trail you came over, but you must not follow that trail, for war-parties are going back and forth on it all the time, and you may meet one. When you are traveling, therefore, keep to one side of this trail, near enough to it so that you will not be lost, but far enough away so as not to be seen. Now, you know that you must travel through some heavy timber, so at night when you stop to sleep, find some leaning tree that has partly fallen down, climb up into it, and sleep in the forks, for there are many bears in the country that you must pass through. Take also this root-digger, and at night when you stop, always put it on the ground with the sharp end pointed in the direction you are going, so that in the morning, even though the sun may not be shining, you will always know which way to proceed. If my people follow you to try to overtake you, you must remember that it is the medicine of the Assiniboines to follow an escaping person for one day only. If they do not overtake him in one day, they return. There is now only one war-party out; if you see them coming toward you, and they pass you, you may then take the regular trail and go on to your home." The Assiniboine woman gave her one of those axes with a round hole in the back and a short handle.[3]

That night the two women left the camp; and the Cheyenne woman started on her way, carrying her boy on her back. She did as her friend had told her, and traveled onward for many days.

She was always watching, and one day she saw people coming along the trail toward her. She lay down in the grass, and remained there for a long time, and when she looked again the people had passed her, and were becoming smaller in the distance. Then she took the trail boldly, and followed it back to the Missouri River. It was in the spring and the ice was about ready to break up, but where the Assiniboines had crossed they had laid poles on the ice, making a sort of bridge, and she crossed there.

Before this she had eaten all her food and was growing thin and weak, but from time to time as she came to old carcasses of bulls lying on the prairie, she cut out pieces of the hides and gnawed on them. At last she came into the Cheyenne camp on the Little Missouri River. When this woman came back to the Cheyennes she told them how the Assiniboines used to make medicine to surround the buffalo, and also about how they chose their chiefs.

Her son, whom she brought with her on her back, they called *Tsĭ nĭm' o*—Tobacco. He became a great Cheyenne chief. He was killed in 1846 by a soldier or a teamster on the Arkansas, below where Garden City, Kansas, now is. The troops had had a little fight with the Comanches near where Fort Larned was built later (in 1859) at the mouth of Pawnee Fork. Tobacco was crossing the Arkansas near the soldier camp. The sentry challenged him, but as Tobacco knew no English, he did not halt nor speak, and the soldier fired and killed him. The place is still known to the Cheyennes as "Where Tobacco Was Killed." When killed he was an old man between sixty and seventy years, and so may have been born 1780-1790.

[3] A "T. Gray" axe, so stamped in the metal—one of the early axes used in the western Indian trade.

OFFENSES AGAINST TRIBE FELLOWS

Crime as understood by civilized people scarcely existed in the Cheyenne camp. Such a thing as theft was unknown. Sometimes it might occur that an individual rode, without permission, horses belonging to someone else. This was seldom done, but occasionally a man used the property of another, and so persistently as to cause a quarrel between himself and the owner. Such a quarrel once resulted in the death, at the hands of the owner, of the man who used the horses. On another occasion the owner of the horses, after fair warning, knocked the trespasser down with a club, and gave him a thorough beating, which ended the matter.

If a dispute serious enough to threaten real trouble took place between important men, the matter was talked about in the camp and, coming to the ears of the head men and chiefs, they discussed it, and perhaps called a council and summoned these men before it in order that their difficulty might be settled quietly. To such a council the men sent for always came. Each stated his case, and the council decided the question on its merits. Very likely they decreed that one of the men should pay something to the other. The council's decisions were usually fair and just, and were accepted by the disputants, but occasionally some headstrong man might refuse to accept the decision, and the trouble continued until a quarrel arose, and perhaps one of the men was killed. If by accident a man killed anyone in the camp—man, woman, or child—the matter came before the council, which decided how much he should pay to satisfy the relatives of the dead.

Public opinion was the law of the camp, and few were bold enough and reckless enough to fly in the face of it. Conformity to the rules of conduct established by custom and enforced by the chiefs was insisted on, and infractions were punished with a severity measured by the injury done, or likely to be done, to the community by violating these laws. As is elsewhere said, offenders often were severely whipped by the soldiers, or their property might be destroyed, their lodge-poles broken, or their horses killed.

On the whole, however, infringement of the rights of others was unusual. Once in a generation, perhaps, a man killed another in a quarrel, or in a drunken row, or in self-defense. The causes of such occurrences were often alcohol or fights about women. Sometimes one murder led to others.

The death of Walking Coyote in 1855 and the events connected with it show something of how quarrels, fights, and killings occasionally took place in the Cheyenne camp.

In the year 1854, White Horse, then chief of the Fox Soldiers, stole the wife of Walking Coyote, who was very fond of her and brooded much over the trouble. He sent word to White Horse to send back the woman, saying that if he did not do so he would kill him. No attention was paid to the message, and after a time Walking Coyote went to Yellow Wolf, who had adopted him, and said: "Father, as you know, White Horse has stolen my woman and I have sent word to him many times to send her back, but he does not do so. Now I intend to kill him, and I ask you not to interfere with my trouble, not to ask me to refrain from killing this man."

Walking Coyote knew that Yellow Wolf loved him better than he did any of his own sons and daughters, and he suspected that Yellow Wolf might ask him not to take revenge on White Horse, and if Yellow Wolf asked this, Walking Coyote felt he must obey him.

One day in the summer of 1854 Walking Coyote with War Bonnet rode up to St. Vrain's Fort (on the South Fork of Platte River in Colorado) from their camp twenty miles below. White Horse was living in a camp of Cheyennes there. Walking Coyote rode into the fort and saw White Horse and his wife—not the woman who had been stolen—sitting on a bench in the hall of the fort. When the two saw Walking Coyote, they arose and walked toward the hands' messroom, and Walking Coyote jumped off his horse and shot White Horse with his gun, the ball passing through the upper part of the chest and killing him at once. Then Walking Coyote and War Bonnet led their horses outside the gate of the fort, and sat down there, and Walking Coyote said, "If anyone has anything to say to me, I am here."

After they had sat there for a short time, Little Wolf, a cousin of Yellow Wolf, came out and said to Walking Coyote, "'This is all over with; you should now go back to your camp." The two men mounted and rode to camp.

Shortly after this the woman returned to Walking Coyote's lodge. After this killing, Winnebago (*Nāhk' to wŭn*) renewed the arrows because of the killing. A little later he stole from Walking Coyote the woman that White Horse had stolen and went up north with her.

Walking Coyote sent word to him, saying, "I am not going to kill another man for this woman, but I shall take your wife, Spirit Woman" (*A sĭ' mŏn i*). Before Nahktowun returned from the North, Walking Coyote went to Nahktowun's lodge, and, entering, took Spirit Woman by the arm and said, "Come along now!" She went with him, for she feared him.

When Nahktowun returned from the North and found what had happened, he was angry, so that night he took his gun, went to the lodge of Walking Coyote, looked in at the door, saw him sitting on his bed, where he was resting after returning from the buffalo hunt, and putting the muzzle of his gun through the door he shot Walking Coyote, killing him.

Next morning he went again to Walking Coyote's lodge, took Asimoni, and made her go back to his lodge.

After the killing of Walking Coyote the arrows were renewed, perhaps by Red Moon.

One day, eight years later, in the spring of 1863, Nahktowun was sitting behind his lodge filing arrowpoints, which he had fastened into a cottonwood stick to hold them. While he was doing this Kutenim came up and began to discuss with him the question of a horse, the ownership of which had been in dispute between the two. Kutenim was a distant relative of White Horse. As Nahktowun was working away, Kutenim became more angry at him and abused him, and finally Nahktowun jumped to his feet and raising the stick which he had been using to file his arrowpoints, struck Kutenim on the head with it and knocked him down. Kutenim jumped up and ran to his lodge, which was near by, to get his rifle, while Nahktowun strung his bow and took a handful of arrows from his quiver. Presently Kutenim ran out of his lodge and fired at Nahktowun, and the ball passed close to his head. Nahktowun drew his bow and shot Kutenim in the left breast. Kutenim dropped his gun, and drawing his butcher knife, rushed at Nahktowun, who ran away, but Kutenim overtook him and slashed him on the arm, and then fell dead.

The men round about, seeing what had happened, did not go near the two. Only old women and old men ran up to them.

The Bowstring Soldiers, who then had charge of the camp, wanted to punish Nahktowun for killing Kutenim by whipping him. They consulted the chiefs, who advised them not to notice the affair at all, and nothing was done to Nahktowun.

The arrows were renewed not long afterward.

In the summer of 1864 Nahktowun was living with the Arapahoes. He had an Arapaho woman, and some people began to talk as if Rising Fire, *Ho ïst o'ha a* (Smoke Rising), were trying to steal the woman. This made Rising Fire unhappy, and the more he thought of it the worse he felt, and the angrier he became toward Nahktowun. Finally he said to some of his friends, "I shall have to kill Nahktowun; he killed my cousin and now he is talking about me."

His friends replied: "You ought to do so, because if you do not kill him, he will kill you. He has already killed two men and is an outlaw, and if he feels like it he may cut your throat or shoot you."

Not long after this, Nahktowun, who was a Dog Soldier, was

GROUP OF SINGERS

invited by one of the Dog Soldiers to come over and eat at his lodge. He therefore moved over from the Arapaho camp near Fort Larned on the Arkansas and camped with the Cheyennes who were on the Saline. On the day of the feast he started, with Little Robe and Good Bear, to walk to the lodge of the host. On their way they passed the lodge of Rising Fire, who was sitting inside looking out the door, and as they passed he shot Nahktowun with a gun and broke his spine. When Nahktowun fell, Little Robe and Good Bear stepped to one side, and Little Robe called out to Rising Fire, "Well, you have begun your work; now come out and finish it."

Rising Fire took an old brass-mounted horse pistol, walked over to where Nahktowun lay, and blew out his brains. *Měh-hǐm' ik* (Eagle's Head) renewed the arrows[4] on the Solomon.

While certain customs and rules prevailed, there was no form of law as we understand it. There was no such thing as a legal death penalty. If a man killed a tribe fellow, he was often obliged to flee, at least for a time, for he was likely to be killed

---

[4] The statement has often been made that the renewing of the medicine arrows was an annual ceremony, something that took place as a part of the religious ceremonial of the Cheyenne tribe. It was not an annual ceremony, nor in any sense regular. It was not like the Medicine Lodge in some tribes, nor like the Green Corn Dance in others.

The arrows are renewed whenever it is necessary, that is to say, whenever anyone makes a vow to renew them. This vow may be made merely as a matter of sacrifice, or it may be made for the general purification of the tribe after the killing of one of its members by a fellow tribesman, or after suicide by a male member of the tribe, or in the case of an accidental shooting within the tribe, whether the victim was a man or a woman. They were not renewed where women hung themselves, as they sometimes did when disappointed in love affairs, nor in any case of suicide where there was no spilling of blood. It was necessary to renew the arrows—in the case of death within the tribe—only where blood had been shed. This blood, as has been repeated, appears on the arrows, when they are opened and looked at, not only on the points, but also on the shafts and sometimes on the feathers. The arrows might be renewed when a man had shot himself, attempting to commit suicide, but had afterward recovered.

The pledge to renew the arrows might not be made by the man who did the killing—who spilled the blood—but must be made by another. Moreover, as elsewhere stated, the renewing of the arrows, while it cleansed the arrows and purified the tribe, did not expiate the guilt of the man who spilled the blood.

by some near relative of the dead man. If he saved himself by flight, the council considered the case, and the chief called in the relatives of the dead man and from them learned how much it would take to satisfy them for their loss. The relatives of the slayer were then called together and the penalty stated to them. When they had paid over this fine to the dead man's relatives, the slayer might return to the camp. Whether the matter was thus settled or not, the man who had done the killing was ostracized by his fellows, temporarily expelled from camp, and lost all standing in the tribe, which he never recovered. He was obliged for a time to camp away from the main tribe, and often he went away from their camp and spent a year or more with some other tribe. A common refuge for Cheyennes was the Arapaho camp, where no guilt attached to them and they were regarded as being as good as anyone else. Lapse of time might cause partial forgetfulness of the event by the people at large, but this forgetfulness never extended to the relatives of the man who had been killed. Their anger flamed hot long after all others in the camp had measurably forgotten the deed and in a sense had condoned it. Nevertheless, the slayer of a tribesman, or indeed of anyone belonging in the camp, even though he might be a member of another tribe, remained all his life a marked man.

The slayer of his fellow might not eat in the same lodge with other people, nor from their dishes, nor might he drink out of their cups. He had a special dish, a cup of his own, and if by any chance he drank from a cup not his own, the cup was often thrown away; if not, it was purified as stated below. No one would smoke with him. He might not receive the pipe as it was passed from hand to hand, but carried his own pipe and tobacco. If unmarried, he probably never took a wife, for no woman would consent to live with him.

If anyone had unwittingly eaten or drunk from the dish or cup that an outlaw had used, and discovered it, he performed a ceremony to purify the utensil, rubbing his right hand on the ground and then over the dish, and repeating the motions with left and right hand again until the dish had been rubbed over four times. The same ceremony was performed in case a man smoked a pipe that an outlaw had used. The stem was held down to the ground, bowl up, the hands rubbed on the earth and then passed over the stem.

It was said that his pipe did not taste or smell as it should, that he was not a fit person to smoke with. The word *ok kli wŭs*, meaning "one who has killed another," carried the idea of decay, putrefaction, rotting.

If people were talking and the murderer came up to join in the conversation, someone might tell him to be silent, that he should not speak. It was supposed that such a man suffered an inward decay, and would ultimately die and blow away. He was supposed to smell bad, either from this decay or from the bad dreams and thoughts that he must suffer. It was believed by some that from time to time he would vomit portions of his own dead and decaying flesh. A part of this old belief was that a man who had done this could never get close to the buffalo, because the buffalo would smell this dead or decaying flesh and would run away.

An outlaw appears actually to have lost his membership in the tribe, and the fact that he was not allowed to camp with it seems to have been a real expulsion. The man was "thrown away." True, after the gravity of the offense had been partly forgotten with the lapse of time, he might come back to the tribe, but could never recover his old standing. Not only was the man himself hopelessly disgraced, but his whole family lost caste. A young man or woman wishing to marry a daughter or a son of an outlaw was felt to have more or less disgraced his own family. It made no difference how prominent the man might have been nor how good his family, the commission of the act of bloodshed cast a stigma over his family and his relations shared in the disgrace. The matter was not only talked about and reprobated at the time, but often the blight remained

355

on the children of the outlaw long after he was dead, and in any quarrel or dispute with other members of the tribe the disgrace was likely to be mentioned and thrown in the face of a child or relation, even when he or she was fifty or sixty years of age.

The killing of one man by another in a private quarrel was extremely rare, but there have been cases where men most eminent in the tribe did this and thereby at once lost all credit and influence. Instances of this are the cases of Porcupine Bear, —the Lame Shawnee—of Gentle Horse, and, last of all, of Old Little Wolf, the greatest of modern Cheyennes. Porcupine Bear, when he killed Little Creek, was chief of the Dog Soldiers; Gentle Horse was a brave of great influence; and Little Wolf, when he killed Starving Elk, was the fighting chief of the tribe. These men by their acts separated themselves from their offices, and became outcasts.

It was not solely the killing of a blood member of the Cheyenne tribe that was regarded as so heinous an offense; the same feeling existed if the man killed had been adopted into the tribe. There were many men in the camp, by birth Sioux, Arapaho, Ponca, or others, who had married Cheyenne women and had Cheyenne children, and who were regarded as Cheyennes. If one of these was killed, the murderer became an outlaw. Such cases were Nahktowun, the Arapaho who killed Walking Coyote, a Ponca; and Gentle Horse, who killed his brother-in-law, a Sioux. The two men killed had married among the Cheyennes and been adopted into the tribe, hence their slayers became outlaws and were treated as such.

The fact that they were outlaws justified the chiefs of the Cheyennes in not allowing Porcupine Bear and his party to count the first coup in the fight with the Kiowas and Comanches in 1838. At the time they were regarded as not being members of the tribe, and the coup was no more to be allowed to them as Cheyennes, than it would have been allowed to the member of any foreign tribe as a Cheyenne.

Those who committed these acts were often men of great bravery, whose success in war and whose standing in the tribe had made them somewhat arrogant and impatient of those who did not do as they had ordered. Such cases were those of Gentle Horse and of Little Wolf. Other men committed murder in revenge. When the crime was committed by a common man in the heat of temper, he had abundant leisure for repentance, and was often in a constant state of nervousness and alarm, fearing that he might be killed by a relative of the man he had slain.

An illustration is the case of Nahktowun who, after he had killed Walking Coyote, as before stated, fled to the Arapahoes and lived with them for some years. On one occasion, with his wife, he went out to kill a buffalo, and while in a stream valley, saw some buffalo approaching. He hastened to intercept them as they came down to water, and finally, to avoid observation, was obliged to get down very low and to creep along the ground. His wife followed close behind him. She happened to look to one side and saw, over a little ridge and close to them, the humps of some buffalo they had not seen, which had come up another way. To call Nahktowun's attention to these, she reached forward and touched him with a ramrod which she held in her hand. Nahktowun sprang to his feet with a scream, and fell backward off the bank. He said afterward that while he was approaching the buffalo, he kept thinking of how he had killed Walking Coyote and that someone was likely to shoot him, and he was very nervous and anxious. The unexpected touch, while in this mental condition, startled him so that he lost all self-control.

Small matters of dispute were settled privately, either by the parties themselves, or by their relatives. The council seldom occupied itself with private quarrels, unless they had a bearing on the general welfare. If, however, a man was worried about some small dispute, he might carry the matter to the chiefs, or to two or three of them, and ask their advice. He invited them to eat with him, stated his case, and asked their opinions as to what he should do.

It will be seen, therefore, that in the government of the tribe there was no tribal machinery for the punishment of crimes against individuals. The soldiers interfered to prevent or punish acts by individuals which were against the general welfare—which seemed to threaten the tribe as a whole; but a harmful act against a person was punished, if at all, by the injured individual or by members of his family.

The references to the killing of one tribesman by another must not lead to the inference that such occurrences happened often; indeed, they were most unusual. The first killing referred to—that by Porcupine Bear—took place in 1836-1837; and the last one—by Little Wolf—in 1879. In other words, there were only five or six such cases in more than forty years.